My Precious Grandangels,

When each of you was born I waited anxiously to hold you. I wrapped your delicate, newborn beginnings in my arms and wept bittersweet tears of happiness, of regret, of hope. Hope that your lives will be as blessed as mine has been. Hope that you will both grow up happy and healthy and confident. Hope that God will guide your steps and be present in your lives as He has always been in mine—even those times when I doubted that presence.

As I savored your perfection and sweet innocence, I realized there is a story I want to tell you. A love story. I promised myself I would begin writing the story within the month. During those many long nights when sleep refused to visit, I wrote the book a dozen times—rehearsing my scattered thoughts into choreographed steps. Unfortunately, life happens while we're waiting for our lives to begin and consumes us in moments, without our awareness those moments cannot be banked, to be retrieved on an "as need" basis.

So the book waited while I cherished your first steps, your first words, and your laughter with a love that loves unconditionally, blissfully. My sweet granddaughter, at age four you reminded me I don't know everything because your mama said it all the time, "Your nana doesn't know everything." And you taught me that broken seashells are nonetheless beautiful. When you were four, my kindhearted grandson, I told you I used to have two little boys just like you. You stared at me with a touch of wide-eyed anxiety and whispered, "Oh, Nana, what did you do with 'em?" Each of you has brought unimaginable joy into my life.

Love, Life, & Broken Rainbows

A Memoir

Love, Life, & Broken Rainbows

Sheila Carroll

Disclaimer:
Events, locales, stories, and conversations have been recreated from memory. Some names and identifying details have been changed to protect the privacy of individuals.

Copyright © 2016 Sheila Carroll
All rights reserved.

ISBN: 1537688758
ISBN 13: 9781537688756

For Barry

Many thanks to those friends
who, through the years, encouraged me to write.

Part One

"We loved with a love that was more than love."

Edgar Allan Poe

CHAPTER 1

Nothing Stays the Same...Or Does It?

Bob Dylan aptly surmised an era in his ballad, "The Times They Are A-Changin.'" It was the turbulent, rebellious, "Swinging Sixties," and times were, indeed, changing. It was the decade our nation mourned the assassination of President Kennedy, whose death ended "Camelot" and hope for our future. The sixties included a space race with Russia, the Cuban Missile Crisis, the Vietnam War, and a diversity of protests connected by the common thread of dissension. In many parts of the country conservative ideals and conformity were the enemies, and societal norms were challenged. The resounding message was "The Establishment" had to change.

However, in a small manufacturing town, once known as a mill town, situated in Northwest Georgia, we were unaffected by those winds of change. Putting a man on the moon or fear of a nuclear war or the spread of Communism or a dysfunctional society were not priorities of concern—not when there were bills to be paid and hungry kids to be fed. Life went on as usual. Although as teenagers we used slang like, "groovy," "far out," "right on," and "let it all hang out," it was only to sound "cool." "Flower Power" meant nothing to us. The psychedelic drug LSD and "trippin'" were unheard of by most of us. Nor would we have ever smoked a "joint" or participated in a nonviolent demonstration known as a "sit-in." The Hippie Movement, with its philosophy of "free love" and "anti-establishment" mantra, didn't find its way to our town.

Nonetheless, Daddy had read an article in *Reader's Digest* and declared, "'em so-called hippies who drop out and live together in communes ain't nothin' but a bunch of deadbeats too lazy to hit a lick at a snake. You and your friends stay away from 'em pot heads."

Daddy needn't have worried about us being exposed to the counterculture population. The closest thing to a long haired, free-spirited hippie we ever saw was the Goat Man. The vagabond rambled around the Southeast in a wooden cart with a makeshift cover, which served as both transportation and his home and was pulled by a couple of his numerous goats. The old man and his goats had a symbiotic relationship. The goats were decked out in bells, and their jingle and the clank of numerous pots and pans could be heard before the man and his entourage actually arrived. But if the wind was blowin' in the right direction the stench preceded the noise. Goats stink, but Lord only knows how long it'd been since the white-bearded man had taken a bath. If any of us could stand the combination of livestock and body odor, we could have a picture taken with the legend for a dollar, if we had a dollar. The Goat Man wasn't a hippie, but we were all limited by our personal experiences.

For example, the Women's Liberation Movement didn't affect Bremen's female population in the least. The majority of them were too busy working and raising families to grasp the significance of empowerment and equality through change. Not only had they missed the feminism train, they hadn't even heard the whistle blow. The "Equal Pay Act of 1963," signed by President Kennedy, was intended to eliminate the disparity in wages between the sexes. As far as women in the workforce were concerned, the bill may as well have been written in sand.

Nor did the Vietnam War directly affect our lives. My brother-in-law was a member of the Green Berets, but he and my oldest sister Frances Jo lived in Fort Bragg, North Carolina. I wasn't exposed to

Love, Life, & Broken Rainbows

his military career often enough to comprehend his role in the army and "'Nam," although I had once seen him pack his parachute. The war that raged in Vietnam and was protested, sometimes violently by those who opposed the war, was happening on the other side of the world—with glimpses provided by the six o'clock evening news. Television broadcasts, especially the *Huntley-Brinkley Report* or *CBS Evening News* with Walter Cronkite, were our windows to what was happening outside of our everyday lives. But as Mr. Cronkite assured us, "That's the way it is."

Newscasts were also our source of information about the Civil Rights Movement and its inherent violence, despite our proximity to Alabama where years of several notable events defined the movement. Discrimination laws were contested by the courageous who sought equality where only inequality existed, inequality based on hate and prejudices that had transcended generations. "Freedom Rides" and black voter registration resulted in riots and police brutality, particularly on "Bloody Sunday" in Selma, Alabama, as witnessed on television. We were strangers to those aggressive, angry protests, as well as the peaceful rallies led by Martin Luther King, Jr. Those incidents were taking place outside the realm of our reality. Integration, however, eventually edged its way inconspicuously, almost imperceptibly, to Bremen and altered our awareness of social constructs.

When the first black students joined our middle school classroom, we comprehended firsthand the impact of the Civil Rights Act of 1964 that made racial segregation illegal. Despite desegregation laws some of those students chose to remain in their own school across town, and there was, for the first year or two or three, a mutual understanding that blacks and whites didn't intermingle. The sign "Coloreds Only" was taken down, grudgingly, from the entrance to the balcony at the movie theatre. As children we'd wanted to sit up there but weren't allowed because we were white. "Spanky's" (the manager's nickname) wife, who sold movie tickets from the tiny booth and ran the concession, had scolded us for even thinkin' about sittin' in the balcony with "'em colored folks."

Change was slow in a small Southern town reluctant to accept change. We sat motionless in the eye of an inevitable storm of political and cultural change while conflict surrounded us. Despite the country's societal breakdown that encompassed a Sexual Revolution, teenagers in Bremen were expected to obey our parents, go to church on Sunday, and stay out of trouble—especially the kind of trouble that could result in an out-of-wedlock pregnancy. *Free love my ass.*

My impression of what was "just not done" was conceived from overheard, whispered conversations between my two older sisters, which, along with thinly veiled tales of love from magazines like "True Romance," passed for sex education in our house. My role models were from a steady diet of "Gidget" and Frankie Avalon and Annette Funicello beach movies, but they taught me nothing about sex since none of them did anything other than kiss. Nor did all those wholesome Doris Day movies provide any guidance. My friends and I had seen *The Graduate* only because none of our parents had a hint in hell the movie contained sexual innuendos, vague innuendos that left us even more confused. Despite that we were clueless, we smiled to ourselves whenever we heard Simon and Garfunkel's "Mrs. Robinson" on the radio, as if we knew exactly what had gone on between the sheets with Ben and his mama's friend.

Unfortunately, sex education at school was restricted to a week's discussion in Home Economics where Miss Habersham* stressed that abstinence was the *only* one hundred percent effective birth control method. Those lessons combined with the fact that Georgia was located in the "Bible Belt," along with our Baptist—or Methodist— upbringing and served as a deterrent for promiscuity. The fear

Daddy would beat the livin' daylights out of me was enough for me to draw the line at innocent kisses.

According to local gossip, which spread like kudzu in our town, a couple of my high school's seniors had gotten pregnant and left school to visit with family, a sick grandparent or aunt who needed full-time care. Those girls returned in a few months, and it was assumed the baby had been given up for adoption. The alternative was to get married and drop out of school; a baby born to an unmarried woman was unacceptable in our judgmental community. The message was loud and clear: sex and pregnancy were for married women.

Mama was forty, and her youngest was almost eight when she realized she would be having yet another baby. I was that baby. When I was born my oldest of three sisters was nineteen and married; my twin brothers, the oldest of three boys, were high school seniors. My siblings had all grown up together, but due to the age gap it was almost like I was an only child. By the time I was old enough to go with them to nearby Oak Lake or the skating rink, they were too old to want to take me with them.

With nothing better to do, I sat propped against a porch post on a humid, shirt soakin' summer evening. I was bored, stuck with Mama and two of my aunts who had parked themselves in large front porch rockers. I swatted at hungry mosquitos while the women were busily snappin' a mess of green beans from Mama's garden. She loved her garden and planted vegetables in a plot of land behind the house and flowers everywhere else, especially rose bushes that surrounded the porch. Mama said workin' in the yard was good for her nerves, breathing space. The trio of women laughed about the delights and hardships of having babies so close together.

Mama and her nine siblings had learned early that life was hard, and they were survivors. They grew up on a small farm in Carroll County where everybody worked in order to have the basic requirements of a roof over their heads and food on the table. The bleakness of the Great Depression hadn't affected their lives in the least because they were already well acquainted with bleakness. Not to mention they didn't have money in the stock market when they'd barely had enough to live on.

They'd managed the farm without Papa for a while when their daddy had worked for the Works Program Administration, which was created by the federal government in an effort to alleviate some of the destitution. Papa had lived in a camp for months with other men who were also desperate for a job. When Mama was old enough she left school to work in a factory out of necessity. Her measly earnings were contributed to the family pot until she'd married in her early twenties and left home.

As I continued to eavesdrop their conversation made it apparent that during, and for a few months after, WWII all seven sisters had shared ration coupons so as to have enough necessities for their ever-growing families. I loved hearing their stories, and one thing I learned growing up in the South was that we loved our family stories. Lord knows, they were told often enough.

I listened again to Mama relate how when my oldest sister was seventeen months old, she and Daddy had been blessed with twin boys. At the time they'd lived on the third floor of an old Victorian, which amounted to one large room that included a small kitchen area and a tiny bathroom. Mama recounted the time Daddy came home from a night at the local watering hole to find their bed filled with wife and babies. He remarked that he didn't know he'd married "a damn incubator" and had pissed and moaned about not having a place to lie down. Mama calmly told him, as she was quoted often in the retelling, "Well, Joe, it looks like you've screwed yourself out of a place to sleep."

Oh well. The sisters' laughter rolled across the porch like thunder on a late, summer afternoon as they reminisced over that remark and other shared recollections. Growing up in a large family that included an even larger extended family involved lifetimes filled with stories. But what I hadn't considered on that muggy, rose scented evening was that one day the stories would be my own.

Although Daddy and Mama were set in their ways, they weren't nearly as strict on me as they'd been with my six older siblings, who referred to me as the "spoiled rotten baby." Or maybe my parents were simply tired by the time I came along. Spoiled baby of seven or not I didn't want to push my luck and risk being grounded for a month for sneaking from the show to a party. Daddy dropped me off to meet my friends Janet* and Diane* in front of our small town's only theatre for Saturday night's Elvis Presley double feature. Plans were that Beth* and her date Steve* would take us all home afterwards as he was seventeen and had a car. Beth was fifteen, but she was in our class because she was held back a grade in elementary school.

I didn't realize until it was too late to back out without sounding like a crybaby that plans had changed. Steve's older brother had told him about a party at the nearby college campus, and I reluctantly climbed into the back seat. Over the radio's beat of The Spencer Davis Group's "Gimme Some Lovin'," I reminded everybody of my eleven o'clock curfew. The party was in Carrollton, a town twelve miles away and home to West Georgia College. It wasn't likely my parents would find out I'd been there.

As we made the trip south on Highway 27, I contemplated my rash decision to let friends talk me into something. I don't know what had possessed me to leave the show with my girlfriends and go to a party. I should have paid the fifty cents for a ticket and gone inside; I really liked Elvis' movies and had seen most of them. And even though Spanky patrolled the aisles like a hungry hawk and Dean the Fiend, a middle aged, bald man who wore black, square framed glasses, sat in the back row, and watched us priss up and down the aisle in our miniskirts, I enjoyed the movies. The portrayals of lives that were very different from my own fascinated me, which is also why I loved to read. Books were an escape to faraway places and exciting adventures.

However, the unplanned "adventure" of going to a party without any adult chaperones, a party where the majority of the teenagers would all be older than my fourteen years, a high school freshman, could be serious trouble. Apparently, my friends had no problem with lying as their laughter indicated, but that delinquency of deception had my stomach in knots. I knew better than to pull such a stunt, and I was sweatin' bullets.

When we arrived and found the right apartment my friends scattered, and I found an empty corner in the dimly lit, crowded room. With resigned acceptance that what was done was done, I kept a close eye on the clock. One of The Rolling Stones' hits from a couple of years ago, "I Can't Get No Satisfaction," was blaring from the stereo. While unfamiliar with marijuana, I was sure pot was the source of the sickly sweet smell coming from one of the bedrooms where some of the local college students had relocated themselves. I was young and naïve, but even I knew weed was illegal.

I'd made a bad decision regarding the party, but I wasn't stupid enough not to realize the consequences of being caught where pot and alcohol were being passed around—whether I participated or not. The party was a definite drag and from the shelter of my corner I nervously peeped around for my friends. It was time for us to leave in case there was a run-in with the law. From what I'd heard through the grapevine, the "fuzz" had been called more than once for disturbances at Brookwood Apartments. My fellow partygoers had disappeared among the seemingly slow motion dancers caught in the eerie strobe light that was set up on the impromptu dance floor.

I was short and stood on tiptoes, but my search was futile. I was about to slip out of the corner to find them when someone's hand casually landed on my shoulder. Startled, I turned my head and saw the most handsome guy I'd ever seen. There was certainly nobody at my high school who looked that good—nobody that would notice me. He was tall, maybe six feet, with broad shoulders and thick black hair that grazed the top of his yellow, button down, collared shirt. He looked into my eyes with dreamy, velvety brown eyes, fringed with dark lashes and gave me a soft, sexy smile that made my heart jump. While I tried to be cool, I couldn't help noticing the fit of his Levi's that weren't too tight but tight enough to show off his muscled thighs and a great ass. Penny loafers, no socks, completed his put together look. He was definitely easy on the eyes.

I had no idea what to say to him, but I wanted my girlfriends to see us standing together and wished I'd had my Polaroid Swinger. I could have used the birthday upgrade from my Kodak Brownie to take an instant picture of the two of us. As the gorgeous fella surveyed the crowd, I checked his wrist to see if he was wearing a watch; he was blocking my view of the only clock in the room. My "coach" wouldn't turn into a pumpkin, but like Cinderella there was a limit to the time I could spend at the ball. I couldn't see the face of his watch in the semidarkness of the room, but I did notice the striking, thick silver banded ring with the chunky, square ruby in the center. The simple, masculine ring caught my eye because my birthstone is a ruby. I wanted to ask if his birthday was in July, too, but wasn't sure I could talk. My pulse was racing, an unfamiliar sensation that left me speechless. I felt an inexplicable inner turmoil that I attributed to the unpredictable hormones of adolescence.

The two of us stood without speaking as the stack of 45s continued to supply the party with music. I noticed several couples dispersing to find some privacy as the Temptations crooned "My Girl." I wondered how many of those girls had gone all the way and if they had "protection" in case their making out led to sex. I dismissed that thought; their behavior wasn't any of my business. My only concern was to be home by eleven. I was torn between getting home on time and staying put when the handsome stranger leaned down so close that I could smell his musky cologne, which smelled much better than the Old Spice Daddy used on Sundays.

Loud enough for me to hear over the noise of the music and the rowdiness of those who hadn't skipped the hunch punch, I heard him speaking to me. "Hi, I'm Barry. What's your name?"

"Sheila," I answered barley loud enough for him to hear.

I was glad I'd worn my favorite white miniskirt, blue peasant blouse, and white go-go boots. Mama had bought me a pair of those new pantyhose, which were much more practical than a garter and stockings. She and I didn't always agree on my wardrobe choices, and she also disliked my popular, Twiggy style short haircut; she thought it made me look like a boy. If Mama had had her way, I would have had a mop of curls. Between the ages of five and eight I was at the beauty school every couple of months for another perm—another attempt for me to have the ringlets of a popular child star, Shirley Temple. Much to Mama's dismay, my hair was too fine and straight and fought the multiple attempts at curling. I ended up with a headful of fluff and resembled a large dust bunny with a face. Mama gave up on curly hair for me and settled for a practical pixie cut. Thank goodness the beauty school closed before I was in middle school, and I got to go to Naomi's Southern Roots Beauty Parlor.

The dark haired young man interrupted my woolgathering, and I jumped at the sound of his voice. "Do you live here? I don't remember seeing you around school."

Still in awe that he was talking to me, I stammered, "No, I'm from Bremen. I was invited to come to this party with some friends of mine."

Although I hadn't seen much of those friends all night, Beth chose that precise moment to rush across the room, grab my arm and sputter, "Let's go. It's after ten-thirty, and even if Steve hauls ass, we'll barely get back to Bremen by eleven."

I briefly explained to Barry that I had to leave because I wasn't supposed to be at the party and had to be home not one minute later than eleven o'clock.

"It was nice meeting you, Sheila. If it's okay, I'd like to call you sometime, maybe for a date."

My "dating" was limited to meeting a boy at the show or for a chocolate sundae at Ma Walker's corner drugstore, with its ice cream parlor ambience. But he didn't have to know that. I didn't want to seem too anxious, so with a shrug I smiled nonchalantly. "That would be fine. My phone number is—"

"Sheila, NOW!" urged Beth while she tugged me along. "Steve has the motor running, and Diane and Janet are already in the car."

I had no choice but to hurry out the door and hope I would run into Barry again somewhere. I threw up my hand and waved a reluctant good-bye. I rode in the back seat of the Chevy SS while Jefferson Airplane's "Somebody to Love" blared from the radio. I thought about Barry, and lines from some of those magazine romance stories I'd read when my sisters weren't around filtered through my lightheadedness. I memorized every detail of our brief encounter, and those thoughts fed the strange sensation of somersaulting butterflies in my stomach. I very much wanted our paths to cross again. With the exception of meeting Barry, my first year of high school was rather humdrum. Then again, freshman year wasn't entirely uneventful.

Less than a month after the party and a few weeks before summer break, I woke up one morning and realized, as milk dribbled down the front of my pajamas, that something was very wrong. There was a lack of movement on the right side of my face, comparable to the numbing sensation after dental work. My right eye felt tight and dry, and I couldn't raise my brow. I put the cereal bowl in the sink and went to the bathroom mirror and was shaken by the image reflected. It looked like an invisible hand pulled my mouth slightly over to the right side, and I couldn't blink; my right eye was stuck in an expression of surprise. I was terrified and immediately called Mama, who'd already left for work and had to be paged to the phone. She assumed I was exaggerating the condition and told me to walk the few blocks to the family doctor's office and to not forget the medical excuse I would need for checking in late at school.

When I arrived, Shirley, the receptionist, dark hair styled in a beehive, noted that I didn't have an appointment. She told me I'd have to sit in the waiting room for a while since I would be a "work in." Then she glanced up and saw my face. She stared at me through lenses held stylishly in place by black, cat eye, frames. "Have a seat, Sheila, and I'll get you in as soon as Dr. Elder has a few minutes."

I picked up an outdated copy of *Life* magazine that was big enough for me to hide from the curious gawkers until I was rescued by the nurse. Dr. Elder had been our family doctor for as long as I could remember and had even made a couple of house calls when I was five or six years old and was too sick to go to his office. He took one look at me and couldn't hide the concern that showed over every wrinkled inch of his face. Without a word he proceeded with the exam, checking my temperature, ears, throat, blood pressure, heart rhythm, and reflexes. It was obvious he was as confounded as I was when I'd seen myself in the mirror earlier. I waited for him to say something, anything.

A few minutes ticked by before he asked, "Sheila, have you had any symptoms since I treated you for the inner ear infection last month?"

"No sir. I finished the antibiotic and haven't had any more pain."

Dr. Elder excused himself and returned moments later with one of his colleagues, Dr. Pritchett. They seemed to have forgotten I was in the room, and they began to discuss a possible diagnosis as if they were two students still in med school confronted with a challenge. I wasn't too alarmed, but I was beginning to worry.

Dr. Pritchett said, "She's much too young for this to be any type of a stroke, and you said her BP and heart rate are normal."

"Yes, she appears healthy, except for the facial paralysis," replied Dr. Elder.

Their confusion and discussion over possible medical causes made it apparent that neither of them recognized what was wrong with me, and I started to cry. I was more upset when no tears fell from my right eye, and it remained opened and dry. My understandable distress interrupted their conversation as both stared at me intently, puzzlement evident on their faces.

I asked, "Dr. Elder, what's wrong with me?" Even as I spoke and felt the words fall from the corner of my mouth, I knew he had no answer.

"We don't know, Sheila, but I'm going to find a doctor who does. Wait here while I have my nurse make an appointment for you." Dr. Elder's compassion was somewhat reassuring.

When I left the office a light spring rain began to fall. I was too upset to finish the day at school. I went straight home, got out of my damp clothes, climbed into bed, and fell asleep. Several hours later I awoke to Mama's voice and her hand shaking my shoulder to rouse me.

"Sit up, sweetie. What did Dr. Elder say?"

I sat up and heard her gasp when she switched on the lamp. "He doesn't know what's wrong with me." I reached over to the night stand and retrieved the appointment card the nurse had given me. "I have an appointment in Atlanta with a specialist tomorrow morning at nine-thirty. His name is Dr. Brown, and his office is at the Ponce de Leon Infirmary. The address and directions are attached to the back of the card."

~

After a restless night my parents and I left early in the morning. The tedious Atlanta traffic was notorious for delays, and we were anxious to see the ear, nose, and throat specialist whom Dr. Elder had recommended. Highway 78-E led us to the interstate access on that beautiful spring morning. Mother Nature had used her palette to create a magnificent display; pear trees were covered in white, fluffy blossoms. Bubblegum pink tulip trees, cherry, and dogwood trees were in full bloom, along with jonquils, tulips, and azaleas in an array of colors. As we approached the outskirts of the city, I noticed that sunlight bounced playfully around the gold-leafed dome of the state capitol. Not even the radiance of the day could lift my spirits.

Love, Life, & Broken Rainbows

We exited I-20 onto the downtown connector and proceeded to Ponce de Leon Avenue. Daddy remarked, "Sheila, there's a Krispy Kreme doughnut shop. We'll stop by on our way home and pick up a dozen. Maybe the sign will be flashing 'HOT,' and we can get a fresh batch."

Krispy Kreme doughnuts, nowhere to be found at home, were one of my favorite, although rare, treats. I wasn't interested in donuts but replied, "Okay. Fine." I'd hardly spoken the entire trip and could think of nothing but that the doctor had to be able to resolve this problem, to diagnosis and treat the paralysis so I would be normal again. It didn't occur to me that Dr. Brown wouldn't be able to straighten my face that very day.

When we arrived the receptionist gave Mama the standard set of informational forms to complete and asked for the insurance card. To her credit, the receptionist didn't even flinch at my bewildered expression and the tightly drawn lip. Thankfully, mine was the first appointment and within ten minutes we were shown to an exam room.

The doctor walked in, shook hands with my parents, glimpsed at me, and without a moment's hesitation said, "You have Bell's palsy."

Mama anxiously asked, "What exactly is Bell's palsy, and how did she get it, and how is it treated?"

Apparently, I was not the only one who had spent a sleepless night, mentally compiling a list of questions. Dr. Brown held up his hand while he reviewed the copy of faxed medical records from Dr. Elder. "Let's take one question at a time, shall we? Bell's palsy is a condition in which the nerve that controls parts of the ear and facial nerves becomes constricted due to inflammation. The nerve, located in the inner ear, is protected by a bony canal, but when the nerve is inflamed it becomes compressed and results in facial paralysis. Bell's palsy is uncommon, particularly in someone her age, but it's not life threatening and is almost always temporary. As for—"

I interrupted his text book explanation. "*Almost* always temporary'? What does that mean? Will you give me a shot or a prescription that will cure this?"

He hesitated a moment before answering, "No, Sheila. I'm afraid there is no quick solution for this condition. Healing is based solely upon nerve regeneration, which takes time."

"How much time? How long will it take for me to be able to smile again?" I felt like the character from *Alice in Wonderland* who'd tumbled down a rabbit hole where nothing made sense. I would have gladly swallowed or eaten any potion if it would have undone the nerve damage, but none was offered. I waited for Dr. Brown to continue.

"Nerves are slow to regenerate, and the length of regeneration depends on the extent of the damage. In your case, I would estimate eight to nine months. I realize that seems like a long time to you, but the process is gradual and improvement will be subtle. I've seen cases more severe, and the patients have had a full recovery. But, as I said, it does take time."

Mama expressed her concern. "Will she be alright? You said Bell's palsy is uncommon but not life threatening. Is that right?"

"Yes, because it can come on suddenly, as it did when Sheila woke up yesterday morning, it's often mistaken for a stroke. I assure you she is healthy, and she will improve. The biggest concern is her right eye. Because she cannot close her eye or even blink, she will need to use moisturizing eye drops several times a day and wear an eye patch at night in order to prevent damage from dust or scratching the eye in her sleep. While I can't guarantee a one hundred percent recovery, the nerve will eventually heal itself. I would like to see her again in four months to assess the progress."

I stopped listening. Dr. Brown wasn't telling me what I wanted to hear.

A few days after the appointment with Dr. Brown, I pleaded in vain with Daddy and Mama to let me move away so I wouldn't have to return to my high school. Of course, transferring to another school was not an option. My real friends were loyal and genuinely sorry and concerned. Several of my alleged friends seemed delighted, and I quickly disassociated myself from them and from their perfect, carefully practiced smiles. Not surprisingly, I was the target of ridicule.

"Look Sheila, I'm Popeye the Sailor." That mimicry from a classmate, complete with closed eye and crooked mouth, elicited laughter from some of the other students standing in the breezeway during break one morning. A few of them had the decency to seem embarrassed as I pushed my way through the crowd, fighting the sting of tears.

I was thankful I'd agreed to live with my sister and her family during the summer and babysit for my young nieces. Pat and Stanley lived in Bowdon, approximately fifteen miles away. The distance made it easier to curb summer contact to my closest friends and a couple of weekend movies in Bremen. Eventually my summer respite ended, and I had to take my one-sided smile to school with me in September. Several of the girls in my class were going steady with their boyfriends, but I rarely had more than one or two dates with the same boy. I was too self-conscious to carry on a conversation. It was easier to be part of a group, as long as the natives were friendly. Some definitely were not.

In mid-October, I was looking forward to the Halloween party and hayride at Gina's* farm. That was until Judy* overheard Janet and me discussing costumes and couldn't resist the opportunity to hurt me. "Well, Sheila, you could always go as a pirate, patch your bad eye…Arrrrgh, Matey," she said from the side of her mouth.

"Or maybe you could find a bushy moustache and a fake cigar and dress up like that old comedian, what was his name? Oh, yeah, Groucho Marx," chimed in Leslie*.

Each malicious comment hurt every time, the last as much as the first. As I'd done many times before I hurried to the restroom, away from their vicious mockery. I heard Janet retort, "Why don't you two bitches leave her alone? As for costumes for the party, you both should go as wicked witches."

―

I made it through the last two classes, and as soon as the dismissal bell rang I walked home the long route and cried; I didn't get home until after five. I went straight to my room and slammed the door. Mama had accepted my bouts of anger and depression, but she waited a few minutes before she knocked on the battered door.

"Go away," I told her through muffled sobs.

Instead, she entered and took a seat on the bed. "What happened this time?"

Between body racking sobs I tried to make her understand. "I was excited about Saturday's party, the Halloween party at the farm, but a couple of girls made fun of me and suggested costumes that would be perfect for me. I'm not going."

"But you've been talking about the party for weeks, and you were happy about your black cat costume."

I was outraged by her complacency and screamed, "You have no idea what this is like for me. Being laughed at in school, using eye drops five or six times a day, wearing a patch every night. Waiting to be rid of this nerve damage and be a regular teenager is horrible. I dropped out of band because there's no way to play the flute with a warped mouth; I won't ever be a majorette. I'm nothing but a joke, a freak, and I hate my life. You don't know or care how hard all of this is for me. I wish I could die!"

My outburst was hateful and unfair, but life had been unfair to me, and I wanted to hurt Mama, to make her feel my pain. While I was not physically bullied, emotionally I was devastated. Whoever made up that ridiculous rhyme about sticks and stones breaking bones but words never hurting hadn't ever been a teenager who'd endured immense pain inflicted by words. Nor did I buy that "pretty is as pretty does" crap. And if beauty was on the inside, Bremen High School didn't get the memo; the pretty on the outside girls had everything.

My sobbing continued, and Mama wrapped her arms around me as she tried to console me. "I'm sorry I can't undo the nerve damage and fix your smile, sorry you're too young to know we all suffer heartaches of our own. And I'm so sorry I can't protect you from the meanness of others." She held me until my crying subsided and stroked my hair with hands that had grown up working on a farm, had held babies and changed countless diapers, had operated the sewing machines of a factory—hands of love that knew a life of labor.

When the tears subsided I pulled away and looked into Mama's watery blue eyes, laced with the remnants of time, and saw the reflection of my pain multiplied by ten. For the first time in my young life, I wondered about her heartaches, her disappointments, her dreams lost. What had she sacrificed to marry and raise her brood of seven? Seven that had been reduced to six by the death of Frances Jo. Mama's silent suffering spoke volumes and I didn't know if she would ever recover from losing her first-born to breast cancer.

In January I had my third and last appointment with Dr. Brown to, once again, "assess the progress." It was a bitterly cold, overcast day—one of those days better spent by the fire with a good book and a cup of hot chocolate. But the appointment made it necessary for Daddy and me to brave the cold as we rode in silence and watched the traffic. It'd been approximately nine months, a very long nine months, since that first trip to the Ponce de Leon Infirmary. Dr. Brown had said recovery could take as long as eight or nine months, and yet my smile remained offset, crooked. I was determined to find out why.

Daddy broke into my resolution from his position in the driver's seat. "I hope the snow holds off until we get back home. The traffic will be much worse if the weather gets nasty, and we don't want to get stranded." He waited for me to say something, but I had nothing to say and continued my blank stare out the window.

Daddy was right about the impending weather. When snowfall was more than an inch in Georgia, the affected areas came to a standstill as we became ensnared by icy roads. Marooned drivers often resembled icicles that clung precariously to whatever their crystal fingers could grab. Surely the appointment would be brief.

We entered an empty waiting room and were shown to an exam room right away. Dr. Brown walked in before we had time to remove our coats. "Hello, Sheila. How are you on this frigid January afternoon?"

I was not in the mood for congeniality and blurted, "It's been nine months, but my mouth is not right. It's impossible to read my lips, and my smile is uneven. Not to mention I look hideous when I laugh."

"Let's see how you've progressed. Blink. Good. How are the tears?"

"Better, but they don't flow the same as they do from my left eye. Another weird thing happens sometimes when I eat. My right eye waters, like I'm crying."

"That's because the nerves are getting mixed signals while they regenerate. It should pass with time. You don't have to use the drops unless your eye feels extremely dry, and you won't need to wear the patch at night. Your eye closes completely now."

He seemed to be ignoring my concern over an asymmetrical smile. "Dr. Brown, it's been nine months. How much longer before my lips match the words coming out of my mouth and my smile curves on both sides?"

After a brief pause he answered, "I didn't promise you would have a one hundred percent recovery, Sheila, because I didn't know. It's one of those wait and see medical conditions, and nerves take months to heal. Unfortunately, in approximately ten percent of Bell's palsy patients the damaged nerve does not fully regenerate. The result is residual paralysis that is permanent. There's a chance improvement will continue, although in my experience if the nerve has not healed within a few months of the onset of symptoms, there will not be a full recovery. I know you're disappointed, and I'm sorry."

Sorry? His words were spoken offhandedly, clinical, and completely detached from the meaning those words held for a fifteen-year-old girl. The outcome for which I'd prayed and impatiently waited wasn't going to be as I had anticipated. Instead, Bell's palsy had left behind an indelible reminder of my teenaged agony.

Daddy and I rode home in the same cloud of silence that had blanketed us on the trip over. He focused on the traffic amid light snow flurries; I focused on the secret dream held in a young girl's heart. I'd deliberately avoided going to Carrollton for fear of running into Barry, something I had previously very much wanted to do. But the last thing I wanted was for him to see me with a twisted face. I'd planned to find him as soon as the paralysis passed—except it wasn't going to pass and my smile would always be crooked. Bitter disappointment was echoed by the bitterness of that gray winter day, and I shed hushed, disheartened tears.

*Name changed

CHAPTER 2

Some Things Were Meant to Be

It was the spring of my sophomore year, another day in the school cafeteria—the same cafeteria where we'd stood in line as children for a sugar cube dotted with the pink polio vaccine. "Simon Says," by the bubblegum band with the weird name, 1910 Fruitgum Company, was winding its way out of someone's transistor radio, which would eventually be confiscated by the lunchroom monitor. Several of us were sitting at a crowded table, discussing what to wear to Saturday's dance in Carrollton at the Pow Wow Room, presumably so named because the West Georgia College athletic teams were the Braves.

As for clothes, Mama shopped for me in town or sometimes at Griffin's in Carrollton or ordered a few things from Sears and JC Penney's catalogs. Some of my clothes were hand-me-downs. Nobody in our clique traveled fifty miles to Atlanta to shop at Greenbriar Mall or downtown at Rich's because working class families couldn't afford to shop at those places. Unless a family member was in the hospital, fifty miles was considered too far of a drive, especially just to buy clothes.

I decided to dress casually for the dance, bell bottoms, platform shoes, and a brightly colored tie-dyed t-shirt with a peace symbol pendant and fringed vest, all ordered from the Sears and Roebuck catalog. As teenagers we wanted to copy the fashions we saw in magazines like *Seventeen*. We weren't permitted to wear pants to school, so we wore our bell bottoms almost every weekend, unless it was too hot, in which case we wore short shorts. Mama needed me to explain the rule about not wearing pants to school although it was acceptable to wear miniskirts that barely covered our butts. She was too old to understand, and I didn't even try to argue with her logic.

As teenagers who wanted to blend in we dressed to mimic current trends and listened to popular music that we added to our collections of albums and 45s without comprehending the lyrics. My older sisters had played Leslie Gore's, "You Don't Own Me" over and over but had no idea it had become an anthem, of sorts, for the Women's Lib Movement. And who in his right mind would have thought Donovan's "Mellow Yellow" was about smoking dried banana peels to achieve a hallucinogenic high? While we were familiar with Scott McKenzie's "San Francisco," encouraging people to go there, we didn't have a clue as to why because we had no concept of a "love-in." Nor had we connected Barry McGuire's 1965 version of "Eve of Destruction" with the violence and injustices that culminated in the sixties. The majority of us didn't grasp that those messages were reflective of times that described a decade.

I was tugged from my musical musings when Debbie* reached across the table for the salt. My heart leapt with recognition when I noticed she was wearing a boy's ring on her finger, held in place by a rubber band. The ring had a broad, silver band with a distinguishing ruby center. It was the same ring I'd seen over a year ago worn by a very handsome boy at a party. But that was before Bell's palsy, and I'd given up any romantic aspirations for Barry and me.

The ring nudged those buried hopes, and I yelled over the noon-day din, "Hey, Debbie, where did you get that ring?"

"Oh, this," she replied loudly as she held her hand up for everybody to see. "I met an awesome guy at Tanner's Beach on Saturday, and he asked me to be his girl."

Love, Life, & Broken Rainbows

Tanner's Beach was a nearby lake with a manmade sandy shore, a family oriented park for swimming and picnics; a concession stand served hot dogs, chips, snow cones, lemonade, and Cokes. Paddle boats could be rented, and there was a kiddie train ride that circled the lake where characters from Mother Goose nursery rhymes paraded along the way. The lifeguards were local teenagers, mostly boys, but there was one girl with ink black hair and alabaster skin. She sat under the shade of a huge, yellow umbrella that was attached to one of the lifeguard stands especially for her. Her name was Nan or Ann or Jan, and she was the epitome of the expression, "If I could buy her for what she's worth and sell her for what she *thinks* she's worth, I'd be a millionaire." Somebody really should have told her she wasn't the only, or the prettiest, pebble on the beach.

The lifeguards sometimes took breaks at a favorite hangout, the Teen Shack, where teenagers could socialize and escape the white hot glare of summer. The Georgia heat could smack you in the face like a skillet of cornbread hot out of the oven. The small, shaded building sat on a hill among pine trees and featured built-in benches under large, open windows, ceiling fans, a jukebox that housed the latest music, and a dance floor in the center. The aroma of Coppertone and sweat permeated the wooden structure.

During the summer months local bands played at the beach pavilion on Saturday nights, and teenagers from surrounding areas gathered sporting shorts, tank tops, flip flops, and suntans. Some girls wore Coppertone QT fake tans and glowed as orange as a harvest moon. But I hadn't bumped into Barry at the lake, a favorite place of mine—whenever several of us could find a ride. However, I'd spent almost all of last summer babysitting my nieces and the better part of this school year at home, in self-imposed quarantine. I wanted to avoid the inevitable questions, "What's wrong with your face?" "Why do you talk out of the side of your mouth?" "Why is your smile crooked?" If I'd known how to cope with Bell's palsy and those questions, I might've already bumped into Barry somewhere. I hadn't, and I wanted to know more about my classmate's encounter with him.

I moved a few chairs over so I wouldn't have to yell. Debbie was a ditz who was notorious for creating scenarios in which she ended up with a handsome boyfriend. The fact that none of us was ever around when those romantic escapades happened didn't deter her imagination, nor her constant chatter regarding the supposed meetings. While she'd obviously met Barry, I doubted he would have given his ring to a girl he didn't even know.

"He was *so* good lookin'." Debbie rolled her eyes dramatically and continued, "Tall, with jet black hair, brown eyes, and a smile that made my heart pound. Oh, sorry, Sheila, about the mention of a gorgeous smile."

"It's okay." By then I'd long grown weary of the snide remarks and references to my lopsided smile. Most of my tormentors had all but moved on to other targets. Her apology was irrelevant as my interest was in the ring and how she'd come to have it.

Debbie was short and slightly overweight, with curly red hair that won the battle with the barrette. A double fistful of freckles was sprinkled across her nose and cheeks. Not exactly the style of the sixties most of us wanted to attain: long, straight hair, miniskirts, and snug pants that hugged slender hips. Nor did Debbie have a winning personality; she was whiny and tiresome and was the first to spread, or start, rumors. Sometimes she was just plain old mean as a snake. Understandably, she was one of the least popular girls in our class, and I usually didn't associate with her.

Still, she might know Barry's last name or phone number. With more than a bit of skepticism I said, "Oh, c'mon, Debbie. Everybody knows you're always makin' things up when it comes to boys. Did that guy really ask you to 'be his girl'?"

She sat maddeningly twirling the ring, playing it up because she had my full attention. I wanted to yank the ring off her finger and demand details. But I remained indifferent. Debbie replied smugly, "Okay, maybe he didn't ask me to go steady, but I did meet him, and I *do* have his ring."

I tried not to seem too engrossed as I picked over the carrots and green peas on my lunch tray. I casually asked, "Yes, and how is it you have his ring?"

"I was at the dance at Tanner's Beach last weekend, and he was there with a few other guys. The band was playing Sly and the Family Stone's 'Dance to the Music.' That's a great song for dancing, and I asked him to dance."

She paused to make sure I was still listening. I was definitely listening and wanted her to get on with her tale. Impatience shimmered through every inch of me as I waited for Debbie to finish the web she was weaving.

"Anyway, after the dance he started to walk away, but I grabbed his arm and struck up a conversation. I asked him about the ring and if I could try it on."

I sat there to process the revelation before I said anything. "He let you keep the ring?"

It was Debbie's turn to hesitate before answering, "He didn't exactly 'let' me keep the ring. He started talking to a girl who interrupted us, and I guess he forgot I had it."

"And you conveniently 'forgot' to return the ring."

Her Cheshire cat grin slid off her face as she stuttered, "Uh, uh, um, yes, but I'm going to give it back to him on Saturday night at the Pow Wow Room. I told him how excited I am that the band Swingin' Medallions is going to be there and that a bunch of us are taking our

45s of their hit "Double Shot' to have it autographed by the band members. I overheard the girl who interrupted us ask him if he planned to be there, and he told her that he might be. He ignored me, and I decided to keep the ring to have an excuse to talk to him at the dance." She paused to catch her breath and to gage my reaction to her tangled yarn.

Janet had been eavesdropping and jumped at the chance to put Debbie on the spot. "You know, Debbie, most of us are planning to be at that dance. Maybe you can introduce him to us. It would be nice to actually meet one of your many male acquaintances, especially one as handsome as you claim he is."

All I could think about was, finally, I would be able to see that attractive guy with the stunning smile again in three days. Would he remember me? Would he be there with a date? What if he was going steady with someone? Those thoughts distracted my attention from Debbie until I heard her reply to Janet's suggestion that she introduce us to her latest "boyfriend."

Although Debbie appeared somewhat chagrined, she met the challenge. "Fine, I would love for all of you to meet Barry."

~

I don't know how I got through those three days before the dance. Thankfully, I was busy with school and homework and a baseball game my girlfriends and I attended, more to be seen in our short shorts than to watch the game. Saturday morning found me too excited to sleep late; I had to get myself ready for the big dance. I wanted to look my best. My excitement was confusing because it was possible Barry wouldn't even remember our brief meeting at a noisy party. Regardless, I planned to be there and hoped to see him again. At least I had plenty of time to get ready.

I was grateful the last of my two older sisters were married. Three girls no longer shared a bathroom (only one for our large family) or

Love, Life, & Broken Rainbows

phone. My phone was an extension, but it wasn't a party line anymore. Because of the nineteen year gap between Mama's first baby and her last, my three oldest siblings had married and moved out before I was old enough to remember them living at home. I was the only one left at home, and the bedroom was, at last, my own. I'd hung posters of the Beatles, the Monkees, Paul Revere and the Raiders, the Beach Boys, Herman's Hermits, Dave Clark Five, and the Rolling Stones. Most of my allowance was spent on records and albums.

We'd always had a console hi-fi stereo in the living room and a record player in our bedroom, but we'd had only one black and white television set. If Daddy was home we all had to watch whatever he watched. He liked television so much that when they were available, we were the first on our block to have a color t.v. set. Mama said Daddy bought it on credit and added, "The man would buy a circus monkey if he could pay five dollars down and five dollars a week."

When I was younger, and my sisters were teenagers, we fought in the afternoons over the one t.v. in the den. Unless I was playing outside I begged to watch *The Popeye Club* with Officer Don, whom I'd seen in person at the local movie theatre. More often than not, and as I was outnumbered, my sisters commandeered the t.v. to watch *American Bandstand*. I was lucky to have a portable t.v. in my bedroom and not to have to watch the westerns, such as *Bonanza*, that Mama and Daddy preferred.

To pass the seemingly endless hours until the dance, I loaded the record player with a stack of my favorite albums, from The Beatles to Creedence Clearwater Revival to The Mamas and the Papas to Sonny and Cher to Paul Revere and the Raiders. With upbeat music to inspire me, I cleaned my room and had all but forgotten the lava lamp lost among the clutter on the dresser—along with several big-eyed Trolls from my collection. Next I tackled my closet, which was a disorganized fashion collage of shapes and hues. In the process I tried on a dozen or more outfits and decided the bell bottoms I'd planned to wear wouldn't do for the occasion. I settled on a sleeveless, lime green, A-line mini-dress with a bright blue daisy in the middle and matching blue, ballet flats. The outfit was similar to one I'd seen Marlo Thomas wear on *That Girl*, although mine was ordered from the JC Penney's catalog. Grandma Pearl had never approved of us girls "primpin'," maybe because pride was one of the seven deadly sins. But primping is exactly how I spent the afternoon.

Hours were filled with a manicure, a long bubble bath, washing and rolling my stick straight, ash blonde hair on giant curlers with Dippity Do to add fullness. I was letting my hair grow long to resemble Cher because I was tired of last year's popular short haircut. I also figured longer hair would help hide the remaining facial paralysis. Those sunny afternoons at the ball field had given me a hint of bronze, and the bright green dress highlighted the promise of a summer tan. I carefully applied makeup; the final touch was a spritz of Ambush cologne and light pink "Barely There" Max Factor lip gloss. Aunt Reba, one of Mama's younger sisters, taught me how to play up my eyes and to use pastel lip hues in order not to attract attention to my mouth.

As I'd heard her often say, "Powder and paint make a woman what she ain't." Reba might've worn more makeup than most women in order to touch up the fading beauty of her youth, but she was still beautiful and glamorous. She was a woman accustomed to attention from the opposite sex, with her long, wavy auburn hair—color Mama said was "straight out of a bottle." She had a full figure accentuated by sexy dresses that caressed curves, and she wore high heels that showcased her shapely legs. She reminded me of Miss Kitty from one of my parents' favorite t.v. shows, *Gunsmoke*, but Reba was married and had two children. I'm not sure if the comparison was drawn due to the red hair and more than a spattering of makeup, or if it was because, according to Mama, they both knew their way around a bar.

In contrast, Mama dressed in a more practical manner and had only four or five "good" dresses. She usually didn't bother with makeup, and when she did it was a touch of rouge and lipstick and a drop of Avon's Honeysuckle cologne dabbed sparingly behind each ear. That hint of makeup and a home perm, combined with a strand of beads and matching earbobs, completed her simple, no frills style for Sunday church. And funerals.

But Aunt Reba's makeup case was a cornucopia of color, and on one of their visits her daughter Teresa and I had helped ourselves to all of those cosmetics. We loaded our eyes with Passionate Purple and Tantalizing Turquoise eye shadows. We hadn't spared the Radiant Rose blush and added several varieties of lipstick that included Chaste Cherry and Sexy Sunset. Our vibrant faces would have rivaled the brilliance of any baboon's ass or peacock ever housed at Grant Park Zoo. When a seven and ten year old finished with each other, we resembled miniature hookers more suited to a corner in Little Five Points instead of little girls in a sleepy town caught in a time warp. We also doused ourselves with her Chanel No.5 perfume, a scent that pervaded the house and made it easy for Reba to realize what we'd been up to. When she climbed the stairs and saw our garish faces, instead of scolding us she laughed until she cried.

I loved my flamboyant aunt and wanted to be just like her when I grew up. When I mentioned to Mama that when I was old enough I wanted to move to Atlanta and get a job like Reba so I could wear lots of makeup and fancy clothes, Mama's response was unwavering. "Like hell you will." Her tone confirmed her outrage. "I love my sister, but no daughter of mine is going to dress like a floozy and work in a bar!" As an afterthought, "Bless her heart."

Mama seemed to have forgotten Reba was a hostess, and occasional bartender, in an upscale restaurant in Atlanta and that she and her husband had invested in several lucrative rental properties. The point was immaterial because the discussion regarding my future career choice was over before it began. Thoughts of Aunt Reba dissolved as I felt the familiar pang of anxiety that came with facing the mirror.

My reflection in the mirror, my worst enemy second only to the camera, looked like any other teenager. Bell's palsy had lessened its grip, and it was not as noticeable that I talked from the left side of my mouth. Though my lips betrayed any attempts to form words that were not slightly askew. Then again, the glass image replicated a more or less normal appearance, even though my smile resolutely declined to comply with my will to curve evenly, to return to its dimpled, pre-palsy normalcy. I let out a habitual sigh of resignation and stared critically at the person who stared back at me.

Maybe the platforms would be a better choice that would add height to my five-foot, four-inch frame. Mama was always nagging me to eat more because I'd been a skinny child and was proving to be a thin teenager, although I'd developed curves. As I was in the middle of indecision about the shoes, I heard the beep of Beth's VW Beetle. Beth was the first to celebrate her sixteenth birthday and was the only one in our clique who had her driver's license and a car.

"There's Beth. Gotta run," I called out to my parents as I grabbed my purse, with the single "Double Shot of My Baby's Love" tucked safely in its sleeve, and hurried out the front door. The screened door banged behind me, and my feet skipped across the porch to the walkway. I slammed the lid closed on the silver Carroll Creamery cold box where the milkman delivered our milk twice a week and picked up the used bottles.

Love, Life, & Broken Rainbows

I loved the porch—with its robin's egg blue ceiling, white rocking chairs, and hanging baskets filled with brightly colored flowers that danced in the early evening breeze. Hummingbird feeders filled with sugar water waited for tiny, winged guests. Beautiful rose bushes sat in rows along the front of the porch railing. Red geraniums rested contentedly in large cement pots on either side of the steps, while marigolds and numerous multicolored petunias moseyed along the walk. Mama always had the prettiest flowers on the street. Everybody said so.

"Be careful and don't forget your curfew." Daddy's voice wafted over the wide wooden planks of the front porch that were replaced a couple of summers ago. When the workmen ripped up the old boards, they found two dust covered bottles of whiskey Daddy had hidden from Mama—back in his drinkin' days.

My curfew was eleven-thirty, thirty minutes later than usual because of the dance. I climbed into the cramped back seat of the Doodlebug and glanced at my watch; I would have less than four hours at the dance. The band was scheduled to start at eight o'clock. With any luck Barry wouldn't wait too late before making it to the dance.

"I see you changed your mind about what to wear," said Janet, seated next to me in the confinement of the undersized seat.

"Actually, I tried on several outfits and liked this one best." Janet and I had been friends since kindergarten, and I'd told her about the ring Debbie confiscated.

"It wouldn't have anything to do with that guy you met last year, would it? The one Debbie said will be there tonight."

"Maybe," I replied before falling into silence amidst their hyped up chatter. I needed the meditative stillness to calm my anticipation, but anticipation of what? Of a chance meeting with a guy I met for fifteen minutes over a year ago? Of the risk of being humiliated if I dared smile at him or, God forbid, laugh? Although the taunts of my classmates had all but subsided, I'd been emotionally traumatized. The insecurity I thought was buried began to surface and threatened to pull me into the familiar darkness of depression.

"Beth. Beth." I repeated myself several times before she heard me over the radio and lively conversation. "Please turn around and take me home. I'm sorry, but I'm very nauseous. Please take me home, and the three of you go without me." She continued to drive as I persisted, "Beth, I'm sick and need to go back home. Please."

Without even slowing down she glared at me in the rearview mirror and said, "No. Not this time, Sheila. We've been planning this night out for weeks, and it's not only about you tonight."

I was stunned. There was no more discussion of my feigned stomach upset, and before I was ready Beth pulled into the parking lot of the T-Burger on Maple Street, across the street from the dance location. She slipped the compact car into a parking spot and again found me in the mirror. "Now let's go in, and find a booth. We agreed to eat here before the dance. Remember, Sheila?"

We all climbed out of the VW and walked inside. Despite the crowd, we found a booth in the back of the restaurant, away from the blare of the jukebox and the Beach Boys' "Good Vibrations," and ordered burgers, fries, and Cokes. While we waited for our food Beth continued her speech. "We, the three of us, have stood by you for months. We've taken up for you, we've sat in your room and let you cry, we've listened to you feel sorry for yourself. We've been your friends, but it's time for you to get over yourself."

Her words were painful because the truth hurt. I remained silent, not sure what to say when Janet faced me and put in her two cents. "We all love you, and our hearts break for your circumstances. But you're not the only one who's had an unhappy sophomore year."

Her words held an underlying message and harsher than I intended I demanded, "What do you mean?"

She flung her long, dark hair over her shoulder before she explained, "Look at me. Do you really think I *want* to wear this pancake makeup? I have to get up thirty minutes early because I need the extra time to put on this 'mask'. This makeup is the only way to cover up my hideous acne. Nobody's complexion is as bad as mine."

"And what about Joan*?" Diane asked. She has to stand in front of the mirror and put on her mascara with a pair of crossed eyes staring back at her. I bet she's cried thousands of tears and would give anything to have healthy, normal eyes."

It was Beth's turn. "You have silky, straight hair that Debbie would love to have instead of her frizzy, curly, red mess. How often has she been teased and called 'Little Orphan Annie'? And do you think the overweight girls enjoy being called 'fatso' or that the kids who wear glasses want to be called 'four eyes'?"

My friends pointed out what was right under my nose, and there was nothing that could justify my thoughtlessness. How could I have been so completely self-centered? What had happened to the bubbly, outgoing, funny teenager I'd been before I allowed Bell's palsy to consume me, define me? I was making myself miserable over something that couldn't be changed—and over a barrage of hateful remarks from a few insensitive classmates. I'd whined about not being able to try out for majorette when in my heart I knew I wouldn't have gotten to be one anyway.

Everyone in town attended the same school, and my friends and I were by no means white trash or riffraff. Nonetheless, cliques were well established, and we were effectively divided by our socioeconomic status. And we all knew it. While my family didn't live in poverty, there was a big, bold line between the "haves" and "have nots" that was drawn in elementary school. Those classmates, who had things I didn't even know to want, were the minority. Even so, peripheries were in place and with few exceptions, only those from the "right side of the tracks" were chosen as cheerleaders, majorettes, football captains, Homecoming Queen, etc.

The ponytailed server brought our meal and when she was out of earshot, I apologized. "I'm sorry. I didn't realize how my selfish behavior has affected all of you. I've been so busy feeling sorry for myself that I couldn't see anything beyond my own misery. Please forgive me. I can't pretend the paralysis doesn't matter, but I promise not to complain as much. Thanks for the kick in the ass I needed."

Immaturity and being the spoiled baby in a large family were my only excuses for not recognizing others' pain and my lack of compassion. For the first time in months I asked with sincerity, "So how are y'all?"

~

Janet, Diane, and I walked across the street to the Pow Wow room while Beth drove her VW over to find a parking spot. As soon as we were in earshot, we could hear Tommy Roe's, "Dizzy" pulsating from the DJ's record collection. Records would be our entertainment before the band took the stage. The parking lot was packed, and I glanced around the designated parking areas looking for Barry's car, although I had no idea what kind of car he drove.

Carrollton was a college town and plenty of older students hung out at the happening dance venue on Saturday nights, which made the "Under 21" stamped in bold, red letters across the top of my right hand necessary. Once inside I strained my eyes in the dim light looking for someone I hadn't seen in over a year. If Barry had gotten there before me, I didn't find him. I stopped searching and concentrated on the music, dancing, and keeping conversation, and my smile, to a minimum. It was almost ten o'clock before I accepted that he wasn't at the dance and was probably not coming. As we lined up for autographs from the Swingin' Medallions band members, I bumped into Debbie and immediately noticed that she was not wearing the ruby ring.

Pretending it didn't matter I asked, "Well, Debbie, did your new boyfriend show up to claim his ring?"

"Yes, but he couldn't stay. He said he had somewhere else to be. I gave him his ring and my phone number and he left."

"Did he ask for your number?"

"Not exactly, but you never know," she confessed with a shrug of her shoulders.

Barry had been there, and I'd missed him. I should have sat by the door instead of dancing. I handed my record to Debbie and asked her to please have it autographed because I was hot and needed some fresh air. I pushed through the crowd and made my way to the deck outside where my disappointment and I found a deserted spot by the railing. There was always a chance Barry and I would run across each other again sometime, but that possibility did nothing to ease the sting of not seeing him at the dance.

I brushed back tears and focused on the beauty of the night. A black velvet sky served as a backdrop for dazzling, infinite stars that hung like diamonds suspended in time. After dancing the Boogaloo, the Jerk, the Swim, and the Twist, the cool breeze was refreshing as it blew my shoulder length hair across my face. I pushed it away and heard someone ask, "Sheila, is that you?"

Startled by the vaguely familiar sound of that voice, I turned around and there he was. It was Barry, standing right in front of me. My heart began to beat double time, a sensation I'd experienced only once before. He was even more handsome than I remembered—raven black hair, brown eyes that seemed to smile even when he wasn't, and those broad shoulders that practically weakened my knees. He was wearing a pink, button collared shirt, sleeves rolled up and tucked neatly into a pair of black and white hounds tooth checked trousers with a cuff that brushed the top of black and white saddle oxfords. He was wearing the ruby ring.

"It is you. I was on my way to the parking lot when I happened to glance over my shoulder and saw a girl I hoped was you. Your hair is longer now."

"Yes, I've been letting my hair grow. I was tired of the short haircut, even though it was much easier to manage." *What was wrong with me?* Why was I standing there talking about my hair?

"I'm glad to see you again. I thought since that girl from Bremen agreed to meet me here to return my ring that maybe you would be here, too."

"Yes, I'm here with some friends. I didn't see you anywhere on the dance floor. Are you here alone?" My demeanor was casual, but I held my breath and waited for his answer.

He seemed embarrassed as he smiled a sparkling smile. "I'm not much of a dancer. I came to get my ring back from that red-haired girl and as soon as I did, I went to the pool hall to shoot a few games. No, I'm not on a date. I was going steady with a girl the night I saw you at that party. Do you remember? Anyway, a few months later she and I broke things off. I made a few trips to Bremen to look for you. I rode by the high school several afternoons, went to the show a couple of weekends, a ballgame or two, the Tastee Freeze and some other burger dive, Hamburger Haven. I even went to all the drugstores in town and sat at the counters drinking malts and Coke floats." His smile competed with the stars. "But I didn't run into you at any of those places, and because I didn't know your last name I couldn't ask around to find you. I finally gave up and decided you weren't really from Bremen."

Yes, I remembered our first meeting. While I'd anxiously searched for him among the faces on the dance floor, he was in the pool hall the whole time. It hadn't crossed my mind to check the pool hall located in the same complex; "nice girls" didn't hang out in pool halls. The idea of him running around Bremen searching for me while I was holed up in my room, a prison of my own making, broke the ice. Without thinking I laughed out loud.

"Wow. That must have been some dental emergency if you found a dentist to see you on a Saturday afternoon. Is everything okay?"

I was so happily surprised to see him I forgot to cover my mouth before the laughter sprang unobscured. His comment about the dentist, although completely innocent, was enough for me to frantically scan the area for the nearest ladies' room—an exit strategy which had been my MO for the past year. Before I could excuse myself, I recollected the advice from my friends earlier that evening. It was time to stop whining and accept what couldn't be changed, as hard as that would be. More importantly, I didn't want to run away, not that time.

"There was no dental crisis. This half smile is the result of Bell's palsy, a medical condition which involves an inner ear nerve and facial paralysis. It's not dangerous, and most everyone afflicted has a one hundred percent recovery, but about ten percent don't ever fully recover. Ten percent seems pretty small, unless you're part of that percentage. I've improved a lot and may continue to improve with time, but there's no guarantee it will ever be any better."

My pulse raced as I waited for him to say something, but he didn't say anything. Not one word as the minutes hung between us. I slung my purse strap over my shoulder and was about to make up an excuse to leave in order to spare him an awkward goodbye. And then he spoke, "Bummer. I'm sorry that happened to you, but I'm glad you're okay now."

"'Okay now'? Do you get that I'm not ever going to have a normal smile and that my words may not ever match my lips? The residual paralysis on the right side of my face is permanent."

With a shrug, he looked at me with nothing but kindness and sincerity in those beautiful brown eyes and said three words I would never forget: "I don't care."

Dumbfounded, I cautiously asked, "Are you sure it doesn't matter to you?"

"Not at all. Now that we've met again, I want to get to know you better. If your friends don't mind, how about walking across the street to the T-Burger with me for a milkshake or a cherry Coke? That is, if you want to come with me."

I was dimly aware of The Association's "Never My Love" playing in the background, as if the DJ had overheard our conversation and foresaw the future. I gave Barry a lopsided smile and answered, "Yes." A hundred times yes. I took his outstretched hand, and beneath a canopy of stars we stepped into the beginning of us.

*Name changed

CHAPTER 3

Young Love

THE ZOMBIES' "TIME of the Season" streamed from the eight track player on that Saturday morning, moving day. Even though the Cutlass was continuously in need of one repair job or another, it was paid for and we could play our favorite tapes when the radio refused to oblige. I pulled the car carefully into the narrow dirt driveway that begged for a new layer of gravel. My brand new husband was on his way, driving a borrowed truck loaded with used furniture scavenged from relatives and second-hand stores. Barry and I followed the path of the majority of young adults in our town: find a job, get married, and raise a family. College wasn't always an option. Most who were couples in high school married each other—all of my six siblings had married their high school sweethearts.

I climbed out of the car and ambled to the concrete walk to take in what would be our first home together. One of Mama's brothers, Carroll, who was named for Grandma Pearl's maiden name and for whom I was named, owned the rental house. At forty dollars a month, Mama suggested it as a place for Barry and me to "set up housekeeping."

We agreed and began married life in a small, white house with redwood shutters and several wide steps that led from the walk to a square porch, also concrete and painted redwood. The risers on each side of the steps were large enough to accommodate flower pots filled with colorful geraniums or petunias, and azaleas would be perfect planted by the porch. Several huge oak trees held arms filled with leaves that would provide much needed shade in the summer as there was no air conditioner.

I followed the steps inside where there was a living room, a bedroom with one tiny closet, a kitchen, and a very small bathroom with a huge claw tub that claimed most of the limited floor space. There was an enclosed back porch with hook-ups for a washer and dryer—if we'd owned those appliances. For the time being the coin operated washers at Scrub-a-Dub-Duds and a clothes line would have to suffice. That was fine with me; I grew up wearing clothes scented with fresh air and sunshine.

My brief tour was finished when I heard the slap of the screened door. Footsteps announced that Barry was standing behind me. He wrapped his arms around me, brushed his lips across the back of my neck, and said, "Welcome home. It's not much, but it's all we can afford right now. We can paint the kitchen cabinets whatever color you like, put down a new linoleum rug, and cover the old wooden floors with carpet rugs. Maybe in a year or two, we'll be able to buy a home of our own, something with more room, a nicer place—"

I interrupted his apology, "It's perfect. Absolutely perfect." And it was.

It wasn't always easy, but we eventually adjusted to married life. However, a young couple who married for love was not nearly as gossip worthy as a "had to" marriage. I didn't doubt the town's busybodies counted months on their fingers and waited for time to confirm there was a bun in the oven. Estelle*, one of our neighbors, was especially vigilant. She kept up with everybody in town as if their business was her business and didn't hesitate to share what she knew, or thought she knew. Estelle wore thick-lensed glasses, kept her hair in a tight bun encircled with a scarf that matched her capris, and thrived on dirty laundry. Mama said our nosy neighbor gossiped because any woman who had time to iron her bed sheets had way-y-y-y too much time on her hands—and Estelle ought to sweep the dirt off her own front porch. Despite the tongue waggin' and speculation, the calendar delivered only disappointment. Barry and I were young and in love and impulsive. But we weren't expecting a baby.

Despite that fact, the meddlers agreed that our teenaged marriage would never last and gave us a snowball's chance in hell. The odds were against us, but the meddlers had underestimated the strength and depth of our love. Nevertheless, our marriage came with the disadvantage of youth, and we were gullible enough to believe "love conquers all." Additionally, I was spoiled and had to grow up before maturity and I had time to become acquainted. Barry worked while I was still in high school, and there was by no means enough money. Living on love proved to be a metaphor that was a rude awakening.

Mostly we lived on cheap meals. Although Mama tried to teach me, I hadn't been interested in learning to cook, As a result, our meals weren't the most delectable. There were burned chickens, squishy pasta, soggy mashed potatoes, undercooked beans, overcooked macaroni and cheese, and biscuits that could easily have been used as hockey pucks. Barry good-naturedly ate whatever I served without complaining. Bless him.

Despite our circumstances we managed to pay the bills and buy groceries, but there was very little left over for luxuries such as new clothes or going to the movies or eating out. Though we rarely fought there were a few arguments, mostly about money. Those arguments were followed by incredible make-up sex and the promise to not ever fight again. It was an impossible promise to keep as we maneuvered the landmine of compromise.

Then one day Janet gave me a new outlook on my marital relationship. Barry and mine's petty arguing and efforts to make ends meet were, in the great big scheme of things, not that bad. My friend's dilemma turned out to be much more serious than ours.

Our conversation began casually enough. "So how's married life?" Janet asked. She and I were sitting in mismatched vinyl chairs at the kitchen table, each enjoying a glass of tea—sweet and iced, of course. The monotonous hum of the window fan stirred warm air.

"Good. Sometimes hard, but I love him with all my heart and don't regret marrying young. I'm sure like most everybody else, we would have gotten married after graduation anyway. Things will be easier when I'm able to find a job."

Janet nervously tapped her fingers on the red and white Formica tabletop before she replied, "You two were destined to be together from the first time you met, and I'm happy for both of you. Y'all are like that Sonny and Cher song, 'I Got You Babe.' You know, poor as a church mouse but head over heels in love. I thought I was in love." She stared blankly out the window. "At least you were able to get a prescription for the Pill because you're married."

The "Pill" was an effective birth control method approved a few years ago and was available by prescription for women who were either eighteen or married. The drug had been credited with aiding the promiscuity of the Sexual Revolution. Thankfully, such contraceptive wasn't around during Mama's reproductive years. Otherwise, the last four of us seven kids might not have been born. As she'd made clear, "Honey, when I had three babies in diapers, if there'd been a pill that could have kept me from gettin' pregnant again, I would have eaten those things like popcorn. I was just grateful when we could afford a television." Mama wasn't one for sugar-coatin'.

My attention had drifted when I was caught off guard by Janet's unpredicted segue, but I picked up my end of the conversation. "Well, yes, thank goodness my doctor didn't hesitate to give me the prescription now that I'm a married woman. There's nothing like a newlywed pregnancy to give the town's busybodies something to talk about."

"Wish it was that easy for us single, underage girls. Sex for us means a condom, every time, or the risk of pregnancy. Or, as Miss Habersham had preached freshman year, 'ABSTINENCE'!" She laughed, but there was an undertone of resentment in her voice.

"Janet, you seem worried and slightly out of sorts. Is there anything you need to talk about?"

There was a long pause followed by an even longer sigh. "Yes, there is. I think I'm pregnant. There, it's out. Except for John*, you're the only person I've told and only because we've been best friends since kindergarten and have shared plenty of secrets. I trust you not to say anything, and when you tell Barry tell him not to say anything, either."

"Oh." Her bombshell made Neil Armstrong's first steps on the moon last year, which Barry's granddaddy swore was a hoax, seem insignificant. I didn't know what to say and waited for her to continue. But she seemed to be lost in thought.

There was a lull in the conversation as I stared at the red brick pattern of the linoleum rug and recalled something Aunt Reba had said the afternoon she stopped by with a wedding gift. She propped herself in the doorway while Barry and I were replacing the old kitchen rug. We chitchatted briefly before she tossed her deep auburn tresses over her shoulder, smiled, and winked at me. "You know, Sheila, that new rug and your new husband have something in common. If you lay 'em right the first time, you can walk all over both of 'em for a lot of years." Her contagious laughter had filled the room with mischief. Lost in unrelated thoughts, I was startled when Janet spoke.

"John won't return my calls. Can you believe that? We've been going steady for the past year and now that it's very likely we've made a baby, he won't even speak to me."

I could believe it. John wasn't my favorite person. I suspected he was using Janet for a dependable date, always at his convenience. I realized it was for sex as well and asked, "Are you sure you're pregnant?"

"My period is over three weeks late, and I'm always as regular as clockwork. And...John and I were careless more than once."

I laid a sympathetic hand on her forearm. "I'm sorry. I hate to ask, but when are you going to tell your mama?" Janet's mama was the receptionist at the Allstate Insurance Agency and knew practically everybody in town. She'd certainly been guilty of her share of gossiping, but the shoe wasn't going to fit as well when it was on the other foot. She was not going to take the news that her unwed, teenage daughter was pregnant calmly. Neither would Janet's strict, tyrannical dad who sold cars at the local Ford dealership. My heart ached for her and I wished I could help my friend, but I had no idea what to do. And the baby's daddy was apparently missing in action.

"Oh, I don't know. Maybe tomorrow, to get it over with. This is not going away, and time will definitely tell. Do you remember when Bonnie* got pregnant and was able to hide it for the whole nine months because she was plump anyway? Her mama took her to the doctor when Bonnie was doubled over with stomach pains. The minute the doctor declared that Bonnie was in labor, her mama hit the floor like a rock, passed out cold." Janet raised an eyebrow and declared, "*That* will be Mama's reaction. She may kill me or throw me out of the house. Or send me to my grandmother's in North Carolina and force me to give the baby up for adoption. Anyway, I would like to talk to John before I tell my parents. With any luck he will want to get married."

I was pretty sure the jackass wouldn't be interested in marrying his knocked up girlfriend—given that the jerk hadn't even bothered to return her phone calls since hearing that Janet was pregnant. But I kept my opinion to myself and asked, "Do you want me to try? Maybe he'll take my call, and I can tell him how important it is that he calls you."

"No, thanks. I'll eventually get in touch with him, even if I have to drive to his house and beat on the door. Stickin' his head in the sand is not going to make this problem disappear. And whether he likes it or not, we're in this mess together."

"Okay." I didn't have anything to add to the conversation and remained silent, but I thought about the high school's bad asses. They were a group of girls who hung out at the campus smokestack with the "hoods" and were known for drinking and sleeping around. Most everybody steered clear of them; they were commonly known as "the whores." Our mamas had taught us the old adage that "birds of a feather flock together." We figured those girls must've always had condoms in their purses because, as far as we knew, none of them had ever gotten pregnant. But "good girls" like us didn't have to worry about an unwanted pregnancy because good girls didn't put out—until we did.

Janet gazed down at her hands and began to fidget. With a wry laugh, "All kidding aside, you know my parents will throw me out for this. Guess I can live in the street."

It wasn't as if Janet was the first of our classmates to find herself in the same predicament. Several had had a shotgun wedding, and several of them had given birth out of wedlock and either kept their babies or gave them up. However, Janet's social climbing parents cared about what people thought of them more than they should have. They would most likely toss their daughter out of the house for disgracing them with her "immoral" behavior. They were, after all, pillars of the community.

I offered what I could. "Listen, our house is small, but if that's what happens you can sleep on the couch. We'll get a portable closet for your things and manage until you figure out what to do. Things will work out."

She interrupted my improvised plan, "I appreciate the offer, but it's not fair for me to crash on the two of you. You're cramped for space as it is. I don't know yet what I'm going to do, but I do know I want my baby. I've already been thinking about what he or she will look like and making a list of names."

Her shoulders were burdened with gloom, and I hugged her tightly before I walked her to the door and down the steps. It was the weekend, and I wondered if Janet would find the courage to tell her parents about the pregnancy. I shared her secret pain with Barry, and he agreed with my opinion of John as a jackass.

˜

Janet gave me a ride to and from school each day because Barry needed the car to drive to work, but she didn't pick me up on Monday morning. Or Tuesday. Or Wednesday. It was not a problem to walk the few blocks to school, but I was worried about my friend and why she'd been out of school for the past few days. When I called to check on her I was told by Sandra*, her mama, that Janet had the flu and couldn't talk to anyone. After a couple more absences from school, I drove the few miles to her house as soon as Barry got home with the car.

Sandra, bleached blonde hair, five o'clock cocktail in hand, answered my knock and repeated that Janet had the flu and was not feeling well enough for visitors. I didn't believe her and pushed my way past her, calling Janet's name. And then I saw it. The *New York Times* had been tossed on the coffee table like the newspaper belonged there, which it definitely did not. It took a moment before I comprehended the significance of the *Times*, and it smacked me in the face. Abortion was legal in New York. Rumor was that termination of an unplanned pregnancy had been the option for at least one of our classmates. I hurried upstairs to Janet's bedroom. Her mother's voice followed, "I did what was best for her."

I stopped in my infuriated tracks and hurled over my shoulder, "No, you did what was best for *you!*"

I knocked on Janet's bedroom but didn't wait for a response before I entered. The room was darkened by drawn shades, and she was huddled on the bed in the fetal position. She moaned when I turned on the lamp and gently touched her shoulder. She slowly sat up, brushed her hair back, and faced me. I was heartbroken at the sight of her red, swollen eyes. I pulled my childhood friend into my arms and rocked her as she sobbed uncontrollably and repeated, "I wanted my baby. I wanted my baby."

Janet survived the decision that had been made for her. She left town as soon as she graduated high school and never looked back. As for myself, I would never forget the traumatic aftermath of that heart wrenching experience. As painful as it had been to see my dear friend suffer her loss, that experience made my news two years later even more of a blessing.

*Name changed

CHAPTER 4

Baby Made Three—and Four

"I'll tell you when you get here. No, I don't want to tell you over the phone," I answered Barry's questions at the receptionist's desk where she sat listening.

We had only one car, and he'd dropped me off at the doctor's office on his lunch break. He couldn't stay because he had to return to work but managed to get off early so he could pick me up when I called him. I waited outside in the early August heat that waved above hot asphalt. I hoped Barry would be as excited as I was when I told him we were having a baby. I suffered migraines from birth control pills, and my gynecologist recommended I stop them for a few months and use condoms in the meantime.

The side effects had disappeared after a few weeks and rather than go back on birth control, Barry and I made the decision that we were ready to start our family. Granted, youth and naïveté were not our best guides in the decision making process. We ignored the voice of reason because we very much wanted a baby. Fortunately, we had the foresight to purchase health insurance that included maternity benefits.

I heard the horn beep and looked up, shielding my eyes against the bright sun, and saw him parking the car and running towards me. "Hi, babe. How are you? What did the doctor say? When are you due? Do you need anything?" His anxious questions made me smile—and love him even more.

"I'm good. Ecstatic. The baby, he or she, is due the first of May. I don't have another appointment for a month, but I need to get a prescription filled for prenatal vitamins."

Barry and I held hands as we walked to the car. He'd bought an old Chevy truck a few weeks ago that waited for repairs until we could afford the parts. Eventually, he would be able to drive the truck to work, and I would have the car as transportation for me and we could stop coordinating schedules. In addition to a second vehicle, we would need a larger place to live.

I was young, healthy, and happily pregnant as Barry and I searched for a new home, although I was reluctant to leave our picture perfect cottage. I wanted to find room for the baby in order to stay there, but there wasn't any extra space. We continued house hunting until we found a three bedroom, white, frame house with forest green shutters. The house rested close to a busy street in town, and we would have to fence in the shady backyard when our baby became a toddler. But the house—with its pine paneled walls and hardwood floors—would comfortably hold our family as two became three. Most importantly, I would be able to stay home with our baby. Although the mortgage loan of twelve thousand dollars came with affordable monthly payments, the hundred and fifteen dollar payment was almost three times what our rent had been. At least property taxes and homeowner's insurance were included.

We spent months working on the house and putting together a nursery; Mama bought a cradle as soon as she found out her baby was expecting a baby. Our nest was ready well before my due date. The finishing touch to our preparations came late one afternoon when I heard Barry's truck pull into the driveway. My heart jumped, as it always did when he came home, and I went out to greet him.

"I have a surprise," he said smiling as he stepped out of the truck. "Look what I traded for today."

I followed his gaze and saw a white washer and an avocado green dryer on the back of the truck, strapped down with ropes. He was tickled pink with his gift. "They're used, but they both work, and I got a good deal. I did some work on a man's car in exchange for the set. I'll get the hand trucks out of the garage and get 'em unloaded and hooked up for you."

Although disposable diapers were available, we wouldn't be able to afford that luxury. I smiled because most women wouldn't consider something as utilitarian as a washer and dryer the most romantic gift. But to a woman expecting her first child and who was plenty tired of draggin' clothes to the Wishy Washy Laundromat, those mismatched appliances were more romantic than all the roses in the Petal Pushers Flower Shop. We were blissfully happy as we anxiously awaited the birth of our son.

We were pretty sure of the baby's sex because my Great Aunt Lou predicted the baby was a boy. She was ninety years old and had outlived three husbands, but she hadn't had children. However, she was a midwife in her younger days and had delivered dozens of babies in rural Carroll County. She was always right when it came to telling an expectant mother the sex of her baby. Aunt Lou could also conjure warts and make them disappear, but Mama said that didn't make her a witch. Not even a witch could have foretold our upcoming dilemma.

When I was in my eighth month I got a call from our insurance agent who was reviewing the backdated claims from my obstetrician's office. Donald hated to have to inform me that our policy had to be in effect for a minimum of three months before conception. He'd checked the calendar and if the baby was born before the fifteenth of May, our insurance wouldn't cover any maternity expenses. The guidelines specifically stated that we were required to be covered for one full year in order to claim maternity benefits. Barry and I had evidently failed to read the fine print when we purchased the health insurance policy.

Of course, our baby boy, Brad, was born when he was ready to enter our lives—two weeks before the insurance would have paid the bills. But as I held my newborn son, with dark brown eyes like his dad's, I was overcome with emotion; medical bills were the last thing on my mind. Barry gently kissed my forehead and wiped away happy tears. I don't know where he found money for the dozen pink roses he sent to the hospital because such nonessentials were not in our budget. Except that it was one of those rare occasions when a woman needed what she didn't need.

While we were both overjoyed with our baby, we had to be realistic about the immediate problem of no insurance and how we were going to pay the medical bills. Per our insurance policy agreement, we were responsible for all medical expenses, expenses our monthly budget couldn't accommodate. I'd already quit my job, and we'd agreed that we wouldn't put our baby in daycare. Cutting corners was everyday territory, but when it seemed our belts couldn't be tightened anymore, I found a note on the windshield of the Camaro that was parked at the Piggly Wiggly while I shopped. I stashed the groceries in the trunk and settled the baby before reading the scribbled note. Someone wanted to buy the car, and the price offered would cover the unexpected medical bills with enough left to pay cash for some kind of a car.

Still, I was reluctant to give the note of interest to my husband. He'd been so proud the day he bought the car, and it was more than being able to afford the car—it was the car itself. It was a used 1969 Camaro SS convertible, the Indy pace car for that year, white with orange stripes, orange and black hounds tooth interior. The car was beautiful and much nicer than the beat up Olds Cutlass we had as newlyweds. Although it wasn't a very practical car for a baby, Barry loved that car.

We made decisions together, therefore, I told him about the stranger's interest. "There was a note left on the car when I was buying groceries. A man wants to buy the Camaro and made an offer. He left a phone number in case you're interested in selling it."

He read the slip of paper I handed him. After a few minutes he said, "It's a good offer. The car is worth about twelve hundred dollars, and this guy is offering eighteen hundred. If we take the offer it'll be enough to finish paying the doctor and the four hundred, sixty dollar hospital bill. There will be enough left to buy another car, something more practical. I might be able to get a deal on a good car that needs a little work."

I didn't answer and cleared the table while Barry fed our infant son his nighttime bottle. After putting the baby to bed, I walked outside to the small patio off the kitchen and sat down in the canopied lawn swing. Chattering squirrels chased each other in the large water oak that would hand us a mountain of leaves to be raked and burned in the fall. I noticed the fading raspberry colored blooms from the cheerful tulip tree and glanced absently at the sun as it kissed another day goodbye. Dusk relaxed into a lavender ambience, and the air was fresh with the renewal of spring and held the sweet perfume of honeysuckles.

The katydids had just begun their nightly serenade when I heard the bang of the screened door. I waited for Barry to sit down next to me before I spoke, "I understand selling the Camaro is the practical thing to do, but you love that car. I can find another job when the baby is older, or I can ask Mama and—"

"No. You and our baby are my responsibility, and I don't want you to worry. Besides, it's just a car." He put his arm around my shoulder and pulled me close. "What I love are you and our son. I'm going to call tomorrow and accept the offer. We need a family car, and I'll start checking around for a used car in good condition or one I can fix up for not much money."

I kissed his cheek and told him what he already knew. "I love you."

We learned from experience and had insurance coverage when our second son was born. We thought it would be nice to have a daughter, but as Aunt Lou accurately predicted we were blessed with another beautiful, healthy boy. For the second time I held wonder and love in my arms, our new bundle of joy, Chuck.

Despite the demands of a toddler and a colicky newborn on different schedules, I was a happy stay-at-home mom. I was the antithesis of the second wave feminism movement that continued from the sixties. Symbolism aside, what woman in her right mind would burn a perfectly good bra? Hell, I only had three or four and one of them had seen better days. No thank you, Gloria Steinem. My choice was to be a "traditional" wife and mother.

But Mama hadn't had a choice. She worked out of necessity and had missed most of her children's school plays, parties, spelling bees, and PTA meetings. As a result I had very much wanted a mama like those from the popular t.v. shows I'd watched as a child, such as *Leave It to Beaver* and *Father Knows Best*. Those perfect, fictional characters were my misguided role models.

Though I quickly figured out being a full-time mom wasn't nearly as easy as those t.v. moms had made it seem. They were always all dressed up, complete with lace trimmed aprons and a string of pearls that hung beneath flawlessly made-up faces with every hair in place—even when they were doing menial household chores. Most days it was all I could do to shower and wash my short, Dorothy Hamill haircut. And I never once saw June Clever or Margaret Anderson slip on a melting Popsicle and slide across her kitchen floor like a greased pig. Nor did their children throw themselves on the floor screamin' and kickin' like a turtle on its back. I'd found the best strategy for a two year old's tantrum was to step over said child and pay no attention to his fit flingin'.

Neither of those make-believe husbands ever stepped on a Matchbox car at three a.m. and let out a stream of curse words that made me glad the kids were asleep. Being a real full-time housewife and mama wasn't always easy, and some days were longer than others. I couldn't imagine how Mama and millions of other women managed a job outside the home in addition to taking care of children and domestic chores. I was thankful that I didn't have to juggle that balancing act. Although we didn't have money for luxuries because our budget was tighter than Dick's hatband, we considered ourselves blessed. Barry worked to support our family, and I savored time with our sons.

On sunny mornings we often left the swing set and sandbox filled with Tonka trucks and walked to the library, which had replaced the old elementary school. The kids enjoyed movie day or story time, and I enjoyed the walk with the baby in the stroller and my three year old riding his training wheeled bike or Big Wheel, serenading us with Glen Campbell's "Rhinestone Cowboy." Sometimes the boys and I treated ourselves to ice cream from the Triangle, a small grocery store that relaxed on a triangular plot of land between the Methodist church and the funeral home and was on our route. A few months ago the owner, George, had done what any one of us had wanted to do at one time or another. He'd pulled out his gun and shot a train.

The incident happened when a train had stretched itself lazily across all of the railroad crossings in the middle of town and lay there like a snake in the sun. The train hadn't flinched when it was hit with the bullet, but George was fined by the railroad company. Talk was he might've had a few nips—or was off his rocker. But George wasn't crazy, not when you considered the varying branches of crazy that could be found in most any family tree, including my own. I don't mean axe-wielding Lizzie Borden or psychopathic Charles Manson crazy. I'm referring to those who were a tad "off," a few cards shy of a full deck. One of several examples was Grandma Pearl. She never went *anywhere* without her pocketbook hooked in the crook of her elbow and was prone to trance-like "spells." However, she and George were harmless, even if he was inclined to occasional fits of impatience, which didn't deter me from stopping by his store.

Sometimes the kids and I detoured from the Triangle and followed the sidewalk downtown, lured by fragrant temptations from the bakery where we enjoyed freshly glazed donuts or a delicious warm-from-the-oven cookie. We leisurely strolled along the cement trail that led past Sam's Barber Shop with its white, red, and blue striped pole that twisted in perpetual motion—and where a flock of retired men gathered like magpies to discuss local politics or hash over the latest gossip. Right next door was the shoe repair shop, and a man could leave his shoes to be re-soled while he got a haircut, unless Mr. Whitton was too busy for same day service.

We ambled past the drugstores that included soda fountains in each of them, the Empire 5&10 and its variety of wares, the shoe stores that displayed feetless footwear, and several clothing stores. On the corner in the middle of town was the Commercial & Exchange Bank where droves stood in line and took care of banking business on payday Friday. The two story building was formerly the Haralson Hotel, and when I was a child several of us had played in the elevator until the manager ran us off. Most of the businesses were the same stores of my childhood where Mama had shopped and where friends and I had enjoyed icy, salty lemon sours and bought candy lipsticks or candy cigarettes for a nickel a box. As the sidewalk curved past one of two jewelry stores, I was reminded that every Friday night after Thanksgiving the high school's band and chorus commandeered the small parking lot to perform Christmas carols which entertained the crowd before Santa arrived atop the firetruck and tossed out candy.

Our lives were busy and happy. Days tumbled like dime store dominos into years filled with babies and first steps and toddlers and bedtime stories and laughter and chasing "flutterbys" and first day of school tears—mine, not theirs. There were birthday parties with cakes that ranged from circus trains to camouflage, complete with a chocolate chip mountain. Halloween costumes included the standard ghosts, cowboys, and Superman to the weirdly funny Kooky Spooks with colored face makeup and inflatable alien heads that tied under the chin. Annual pictures with Santa where secret wishes were whispered in his ear brought squeals of delight on Christmas mornings, thanks to Santa and his Sears credit card.

Our kids also loved animals. Therefore, added to our family were various pets because children always *promised* to take care of them, and they did for about two weeks. Included in our menagerie was a velvety, white bunny left by the Easter Bunny one year because sometimes the Easter Bunny screwed up. The boys named their new pet Mr. Rabbit, and he lived in a large box in the laundry room until he was big enough to climb out, hide under our bed, and scare me half to death. He was moved to a cage behind the garage until he outgrew that. Eventually, after Barry secured the small open gaps in the fenced backyard, the large rabbit lived there 'til the day the neighbor's child accidently left the gate open, and Mr. Rabbit made his getaway. And the neighbor's dog promptly enjoyed fresh rabbit for lunch. His death was hard on all of us, especially the boys. We couldn't even have a proper funeral for him because, well, other than the poof of a tail, there wasn't anything left to bury. Most days didn't hold the drama of losing a beloved pet.

Bremen was a comfortable little pond for a few big fish, and life happened at a simpler, slower pace. It was a contented town in which to live, our very own "Mayberry." I appreciated that my sons would grow up wrapped safely in the arms of that continuity of innocence. Despite the previous decade's restless demands for change that altered acceptance of what had long been accepted, Bremen had pretty much remained the same during the tumultuous sixties. The status quo continued as usual in our small town during the seventies. We weren't exactly Woodstock.

The seventies was the decade that not only gave Barry and me two sons but was host to the Watergate political scandal that led to the resignation of President Richard Nixon, higher gas prices and shortages, and an end to the Vietnam War, although not to the hostility towards returning vets. Abortion was legalized throughout the country as a result of the Supreme Court's Roe v. Wade decision in 1973; however, the dispute between pro-life and pro-choice advocates was far from over. In 1976 Jimmy Carter, Georgia's governor, was elected as President of the United States.

Like most decades the seventies was a unique time capsule. Tupperware was king and sales parties were an almost weekly event. Housewives were convinced they couldn't manage without the organization brought by sealable, plastic containers that came in all shapes and sizes and would last forever. Other trends included disco music, hot pants, Candies shoes, and mood rings. Four-year-old Brad and I loved the movie *Star Wars*, but I wasn't certain it would be everybody's cup of tea. On the contrary, the movie's universal theme of good vs. evil that took place "in a galaxy far, far away" combined with awesome special effects to make it a pop culture megahit.

But not everything was all the rage. Along with the ridiculous Pet Rock, another less popular, short lived fad in the seventies was "Streakers" who often eluded capture as they ran buck naked in public venues. For those men who preferred to remain dressed, fashion for men rebelled against formality as evidenced by the popularity of the more casual polyester leisure suit, with its four pocketed jacket. The suits were available in an assortment of colors, including salmon, baby blue, and mint green; many were manufactured in Bremen. Fabric from around the world was transformed into suits, sports coats, dress slacks, and shirts that were shipped throughout the country. As we were the "Clothing Center of the South," most residents were employed in the various clothing factories where sewing machines hummed like busy bumblebees.

However, Barry worked for a local mechanic shop because that was where his experience led—and where somebody always had a used vehicle for sale. We sold our older, yellow with wood grain station wagon and bought a newer model, although used, light blue van. It was a customized van with diamond cutout windows in the back corners, floor-to-ceiling blue shag carpeting, and four comfortable captain's chairs. If there were four adults who needed the seats, we threw a couple of bean bags into the back for the kids.

On summer afternoons I loaded the boys into the van, and we spent many lazy hours enjoying picnics at Tanner's Beach or at city pool where I swam through childhood summers. We kept the van for practical reasons, but eventually we purchased our first, brand new vehicle. Barry chose a blue and orange, limited edition Jeep, a 1979 CJ-5 right off the showroom floor. The Jeep was more for fun and family outings than anything else but proved to be serviceable on more than one occasion.

⁓

One winter a rare snowstorm left behind three inches of snow that covered a thin sheet of ice like a white blanket, and the Jeep was our only mode of transportation. We, along with my cousin Cathy and her husband Bill, piled into the four wheel drive Jeep with our two young boys and the rarely used Radio Flyer sled. We agreed the deserted, slopped high school parking lot would be a perfect place for sledding. Besides, hospital hill, a popular place to play on snow days, would be too crowded with kids using everything from sleds, trash can lids, and plastic wading pools in their race downhill. Brad was excited about the outing and was bundled up to the point that he resembled the Michelin tire man. Chuck was too young for sledding and was left snuggled in the warmth of my mama's arms with his "bestest" books. They had plans to make chocolate teacakes, my favorite second only to her sweet potato cobbler.

While the five of us carefully made our way a block down the road, Brad pleaded to be first to ride the sled. I agreed—because what could possibly go wrong? Barry put him on the wooden sled, flat on his stomach, and showed him how to steer the sled left to right. Suddenly, I had a flashback to the day I'd wanted to be the first one to jump off the house with Daddy's oversized umbrella after a bunch of us kids had seen the movie, *Mary Poppins*. Contrary to my expectations, I didn't float daintily to where my friends anxiously waited. Instead, the umbrella turned inside out, and I hit the ground like a cement block. Friends and cousins gathered round, and one of them asked, "Do you think she's dead?"

Clarity hit like a bolt of lightning, and I yelled out in caution. But before he heard me, Barry gave the sled a gentle push. I would like to blame the incident on our lack of sledding experience, but it immediately became apparent that we, as parents, had done something stupid. Really stupid. Our child was speeding downhill, alone on a sled that flew over the snow and ice.

As the sled gained momentum Cathy asked, "Does he know how to stop that thing?"

I pushed panic out of my voice and faltered, "He knows how to ride a bicycle without training wheels."

Her sarcasm confirmed that my reply was absurd. "Oh, well, then stopping a sled racing out of control on an asphalt slope layered with snow and ice should be a piece of cake."

We stood with our feet frozen in place, like human sculptures against the wintry landscape, and watched as the metal runners continued to gain speed with our five year old hangin' on for what appeared to be dear life. All we could see were his red snow boots that bobbed and dangled from the sled. Barry was the first to catapult into action, making his way toward the runaway sled as it approached the pine trees laden with ice and the street on the other side of the ditch. Due to the condition of the roads, no other idiots attempted to maneuver the hilly, dangerous streets, so dread of Brad being hit by a car was not one of our concerns.

But we were terrified of an impending crash. The three of us followed Barry across a parking lot that was slicker than owl's shit and struggled not to fall on our asses. Amazingly, the sled missed the trees, jumped the ditch, slid across the street, continued over the sidewalk to the gym, missing the posts that supported the awning, and came to an anticlimactic halt at the athletic field house. Barry and I reached our laughing son as he hopped off the sled and begged for another turn. I hated to poop in his Easter basket, but there was no way that wild ride was gonna happen again.

Cold and tired of snowball fights and pulling Brad around on the sled, we returned to pick up Chuck. Mama welcomed us with homemade vegetable soup, hot cornbread, and teacakes. I cautioned the others not to mention our what-could-have-been a serious error in judgment to Mama. I was afraid she would take my children away from me.

Six Flags, Grant Park Zoo, Stone Mountain, and hiking at nearby Cheaha Park were occasional day trips. When we could afford a vacation the first choice our budget would permit was the white, sandy shore of Panama City Beach, Florida. Although the movie *Jaws* had scared the shit out of me, I loved those carefree trips to the seashore. We spent hours building sand castles and playing in the surf. Our two little boys were toasted brown by the sun until they resembled a couple of Pop-Tarts. One summer we took a "magical" vacation to Disney World where Brad got to ride Space Mountain—whether he wanted to or not.

After countless commercials promoting the roller coaster, listening to him beg for months and then for more than five hundred miles his, "I can't wait to ride Space Mountain," we waited in line for more than two hours. But when it was our turn to board, Brad sat down like a donkey and refused to climb in. In my son's defense, the t.v. ads that revealed the "mountain's" dark interior that simulated a ride through a night sky filled with stars, planets, and spaceships appeared to be more fun than scary. The real thing was frightening, but with an annoyed sigh Barry picked up our son, put him in the "rocket" with us, fastened the seat belt, and told him to enjoy the ride. I was sure Brad wouldn't forget the lesson to be careful what he asked for. He sure as hell wouldn't ever forget Space Mountain.

But life was a roller coaster, and change was a given. We were due for another change that affected our lives in a positive way. One night after tee ball practice, homework, and baths, Barry sat down at the kitchen table while I put away the dishes. He wanted to discuss a business offer he'd been made. There was a local oil company that owned a service station in town, in a prime location. The company needed someone to take over the station from the prior owner who was retiring at the end of the month.

I pulled out a chair, sat down at the table, and listened as Barry began his rationale. "We'll have to take out a bank loan for the equipment and stock, but in the long run I believe opening my own business is the best solution for us. I've thought it over from every angle, and I'm a good mechanic. With gas sales, I'm sure I can make an already good business more profitable. You've said, several times, that we're gonna need a bigger house soon. The boys are almost seven and four, and Brad wants a place to ride his minibike without you having to load it in the van and take it to the dirt track over at the elementary school." He made his final point. "We can't move to a nicer house in a better neighborhood for the kids unless I can make more money."

I hated the added responsibility of another monthly payment, but Barry was certain the offer was the right thing for our family. I hesitated before I replied, "I know you think this is a huge opportunity, but I'm worried about borrowing more money. We're finally in a good place, a place where the bills are paid, household expenses are not a worry, and we have a small amount left over for a few extras and for our meager savings account. At last we're taking two steps forward and only one step back."

I wanted to snatch those words back when I recognized the look in his eyes. The look that meant even though it was something he wanted, he wouldn't pursue the venture unless we were in agreement.

How could I not agree when he worked hard and had always provided for his family? With a leap of faith we gave up the security of a weekly paycheck and jumped into our own business. The mutual decision was a good one. As our younger son would be attending preschool, it was time for me to go back to work full-time.

Mama was retired and babysat while I worked as a part-time substitute teacher. I had my foot in the door and was fortunate to be hired as an assistant in the library at the high school. Jim, a former football coach for Bremen High School, was the principal and recommended me for the job. He was a good, down-to-earth man who didn't tap dance around situations. I once overheard him tell an irate mother that contrary to her belief that her son could do no wrong, there was only one "perfect" son and He had died on the cross for all of us—even her and her not-so-perfect son.

Jim's wife was just as outspoken and could come off as abrasive and bossy. Emily could best be described as the uncompromising Ouiser Boudreaux from the movie *Steel Magnolias*, played by Shirley MacLaine. Both that character and Emily had a good heart wrapped in barbed wire. Despite the differences in our ages and backgrounds, Emily and I fell into an unlikely friendship.

She proved to be a friend through rain and shine, and our friendship was an unexpected bonus to a paltry salary. But additional benefits that included health insurance and a schedule that matched that of the boys compensated for my skimpy paycheck. The timing couldn't have been better because we were ready for a new home. We found that home in a pleasant, reasonably priced suburb, Treetop.

CHAPTER 5

Boys Will Be Boys

It was mid-August, and I didn't need a weatherman to convince me that 1980 was one of the hottest summers on record. Barry and I were standing in the driveway of our new home, and despite the lazy breeze it was hotter than a whore house on dollar night. We were able to afford the house because we used the equity from the sale of our smaller house as a down payment, even though interest rates for a mortgage were at a record high due to runaway inflation. The bigger house wasn't the two-story Cape Cod with a bay window that would have been my first choice, but the one big attraction was that it fit our budget. The house met three of our requirements: a big yard, a full basement, and a large family room with a fireplace.

Treetop was a subdivision a couple of miles from town where the houses were similar but not the cookie cutter dwellings of the post WWII era. Those prefabricated cutouts were planted like fields of cotton, row after row, in suburbs of large cities to meet the demands of returning vets and economic growth. They were the homes where "Rosie the Riveter" had hung up her hard hat and donned an apron, an apron that didn't fit well for some of those women. Thousands of women picked up the slack while husbands fought in the war. Thus, many experienced their first taste of independence provided by their hard earned paychecks, and some were reluctant to return to the hearth. Their dissatisfaction led many of them to cry foul and had sown the seeds of change.

Barry disrupted my contemplations when he put his arm around my shoulders. "Welcome home, babe. I'm gonna need to buy a riding lawn mower to keep this big yard cut. Wish there weren't as many pine trees to cut around, but we can use the straw as mulch for the shrubs and islands. Think you'll be happy here?"

I brushed my short, tousled, and sweat-drenched hair away from my face. "Yes, it's a nice place to live, a good neighborhood for raising children. Anyway, it's not forever. One day, when the kids are grown, we're going to build that cabin on a lake somewhere. But for now it's exactly what we need. Central air conditioning will be a luxury!" We'd not ever had central air—or heat.

Barry was right about the trees, but their shade couldn't buffer hundred degree temperatures. There were plenty of them, mostly tall pines that swayed as one. I surveyed the neat houses and well-kept lawns; kids rode bikes and ran through water sprinklers, dogs barked. The images seemed idyllic and "Norman Rockwellish" on the surface. But I wondered what secrets remained hidden behind each of Treetop's smiling doors. Even in our small town, some skeletons in the closet stayed in the closet. There was really no need in confronting family problems when it was often better to let sleeping dogs lie. And nobody wanted to open Pandora's Box and reveal the goings-on of Bremen's very own *Peyton Place*.

In spite of my speculation that all might not be as it appeared in our town or the neighborhood, many of the neighbors were in our age group, with children approximately the ages of our boys. Treetop was reminiscent of the neighborhood where I'd grown up, where kids rode bicycles, played freeze tag or hide and seek until the street lights came on and signaled us to go home. Another plus in our decision was the open field located across the road from the neighborhood's entrance, complete with trails and a creek where the boys and their new friends could ride their three wheelers and dirt bikes. "Plus" may have been subjective.

Barry grew up with and around dirt bikes and motorcycles, and he saw no reason for our sons not to have one, as long as they wore a helmet and didn't ride alone. Brad loved his dirt bike, but Chuck was more comfortable on a three wheeler. Within a few weeks they were allowed to cross the main road to the welcoming arms of wide opened spaces. There were some minor accidents, but nothing more serious than a few stitches and a broken arm. Once, after days of heavy rain, Brad thought he was Evel Knievel and could jump a large mud pit. He couldn't. His new dirt bike was buried so deeply that the only way he and his dad found it was when the sun glinted off the chrome front brakes handle. Sometimes my boys came home completely covered in red mud and resembled swamp monsters.

With friends who also had motorized toys, the boys spent countless hours exploring the terrain, climbing hills, and plowing through the creek. When a half dozen or more of them rode together they rumbled through the neighborhood like pint-sized Hells Angels. While the riders were not nearly as loud or rambunctious as the Hells Angels gang, they made enough noise to awaken sleeping babies and, therefore, endeared themselves to several mothers.

But there were no complaints as we settled into our new home. It took weeks for me to adjust to the silence that fell in the middle of the night, especially the lack of the beckoning wail of trains which could be heard only on very still, cold nights. Trains were a constant in Bremen and having never lived anywhere except town, their lonesome horns were ingrained in my soul. As children my friends and I had sat on the bench at the train depot and made grandiose plans for all the places we would go when we grew up.

I was fascinated by the windows of nameless faces traveling on Amtrak and fabricated stories about where they were from and where their travels would take them as they clickety-clacked along the tracks. My knowledge of travel had been limited to summer vacations at nearby destinations such as Panama City or the Smokey Mountains of Tennessee and those every other summer trips to Texas to visit Daddy's relatives. I planned to one day escape the boundaries of my childhood and venture into the unfamiliar, to experience life outside of a fish bowl. I'd envied those fortunate travelers who rode the rails or utilized Greyhound. They used the corner bus stop only to get a bite to eat and to stretch their legs before they continued on their journeys, what I imagined to be exciting journeys that didn't end in Bremen.

While the bus station and train depot were long gone, I—like George Bailey from *It's a Wonderful Life*—remained firmly planted in my hometown. The unexpected fairy tale of falling completely and hopelessly in love had changed everything, including my perception of the life I wanted. I realized Dorothy was right, "There's no place like home." Even if that home was not yet fully furnished and held a couple of empty rooms that begged for furniture.

The house was larger, and we didn't have enough furniture to complete the living room and dining room. Although we had a small dinette that fit perfectly in the breakfast nook, I was anxious to buy a set for the dining room and found one at It's a Suite Deal furniture store. I started dropping hints well before Christmas and making comments referencing exactly which dining room set I wanted. On Christmas Eve I waited expectantly all day for the delivery truck that didn't come.

Christmas Day was always filled with predawn shrieks of glee, followed by big family dinners at our parents' homes and a cacophony of commotion as gifts were exchanged among family members. Hence, Barry and I began a tradition of exchanging our gifts early. On Christmas morning he handed me a small silver box with red curly ribbons, and I was convinced it was an elaborately wrapped check for the dining room set. But when I opened the box I blinked twice as the solitaire diamond ring, snuggled in its bed of deep blue velvet, blinked back.

"Oh, Barry, it's gorgeous. It's…it's a complete surprise."

"Good. I wanted to surprise you." He took my hands in his and kissed my fingertips. "I didn't have enough money to give you a diamond ring when we married, and you've not ever complained about the cheap, plain wedding band that was all I could afford. You're long overdue a diamond ring."

His dark brown gaze still melted my heart, and after a long, lingering kiss he slipped the ring on my finger. I'd never felt more cherished and completely forgot about the more practical dining room set. Though I felt somewhat less cherished a few months later when Barry brought home another surprise that wasn't nearly as nice as the ring had been.

I was loading the dishwasher when I heard a motorcycle pull into our driveway. The horn beeped a few times, and I tried to remember who we knew that drove a motorcycle. I pushed "start" on the dishwasher and moseyed outside to find my husband straddling a red Honda Shadow 1100, smiling like he'd won the state lottery.

"What do you think? Do you like it?"

Hesitantly, I asked, "Does it really matter whether I like it or not?"

"Well, considering I just bought it, I would like for you to like it. It's not a Harley, which I will own one day before I die, but I got it for less than book value. One of my customers lost his job and was in a bind."

"You bought a motorcycle without discussing it with me?" I couldn't believe he would spend that amount of money without talking to me first. We'd always made decisions together, especially with all big purchases. For him to blow several thousand dollars before we'd carefully considered spending any extra money threw me for a loop.

Sensing that I was not as thrilled as he was, he chose his words carefully. "Okay, I should have talked it over with you first, but the guy needed cash and was going to move on to the next interested buyer. It's a good deal, and I could sell it tomorrow and make a few hundred dollars. You know I wouldn't have bought a bike if we couldn't afford it. C'mon, it's a great afternoon for a ride."

I stood in the sunshine, hands defiantly on my hips. I was angry about the motorcycle, and when he offered me a helmet and told me to climb on I didn't budge. "No, I don't want to ride. We should have talked it over before you bought a motorcycle."

He knew from my tone that I was mad, but he didn't bother to mince words. "I get that you're pissed off, but let's be fair about this. I work hard to take care of you and the boys, and this bike is something I wanted. Let me remind you that I pay the mortgage, my truck and your car payments, all utilities, taxes and insurance, and I buy the groceries every week. If you need extra money for you or the boys, I don't argue or question you about it. So, Smurf feet, you can keep that fine ass of yours on your shoulders, or you can park it on the back of this motorcycle and enjoy a ride with me. You're wearing jeans, but since you've got on flip flops we'll make it a short ride to town and back." He smiled coaxingly. "C'mon."

I stared down at my flip flop clad feet and was glad to see the color was fading. A few days ago the toilet in the boys' bathroom had overflowed, and by the time I figured out there was a shut off valve on the back of the commode, I was ankle deep in blue water. Dark blue water to be exact. The Ty-D-Bowl cobalt cleansing fluid that kept the toilet fresh had burst and dumped its contents into water that was swimming out of the bowl and onto the tiled floor. The dye stained my feet a deep shade of blue, hence "Smurf feet." The three males with whom I lived had found the whole incident very funny. Barry interrupted my analysis of the blue feet condition. "Sheila, did you hear me?"

As I considered my decision Mama's voice wandered by on legs from my childhood. "Don't cut off your nose to spite your face, Missy."

I'd been a stubborn child and the adage not to cut off one's nose to spite one's face was a hard lesson for me to learn, but I'd finally grasped the concept. I briefly pondered my limited options. I wavered for another minute or two before I replied, "Yes, I heard you." And with a smile, "Sure hope my helmet fits."

Home truly was wherever family was together, a place where the ups and downs of life happened and where boys grew like weeds. Barry didn't worry about the lawn because he said we were raising boys, not grass. Depending on the season our yard was used as a baseball field, a football field, or a place to pitch a tent for campouts. And on those rare, enchanted snow days, the slope from front yard to back became a place to sled until frozen noses and toes demanded the warmth of hot chocolate by the fire.

One such winter day in January of '86, there was a NASA tragedy when the space shuttle *Challenger* exploded a few seconds after launch. Christa McAuliffe, the first teacher in space, was among the seven astronauts who lost their lives that day. The boys and I were home enjoying the gift of a snow day and watched the live broadcast, along with most everybody else in America. Our country was collectively shaken and mourned the loss together.

Usually there was no television because the power went out if there was snow or ice or the wind blew too hard. Firewood was brought in; blankets, lanterns, and flashlights were retrieved. Many hours were spent by a cracklin' fire playing cards and board games. Thus, home was also the place where memories were made, but not all memories would be pleasant ones. Raising boys proved to be a learning experience, with a steep learning curve.

Chuck was five years old, a plump child who very much resembled Adam Rich, the youngest character of the eight children on the popular t.v. series *Eight Is Enough*. On a typical sweltering summer day I noticed my younger son scratching his privates and walking like a bow-legged cowboy. I took him into the bathroom to assess the problem. His privates were indeed red and irritated. I reached for my "go to" solution, a spray bottle of Bactine, which I applied to the area. What happened next shocked us both. Chuck screamed, yanked up his shorts, and ran out the back door like a fire had been lit under his ass—which, maybe, there had been.

With twenty-twenty hindsight I realized Bactine wasn't the best choice for whatever was going on with my son's business. Apparently, when a boy's scrotum was on fire, his instinct was to run. And run he did, like a bat outta hell. For a chubby kid, he could move faster than I would have bet. It took several minutes for me to corral him in a tub of cool water before I called his dad to discuss the mystery condition.

I relayed what had transpired, and Barry was, surprisingly, mortified at what I'd done. "Why didn't you just throw kerosene on his privates and light a match? The poor kid has jock itch, which as a matter of fact I had when I was about his age. What were you thinkin'?"

"What was I thinkin'? I was thinking I didn't have a hint in hell what was wrong with him. And since I was a scrawny *girl* child, jock itch was not a problem."

"Okay, you didn't intentionally light him up. I'm about to close the shop and head home. I'll stop by the drugstore and pick up a can of what you should have used."

Chuck was, understandably, a bit skittish when his dad got near his privates with the appropriate remedy. He wore the expression of a cornered squirrel as Barry coaxed him into letting him apply the soothing spray. Thankfully, the rash healed in a few days.

My son survived my sketchy nursing skills. And I learned a valuable lesson: Bactine was not a cure-all. My discoveries in raising boys continued as the kids grew, as did the scope of my education.

Springtime and baseball were old friends, and Brad was excited to be assigned the position of catcher on the team. As we were leaving the practice field, his coach called out, "Don't forget Brad will need a sports cup. Have his dad pick one up before tomorrow's practice."

Barry would be at work until after six, and Sports WearHouse would be closed; anyway, it was on our way home. The boys and I entered the store and greeted Marty, the owner and a former classmate of mine, "Hi, Marty. I thought we had all the equipment we needed, but Brad's coach said we should pick up a sports cup. He's the catcher this year. If you'll show us where they're located, he can pick out the team he wants."

Turning to face my older son, I reminded him not to choose a popular team. "Don't pick the Atlanta Braves because most of the boys will get that one, and there's no tellin' whose cup you'll be drinkin' out of. It's bad enough I have to worry about head lice, what with y'all passing the battin' helmet around like yesterday's news."

Chuck was pilfering around the store and, for whatever reason, Brad took my instruction about selecting a cup as his cue to disappear among the neatly arranged gloves and bats that waited patiently for the right boy or girl. Marty was doing a piss poor job of suppressing his laughter before he spoke, "Sheila, a sports cup is not something you drink from."

I stared blankly at him. "Then why does he need one?"

"Didn't you say he's the team's catcher? Well, he's gonna be in a squatting position directly behind home plate, you know, where the ball will be thrown to the batter."

The brief pit stop was taking longer than I expected, and I didn't have time to fiddle-fart around. Still not following his line of reasoning I said impatiently, "I do know something about baseball. The boys have been playing since they were old enough for tee ball." I purposely glanced at my watch. "What's your point?"

He was beginning to seem slightly uncomfortable as he continued to convey his advice regarding the sports cup. "Let's review. Your son will be in a squat, legs apart, glove in hand, waiting for a speeding baseball. Should that baseball miss both the bat and the glove, there's a chance it could hit..."

Ouch. The light came on as I connected the dots and comprehended the importance of a sports cup. I made the "one-size-fits-all" purchase and thought maybe his dad should have taken him. Be that as it may, Barry was absolutely the one to handle the looming fire fiasco.

It was an ordinary Saturday afternoon, summer in the suburbs. The smell of freshly cut grass combined with the scent of burgers on charcoal grills as lawns were mowed and dads flipped lunch. Kids were playing ball or cooling off in wading pools—or setting the woods on fire. We'd barely finished lunch when the doorbell rang repeatedly, with a sense of urgency that irritably demanded to be answered. I opened the back door to find a sweaty, out of breath, disheveled nine year old Eddie* standing on the carport anxiously wringing his hands. His freckles popped almost in 3D in sharp contrast against his pale face. Between gulps of air Eddie managed to say, "Oh, hi. Can you *please* tell my dad I've been at your house playing with Chuck? If he asks tell him we were playing in the basement, you know, because it's so hot outside."

He had evidently thought his story through on his sprint up the street from his house to ours. I didn't interrupt as he continued, "Maybe you can tell him that me and Chuck were playing with the Hot Wheels track or the GI Joe stuff or Pac Man or Frogger on Atari or any other game inside. You know, because it's so hot outside," he repeated nervously.

I was about to ask him why he needed an alibi when I heard the shriek of sirens. I scooted past Eddie and ran out to the driveway, saw the billows of smoke coming from the wooded area at the end of the street, and shouted for Barry. He, followed by Brad, Chuck, and Eddie, came rushing around me. Barry jumped in his truck and squealed out of the driveway, right behind the firetruck that wheeled its way into Treetop. He knew it would take several men to control the blaze because, unfortunately, that wasn't our first neighborhood fire.

With a sigh I looked at Eddie, who had a penchant for matches, and asked, "What happened this time?" Although an explanation wasn't really necessary. He'd set their kitchen on fire when he attempted to burn the trash while it was still in the trash can. Then there was the campfire that had blazed rampantly because neither Eddie nor Chuck considered the danger of building a campfire next to the woods, in the middle of a drought. I was relieved Chuck was not his accomplice on that particular day as the weary firetruck lumbered back to the station. Little wonder that each summer Eddie's mama and I registered our boys for rec baseball, swimming lessons at the city pool, and every Vacation Bible School in town. But if it wasn't the fire, there was always something else that kept us on our toes.

Such as the morning I forgot Barry's old work truck was parked parallel in the driveway, a few yards behind my car. In my haste to get the boys to school and myself to work I rammed the rear fender of that Mercury Cougar into the passenger door with such force that it caved in the truck door and rattled my teeth. For a few seconds the boys looked like Bobbleheads. We were okay, but the passenger door on the truck remained stubbornly in the closed position, and Barry said it wasn't worth fixin'.

As luck had it the truck door wasn't completely locked into place, as we found out a few weeks later when Barry and Brad went to cut a load of firewood. Barry came into the house wearing a panic-stricken face; he was as white as a ghost. When I questioned him about what happened, he mumbled that he'd thrown Brad out of the truck. I let a frustrated sigh escape, but I couldn't very well damn the man—not when I'd been tempted, on more than one occasion, to toss the kids out of the car myself.

However, Barry had actually, although unintentionally, flung Brad out of the truck when he made a left turn. The crushed truck door swung open, and Brad skimmed butt first across the ditch like a flat rock on a calm lake. Barry said he'd jumped out of the truck while it was still in motion and rescued our uninjured son. Thank goodness the truck had veered off the edge of the road and was stopped by a small pine tree. Brad was on the driveway shooting hoops and acted as if nothing out of the ordinary had happened. Children were amazingly resilient.

~

There was no denying that children were also mischievous, and ours were no exception. One day they shouted for me to hurry downstairs when they'd laid a large, rubber snake on the bottom step. Twice Barry had found a lifelike, plastic tarantula in his tool box. Another of their pranks took place the night Barry and I had gone out for dinner and a movie. When we returned home my niece Kim, our teenage babysitter, and her anger were waiting for us. Her dark brown eyes flashed with indignation as she yanked open the back door. We were barely in the house when she pounced like a tiger.

"Don't dial my number again, and I mean it this time. The last time I babysat your two hooligans, they tied my boyfriend to a post in the basement where he stayed until I got back with the pizza and heard him yellin' for help. But this stunt was worse. Much worse. I've had it with those boys. The little shits were laughing their asses off while I was hopin' I wasn't having a heart attack. I thought they'd blown up the damn house. No, don't ever call me. You couldn't pay my enough to babysit them again."

She hadn't even paused for a breath. Exasperation was scrawled across her face in red as she grabbed her keys and peeled out of the driveway. My children could sometimes be a handful. But in their defense when two young boys holding a rope had innocently asked Kim's sixteen-year-old boyfriend if he wanted to play a game, well, he really should have seen that one coming. Through her latest explicative tirade and careful interrogation of my "hooligans," I was able to piece together the events of their most recent escapade.

Love, Life, & Broken Rainbows

Kim had assumed the boys were tucked in and sleeping and decided a make-out session in front of the fire with her boyfriend would be very romantic. However, the boys weren't asleep. With the stealth of Navy Seals our nine and six year old sons had slinked on their bellies, undetected in the darkened room, to the fireplace. They tossed in an entire pack of Black Cat firecrackers leftover from their Fourth of July stash. Needless to say the rat-a-tat-tat machine gun sound of firecrackers exploding in a confined space put an abrupt end to the couple's canoodling—and to Kim's babysitting services.

But in a blink there was no need for a babysitter; their teenage years snatched them from childhood. Dukes of Hazards figures and cars, GI Joe, He-Man, and Star Wars collections were packed away and forgotten. Dirt bikes were eventually abandoned for trucks. And the "I'm *never* going to like girls" pledge of their grade school days was replaced with girlfriends. Additional fears were added to my inventory of worry when they each reached sixteen. I'm not sure if it was the fact they were driving or the fact they were dating that scared me the most. There were a lot of "easy" girls out there, and I cautioned each son to have enough self-respect to not sleep around. Barry was more realistic and instructed them to always wear a condom, which was how I learned the meaning of "wear a raincoat."

It could have been that Emily had the best advice for sons. "Tell them not to get crazy the first time they get laid because we all have one and it won't ever wear out. And I don't give a rat's ass what girl they're screwin' as long as they know she doesn't have a monopoly on the booty market." Emily had a way with words and expressed her opinion on everything—whether you wanted it or not.

Yet her well intentioned advice usually cut to the chase, and as a teacher she knew the workings of adolescence. She reminded me that nobody's children were perfect. Although several of their mamas thought the sun rose and sat on her child's ass. I, however, wasn't one of those mamas, and I'd never once uttered the words "my child won't ever…" Because sometimes my child had, and I had learned to pick my battles. Even so, there were some challenging, even rebellious ordeals that pushed Barry and mine's patience to the limit.

At sixteen Brad was picked up by the local police one night for trespassing on city property, a minor offense, when he and some friends were at the construction site of the new recreation department. The boys laid odds as to which one of them had a truck that could climb to the top of a large hill that dared them to try. Brad had to call his dad from the police station…but he'd made it to the top.

Our first experience with direct disobedience, that we knew of, came when Chuck was fifteen and was grounded for missing curfew no less than a half a dozen times. However, Chuck had already made Saturday night plans with friends before his detention was levied. Too bad. We told him he would have to cancel those plans.

Chuck's solution to his "mean and unfair" parents was to wait until we were in bed, sneak out of his bedroom window, and hitch a ride with a friend who waited on the corner. Several days of rain had transformed familiar dirt trails into mud pits that beckoned all four-wheel drive trucks to come out and play. From our bedroom we heard Chuck's window open, heard his breakout when he fell into the shrubbery, and heard the loud truck his friend drove as it squealed out of the neighborhood. It didn't help the escapee that his friend's jacked up truck had spotlights that crouched across the exterior of the cab like a row of prison search lights. Houdini he was not.

I was furious and ran around like a chicken with its head cut off. I was ready to get dressed, track down my youngest offspring, and drag him home by his ears. Barry convinced me to calm down and not to launch a manhunt—and climbed into Chuck's bed to wait for him to sneak back in the window. That episode convinced me that God programmed us parents to fall completely in love with our babies so we would hold onto that love when those adorable babies became not quite as adorable teenagers. And then they were teenagers no more.

I discovered that raising children meant having to let go while wanting to hold on. Barry and I had done our best in guiding our sons as they navigated their way towards manhood. Regardless of the difficulties that were inevitable in childrearing, the love, laughter, and happiness they brought to our lives far outweighed the minor misadventures. Without a doubt, raising our boys was a wonderful, unpredictable, ride. And we considered ourselves fortunate to have been along for that ride—a ride that ended much too soon.

*Name changed

Part Two

"The web of our life is of a mingled yarn, good and ill together."

WILLIAM SHAKESPEARE

CHAPTER 6

There Must've Been a Mistake

It was a late November afternoon in 1995, the Monday after Thanksgiving. The sky was a cloudless, deep blue, and the air was brisk. Although most of the leaves had succumbed to the inevitable, those remaining clung tightly and wore their brilliant oranges, reds, and yellows in defiance of the approaching winter. The sun was beginning its descent into the horizon, taking any semblance of warmth along with it. I pulled my jacket closer as we walked arm-in-arm from the parking lot towards the medical building for the follow-up appointment. There was no foreboding of what was awaiting us, no premonition that warned me to run. Or had I ignored the secret whispered among rustling leaves as they tumbled along our path and crunched in harmony with our steps?

Although Barry and I were apprehensive about last week's biopsy results, we were confident nothing serious would disrupt our hectic, happy lives. If anything, this would be nothing more than a minor bump in the road, a slight detour to be traveled together. We shared the good times and bad. Our marriage hadn't been a bed of roses, but neither had it been littered with thorns.

We arrived a few minutes early for our rescheduled five-thirty appointment. The perfectly groomed receptionist who had called and asked us to come in later showed us immediately to an exam room to wait for the doctor. Walls of stark whiteness were interrupted only by the soothing pastels of a Monet print. Barry and I discussed holiday plans and Christmas shopping to be done, small talk to fill the wait. A purple dusk peeped through the half opened blind that covered a grimy, fourth floor window.

Our laughter over some shared memory, one of many after more than twenty-five years of marriage, was interrupted by a knock, followed by the sharp click of the door as the doctor stepped in to invade our cocoon. Dr. Seeman was wearing the standard issue, impeccable, white lab coat, his name embroidered over the left pocket, and a stethoscope that doubled as a necktie. He held a thick folder in his hand. His dark eyes met my gaze with an expression I couldn't read, an expression that gave my heart cause to beat slightly faster— as if it already knew the impending outcome of the biopsy.

He closed the door behind him, shook hands with my husband, and addressed us both in his best bedside manner voice, "You are my last appointment of the day. We have plenty of time to discuss options."

The small room became smaller, and the air was heavy with dreaded anticipation. I couldn't breathe. In that moment, in the harsh glare of fluorescent lighting, I understood fully that our lives had changed forever.

CHAPTER 7

Wake Me Up, Please

My husband was the first to speak, "I'm guessing the news you have to tell us is that the tumor in my stomach is cancer."

Dr. Seeman cleared his throat before he answered, "Yes, Barry, I'm afraid so. I suspected as much during the biopsy procedure, but there was no reason to ruin your Thanksgiving before the lab results confirmed the diagnosis."

"What's next? Will you be able to treat me?"

I was blindsided by the diagnosis and stammered, "I don't understand. How can the tumor be malignant? He hasn't even been sick. I admit he's lost weight, but he's been trying to lose a few pounds." I could feel the panic rising, along with the escalating tone of my voice.

The doctor paused before he continued, "He's lost weight because the cancer formed a constricting ring around his stomach, which made it difficult for him to eat more than a few ounces of food at any one meal. The tumor is localized at the GI junction and is approximately the size of a small fist. The pain he has been experiencing is the result of the tumor pressing against nearby lymph nodes."

I stared at my husband. "Pain? What pain? Why didn't you tell me you were in pain? Why didn't you tell me you couldn't eat a full meal?"

Barry recognized by my tears and near hysteria that I was on the verge of a total meltdown and tried to calm me. "Sheila, it will be alright. I didn't think much about not eating more because I've been dieting and figured my stomach shrunk. As for the pain, I didn't want you to worry unless there was a reason to worry. Since I was due for a complete physical, I decided to wait and find out what the doctor had to say before I complained."

He was being his usual, calm, logical self, but had I known he was in pain, I would have scheduled the physical sooner. Dr. Gordon, who ordered the upper GI, could have found the source of the pain and referred Barry to Dr. Seeman. The biopsy could have been done weeks ago, but instead he'd waited in order to spare me worry. I'd loved him for so very long, since high school. Why hadn't I realized he was suffering? Why hadn't I noticed he'd lost too much weight in only a few months? How had I missed his symptoms? Those questions were painful to contemplate.

Barry continued with his reassurance. "Dr. Seeman will take good care of me. I'll be fine." He lifted up my chin and looked into my eyes in an effort to soothe me. "Everything will be okay."

"Actually," Dr. Seeman interrupted, focusing his attention on my husband, "I'm going to recommend a surgeon at Crawford Long in Atlanta."

"Why? I trust you to take care of me." Barry was more coherent than I was.

"That's exactly why I'm referring you to Dr. Miller. As a gastroenterologist my treatment is limited when it comes to malignant tumors, and your cancer is very aggressive. The sooner treatment is begun, the better your chances. Dr. Miller is the only surgeon in the Southeast who has the necessary experience and has, in fact, devised a surgical technique for successfully removing this type of tumor. He may, however, refer you to an oncologist first to review your file, and they could decide to begin the treatment regimen with chemotherapy."

That new information was almost too much for me to process, but I comprehended the urgency regarding treatment. "When can we schedule an appointment with the surgeon you're recommending?"

"I'll contact Dr. Miller's office, but they may already be gone for the day. If so, I'll have my receptionist call you first thing in the morning regarding an appointment. I've already discussed your case with him, and he's in agreement that we need to get the ball rolling as soon as possible. He will most likely want to see you tomorrow or the day after at the latest. Will either of those dates fit into your schedules?"

"Yea, Dr. Seeman, sure," mumbled Barry.

"Good. If you'll excuse me, I'll call Dr. Miller's office."

As soon as the door closed behind him, I wrapped my arms around my sweet husband and felt the rapid beat of his heart against my chest. Fear draped him in a cloak of pretense, and I was selfish in not realizing the impact the diagnosis had on him. All of our lives together he was the strong one, the one who took care of me and our sons. He was the one who always seemed to make the right decisions when my indecisiveness stalled our lives. Now it was my turn to be the stronger of the two, my turn to make decisions and take care of him. I prayed a silent prayer and asked God for strength and guidance, and held my husband closer.

"I love you," I murmured in his ear. "You're right. Everything will be fine."

In a matter of minutes Dr. Seeman returned and told us he was able to reach Dr. Miller's receptionist and that we were scheduled for nine a.m. day after tomorrow, on Wednesday. "You'll need to go to the hospital before the appointment to pick up the x-rays and pathologist's report. Dr. Miller asked that you bring them with you in order to save time, and there's no need in duplicating expensive tests. If it's more convenient you can stop by the hospital when you leave my office. The outpatient department has been notified to release the records to you. My receptionist has the directions and contact information for Dr. Miller's office that you can pick up on your way out. Do you have any other questions?"

I sat in a cloud of confusion and wanted to scream, *"Do we have any more questions?"* I had about a hundred more questions. For starters, how did cancer happen to someone like us? The scenario was dreamlike, as if this must be happening to someone else, that the test results had been mixed up, or that the doctor was holding another patient's file. It was true what people say, cancer was supposed to happen to *other* people. And yet, less than an hour ago *my* husband was diagnosed with the "Big C." I felt like I was going to either pass out or throw up, and I leaned on Barry as we walked out of the building.

～

We pulled into the well-lit parking lot of the hospital to pick up Barry's records, and he reached for the door handle. I put my hand on his arm and said, "I'll go. You wait in the car where it's warm." I kissed him on the cheek. "I'll be right back"

I grabbed my purse, hurried up the steps, and followed the signs to the designated area where the second shift clerk would have Barry's medical records. My mind was contesting the news, and I had to struggle against tears and what I was sure was an oncoming anxiety attack—although I hadn't ever actually experienced one. I passed a pay phone, paused, and retraced my steps to the phone. I didn't know if the echo was from the clicking of my boots on the tiled floor or from my pounding heart. I dug a quarter out of my purse and called one of my best friends, BJ, short for Betty Jane. The minute she answered the phone, words were replaced with gasps as I fought to control tears that loomed like Niagara Falls.

"Hello. Hello? Hello, is anyone there?"

She must've thought someone had dialed the wrong number when she heard my barely audible, "BJ. BJ, it's me, Sheila. Listen, I have only a few minutes. Barry is waiting in the car"

The tense, controlled distress in my voice let BJ know something was very wrong. "Sheila, what's wrong? What did the doctor say? Where are you?"

"Barry has cancer, and I can't talk to you or anyone else right now. He's in the car, waiting for me to pick up his medical records to take with us to Atlanta day after tomorrow, to our appointment with a surgeon, or maybe an oncologist. Or both."

"Oh, God, Sheila. What can I do? How can help?"

"Pray. And please call my sister Pat and let her know the diagnosis, but make it clear to her that I cannot discuss this situation now. I'm hanging on by a thread and can't handle explanations tonight. I'll have to call Barry's parents, but that can be put off until in the morning. Or maybe Barry can tell Carl and Melba. They have to be told." I'll talk to you and everyone else when I can, as soon as I'm able. I have to go. I'll be in touch soon. Thanks, BJ."

I didn't give her a chance to open the conversation as I replaced the receiver. I continued down the hallway in a surreal fog to retrieve his records that were ready for me when I arrived at the desk. I thanked the night clerk and made my way towards the exit. My next thought made me feel lightheaded. How was I going to tell our sons? Thankfully, they were young adults and old enough to grasp the seriousness of their dad's disease. I sighed heavily and felt I was having an out-of-body experience or a bad dream. But the huge manila envelopes in my hand confirmed that I wasn't having a nightmare, and I hurried to the car.

I wondered if Barry had spent the past fifteen minutes alone thinking about the cancer, growing inside him, taking his life away from him. He had to have known something was wrong with him. The fatigue, the weight loss that came much too easily, the pain in his stomach, the fact that he couldn't eat any more than a handful of food at any one meal—all symptoms he, we, had ignored. While he may not have been caught completely off guard by the diagnosis, hearing the word "cancer" must've hit him like a Mack truck.

Barry was my "one," and he loved me, had loved me unconditionally, almost from the first moment he saw me—as I had loved him. We were young, but he'd promised Daddy he would take good care of me, and he had kept that promise. But due to recent circumstances beyond our control we both had to accept the fact that he might not be able to take care of me for the rest of my life. I climbed into the car where I refused to let that thought, the one that lurked somewhere in the shadows, control my emotions. If I allowed that thought to surface, the one that he wouldn't live, then I would be lost. The very idea of a world without him was unimaginable, and I slammed the door on both the car and the notion.

"Ready to go? Are you hungry?" I asked, as if everything was still normal. We'd planned to have dinner out when we were finished with the doctor's appointment, but after hearing words we never thought we'd hear, neither of us had an appetite.

"I'd like to go home now, if that's okay with you," he said quietly.

"Alright. I'm ready to get home, too."

We rode in silence. I wanted to say something, but there were no words to be found. The radio was set to an oldies station, and The Associations' "Never My Love" floated from the dashboard. Our song. I snapped the radio off and fought back burning tears that would drown me if I let them. I couldn't listen to the song from our happy, healthy past when our path was paved with the shared dreams of youth and optimism. I was preoccupied with thoughts of cancer, an unwelcome hitchhiker.

A few miles from home Barry's memory was jogged, and he asked, "Hey, what about your class? Isn't your final on Wednesday night? Depending on how long we're in Atlanta and the traffic we may not be back in time, and I know it's important to you."

Important to me? That morning it had been important to me, but now my college class at the local university had dropped to the bottom of my list of priorities. I worked full-time and attended classes at night, as a part-time, "nontraditional" student, which was a more professional way of saying "older" student. I didn't have any particular goal other than to earn a degree and had made the decision a few years ago when our sons required less of my time.

Being employed at the high school proved to be the ideal environment for a college student; I had tutors for almost every subject. Carla dragged me kickin' and screamin' through my required math courses, and Carol was especially helpful with my major, history. My coworkers were also friends who were more than willing to offer their knowledgeable assistance. Additionally, the majority of my professors and my advisor were very supportive of my decision and encouraged me to excel as they guided me through an unfamiliar maze of academe.

But why was I burning the candle at both ends when I had no specific objective other than to graduate? Was it because I'd married while still in high school and had had no interest in college? Maybe that degree was important to me because I felt restless and needed something more, something for myself. Or it could have been that it took almost thirty years for the Women's Lib Movement to influence me. I could have wanted an education because I considered, as I'd done all those years ago, the sacrifices Mama had made growing up on a farm and later working in a factory while raising her seven children.

Or maybe it was because I was inspired by Reba McEntire's video "Is There Life Out There?" Whatever the motivation a degree was something I wanted, needed. Sometimes I had too many irons in the fire, but I flourished in college and was determined to graduate. Barry encouraged me one hundred percent. But I was so stressed and so busy that there wasn't time for one more damn thing—until that one more damn thing was cancer. Nothing else mattered.

"Sheila, are you listening?"

"Yes, I'm listening. The college class is the last thing on my mind, so you don't need to let it worry you. I'll call my professor tomorrow and explain the…the situation. Whether I attend the last class or not isn't important. As a matter of fact, I'm glad you brought up my college class. I'm going to make an appointment with the dean and find out what I need to do in order to take some time off, my last couple of quarters, without falling under new catalogue graduation requirements for my degree. I need a break."

"A semester off! Are you out of your mind? After all your hard work, hours at the library, weekends spent studying or writing papers. You're so close, two more quarters of Spanish, and you'll finally have the college degree you want. Sheila, what is the matter with you? Why would…" His voice trailed into the realization that I was doing this for him. Because a couple of hours ago we'd learned he had cancer. "Sheila, I don't want you to give up this dream, not for me, not because of the cancer. Please."

"I've already made up my mind. You're more important than anything else, and you and I are going to need every minute and every ounce of strength we have for whatever lies ahead. I can, and will, finish school when all of this is behind us, when you are cancer-free. No more discussion about this matter."

He realized my decision was not debatable and had often asked me if my middle name was "stubborn." Our chat was a short-lived reprieve from the cancer that should have been a mistake. Except that it wasn't.

~

We turned off the main road into our neighborhood, our home for the past fifteen years. As we pulled into the driveway I was relieved to see neither son's truck was there. I could postpone until morning the news that their dad had cancer. Once inside I threw my jacket onto the hall tree, walked into the den, and noticed the red message light on the overwhelmed answering machine that flashed impatiently. For some absurd reason the sixties song, "Western Union" by the band Five Americans, popped into my head. BJ had apparently done as I'd asked and notified several family members and friends of the news, like a telegram: "Barry has cancer. STOP. Not sure about prognosis. STOP. Will know more after Wednesday's appointment. STOP. Keep them in your prayers. END." Suddenly, I was mentally, emotionally, and physically exhausted; the messages would have to wait until tomorrow.

Barry was standing behind me and spoke softly, a whisper on the back of my neck. "I'm sorry. Sorry that I have cancer and that our lives have been turned upside down." He wrapped me in his arms and held me close. There, in the solace of his arms, the dam broke.

Between sobs, "Don't you dare apologize for the ugliness of cancer! But why us? Why did cancer find you? It's not fair! You, we, don't deserve this."

He pulled me closer, planted a kiss on my forehead, and tried to console me. "Sheila, nobody deserves cancer, and it didn't 'find' me. I'm not any better than the next man to be diagnosed with cancer. And you learned a long time ago that sometimes life's not fair. We've been in love since high school, and other than a few minor financial worries, life has been good. We've raised two healthy kids, we have a comfortable home, and until now, we haven't had any serious health problems." He wiped away my tears. "We're both tired and need to rest. Things will work out. They always do."

I looked into his beautiful brown eyes filled with love and knew that he was right. Nobody deserved cancer, and cancer made no discriminations. Up until then, life had been gentle with us. Entwined in each other's arms we walked to our bedroom and crawled under the comforter where his goodnight kiss made my heart race, even after all of our years together. Snuggled in our familiar spoon position, I tried to concentrate on the wall of shadowy tree branches that chased each other in moonlight that crept through the blinds—anything to distract me from thoughts of cancer. Tears and prayers silently filled my soul, and I was unable to escape my anxiety.

Barry's deep, even breathing assured me that he slept. But for me sleep was a stranger, and I lay awake long after the boys came home. My heart filled with dread, and the thought of telling them of the diagnosis made sleep impossible. When the house had settled into slumber, I slipped out of bed and into my flannel robe and fuzzy bedroom shoes. I padded quietly down the carpeted hallway and out the French doors to the porch.

I'd always found solitude on the screened porch, my favorite retreat. Liquid moonbeams poured through the screen and splashed across the wooden floor like spilled milk. I tried to relax on the chaise, but I wanted my mama and wrapped myself in the comforting warmth of the afghan she'd knitted for me. I was her baby, and even when I was forty she continued to refer to me as "my baby." I needed her to hold me and assure me that my husband would be alright and that this crisis would pass, but she'd died of a heart attack a few months ago. My broken heart had not yet healed, and fresh tears blurred the moonlight.

But my heart ached more for a husband with cancer. The possibility that I could lose him compelled me to recall memories from almost three decades ago. Although Barry and I grew up in separate towns less than twenty miles apart, it was fate that brought us together, a fate that began at a long ago party where our paths had first crossed. Warmed by the afghan and bathed in silver moonlight, I couldn't leave the porch—or the pages of our lives.

At seventeen Barry was estranged from his parents because he and his dad, who was in one of his unpredictable rages, had come to blows. As a consequence Barry was thrown out of the house to fend for himself. Fortunately, he was able to stay in a friend's parents' tiny garage apartment. But Carl hadn't allowed his son to take the turquoise '57 Chevrolet Bel Air that Barry worked on rebuilding, spending every spare minute and dollar in the process. It was a four in the floor, a Hurst shifter, which he patiently taught me to drive, although he had to replace the clutch two or three times.

That car had sentimental value to me because I'd lost my virginity cradled in the big, vinyl embrace of the '57's back seat. Barry and I usually made out at the drive-in, but on that moon-drenched night we parked on the ridge at Oak Mountain. We'd been going steady for almost a year and always stopped ourselves from going all the way. But our passionate kisses and gentle caresses passed the point of no return. We were seduced by the softness of an early spring evening, the air lush with the sweet, intoxicating fragrance of magnolias, and Bobby Vinton's velvety voice that slid one of his hits, "I Love How You Love Me," effortlessly from the radio—and we were horny as hell. Clearly, the heat of my ass had burned up my brain. Afterwards, Barry tenderly kissed away my tears as we clung to each other and promised we would never be apart.

But less than three weeks later our promise was threatened by the indifferent grip of the federal government's Selective Service System and its recruitment of eligible men. Barry's part-time job at a gas station became full-time after high school because college was not on the agenda. And neither was a student deferment from the military. Registration was required at age eighteen, and after compliance Barry waited for the inevitable. It was six months before the mandatory draft notice arrived, with the date and time he was to report to an army induction center in Atlanta. He dreaded telling me the news but broke it to me while we were sitting in the front seat of his red, 1964 Cutlass he was able to afford because it needed mechanical work he was able to do himself.

The car was a two door with bucket seats and a floor console with an automatic transmission, much easier for me to drive than a stick. We were parked next to an intercom at the A&W Drive-In where the carhop skated over with our frosty root beer floats. When he told me about the letter, I almost dumped the icy mug in my lap. In a lightening flash of fear I understood anti-patriotism: draft card burning protesters and deserters who fled to Canada in order to evade being sent against their will to fight a war that wasn't theirs to fight. No longer just a song on the radio, The Temptations' anti-Vietnam War soul song, "War," held new meaning. The lyrics hit home when the bodies of two of my high school's graduates were shipped home in boxes to devastated families. Would Barry be next? Inconceivably, the tentacles of Vietnam had reached across the North Pacific to the corners of the Deep South and found my heart.

There was nothing Barry could do except obey the summons. He rode a bus filled with other young men who were transported to a facility in Atlanta. I was waiting, pacing on the porch when he returned from a day spent being assessed by the military. As soon as I saw his car at the corner, I ran into the cool April rain to meet him at the curb. I was soaked and chilled to the bone, but I didn't care. He jumped out of the car, took me in his arms, and kissed me over and over. I feared the worst. When he let me go, he explained that he had no inkling he had hypertension. At first I hadn't comprehended the significance of high blood pressure, but his smile told me it would spare him from the hostile jungles of Southeast Asia. I thanked God that Barry's blood wouldn't be mingled with the red stain of thousands who had fought and died, by choice or by force, in a war that divided our country.

Rain, relief, and love washed over us and between kisses, he asked me to marry him. He held me close and whispered that he'd wanted to ask me the minute he received the notification, but didn't think it would have been fair, in case he didn't make it back home. I shuddered at the thought and although I was still in high school, I didn't hesitate to accept Barry's marriage proposal. I couldn't have turned down his promise to love me longer than forever, not when I loved him so much it ached to be away from him. We eloped and were married in a courthouse in a neighboring state. Strangers were our witnesses as his high school class ring was replaced with a simple, inexpensive wedding band.

That chapter was written long ago by teenagers in love. Our marriage vows had since sat on a shelf for many years, collecting dust like faded, forgotten photographs. But our love had been strong enough to beat the odds that most teenaged marriages ended in divorce. In retrospect, the "poorer" promise wasn't all that bad. We had everything we needed, with a few "wants" sprinkled in.

My stroll down memory lane was halted by barking dogs. The moon hid behind clouds, and a damp chill settled into the night air. I pushed the afghan aside, left my sixties reverie on the porch, and retreated to bed where I tumbled into a restless sleep. As daylight soundlessly crept over darkness, I lay perfectly still so as not to awaken my husband and thought about what the day held. We had to break the news to our sons; phone calls had to be returned; job responsibilities needed to be worked out in order to accommodate the intrusion of cancer into our lives. Together, we would have to face the unknown challenges cancer would bring. I let out a long sigh.

Barry rolled onto his side and propped himself up on his elbow. His thick, tousled black hair, with only a few strands of gray, made him appear younger than his forty-five years. Although he seemed relaxed, there was an uneasy air about him—as if he'd had a bad dream from which he couldn't awaken. His soft brown eyes trustingly sought mine. "Do I really have cancer?"

Reluctantly, I clarified his sleepy confusion. "Yes."

He flipped over onto his back, arms stretched above his head, and stared at the ceiling. "I'm scared shitless."

"Me, too."

CHAPTER 8

Crumbs of Encouragement

THE LATE FALL rain tap danced softly on the windshield as we made our way into Atlanta to meet with Dr. Miller. Someone from his office called the day before and recommended I pack a bag for my husband. She explained that Dr. Miller would most likely admit Barry to the hospital to begin tests before chemo. I packed two bags, his and mine. I didn't know what the hospital's policy was about spouses staying overnight, but I had no intention of leaving him alone and would sleep in the waiting room if necessary. The rain and rhythmic swish of the wipers had a mesmerizing effect; I replayed the events of the previous day, along with memories of days gone by.

The day was not an easy one for any of us. We told our sons together, and they were shocked and upset. I had a feeling that most of their distress was held in check for their daddy's sake. Even though they were no longer children, I wanted to grab them up like I had when they were small and got a new boo-boo, and I could console them with a hug, a Superman Band-aid, and a Popsicle. I hadn't realized I would miss nursing colds and tonsillectomies and chicken pox and bouts of stomach viruses. Not to mention the trips to the ER where we had our own parking place and where the boys were treated for minor accidents. I even missed the "Stop fighting with your brother," and "If I have to stop this car, it's not gonna go well for either of you," and "Good Lord, learn to share!"—all punctuated with a couple of sharp finger snaps. Sometimes I'd felt more like a referee than a mother. But I longed for those years and wished I could have stopped time and held my children close for a little while longer. Their childhoods had passed much too swiftly, and they were grown years before I was ready to let them go. However, as adults they were old enough to understand cancer and the pain it brought to our lives.

Barry told his parents of the diagnosis in person rather than over the phone. He came from a small family; he was the oldest of three sons. His daddy was an only child, and his mama was one of two girls who'd lost her older sister to childhood leukemia. However, he knew from the get go that I was the youngest of seven, but maybe he hadn't considered the dozen nieces and nephews. Holiday family gatherings could be daunting, and Barry probably didn't realize that men don't only marry the woman, but her family as well. Though he would seek solace in the midst of our family congregations by retreating to the front porch or a quiet corner, my big family hadn't discouraged him from marrying me. Maybe he loved me enough that the clamor and commotion that were part of the package were acceptable. To his credit, Barry did his best to blend into the melting pot of personalities. Or as my brother Donnie jokingly referred to us, "a can of mixed nuts."

I offered to go with him to tell his parents, but he felt he should go alone. His mama and daddy hadn't accepted the news of their son's cancer calmly. Perhaps some of their sorrow, specifically his dad's, was the result of guilt over throwing his son into the street all those years ago. There had been no contact between them for a few years, and reconciliation was slow. It was Barry who took the first step in repairing the damaged relationship. He'd extended the olive branch when we were expecting our first baby.

While Barry spent the morning with them, I returned the calls left on the machine, calls that pleaded to be answered. And due to a meeting that couldn't be rescheduled, it was necessary for me to go into my office for a few hours. My boss, whose wife was a breast cancer survivor, was very understanding and agreed to a flexible schedule that would allow me to be with my husband when necessary and still meet my job responsibilities. I was promoted several times over the years and had gladly accepted the increased work load that came with a raise in salary.

During our discussion Mr. Rogers* shared some of the side effects of chemo his wife had experienced. I concluded that to watch someone we love endure the unique misery of chemo treatments would be as close to hell as any of us would ever want to come. I thought again about how unfair life can sometimes be, to all of us.

The next order of business was to call my college professor and explain to her why I wouldn't be attending the last class and, therefore, would be unable to present my final term paper to the class as required. Dr. Mitcham* was sympathetic and supportive and reminded me that I hadn't been absent all quarter, and missing the class wouldn't affect my grade. I promised to mail my paper to her office and, given the circumstances, she agreed to accept the paper without the presentation. She also agreed a hiatus from college classes would be in my best interest. I then made a note to schedule an appointment with Dean Richards to discuss delaying my graduation date.

As the morning progressed I had an unexpected visitor. For the first time in the sixteen years that I'd worked at the high school, Daddy showed up, nervously twirling the narrow brim of his ever-present fedora—straw in the summer, felt in the winter—in aging hands. He was tall, over six feet, and had always stood proud, but now his shoulders slumped. There were both agony and compassion in his aging blue eyes that brought tears to my own.

"Now, sugar, Barry's gonna to be fine. He's a young man whose gonna beat this," he muttered. To someone from Daddy's age group, any diagnosis of cancer was an automatic death sentence. Though he tried not to show it, his words were filled with anxiety.

I crossed the room and reached up to put my arms around him. Although he'd come to offer comfort, I did my best to comfort him. "Yes, he will, Daddy. Thank you for stopping by to check on me."

"Well, it was your mama who always took care of you kids, and she would be better at this than I am. But she's not with us anymore, and I needed to come by and let you know I'm praying about this situation. I called the preacher, asked him to add Barry to the prayer list. Barry's gonna be fine," he repeated with feigned conviction.

"Thank you, Daddy. We need all the prayers we can get."

He was right in that Mama had been the primary caregiver. He hadn't been very involved in our lives except when it came to disciplining my older brothers. Men of his generation believed child-drearing was "women's work" and to offer a hand or show loving emotion would be a sign of weakness. And from what I'd gathered, his mama, who'd died before I was born, was a critical, cold-hearted, bitter woman made more so by farm life on the harsh plains of Texas. Supposedly, my paternal Grandma hadn't ever shown love or an ounce of kindness, or even a smile, towards anyone. In his early twenties, Daddy left the detached environment of his childhood to find factory work in Georgia, where he and Mama eventually met.

Although displays of affection between my parents were rare, when Mama died Daddy wasn't able to suppress tears that slipped down his cheeks as he sat beside her coffin. I overheard him tell an old friend she'd been his wife for sixty years but that it wasn't enough. His heart could have been broken not only by her death, but remorse for years wasted drinking and womanizing. I sometimes wondered if regret was his companion in old age.

Until I was about six or seven years old Daddy was a "functioning alcoholic" who often worked two jobs to support his big family. But weekends were spent losing himself—or looking for himself—in the bottom of a bottle. Mama had said that Daddy came home several times drunker than the infamous Cooter Brown. In years past, more than once, she'd had to track Daddy down at the VFW and demand he hand over his weekly salary. Women weren't allowed at the club except for the Saturday night dances, so she'd always taken one of my older brothers and a big hammer with her. Once inside, she took his cash and gave Daddy the allocated five dollars, which was all they could afford for him to throw away on liquor. Mama was fit to be tied, but Daddy's only defense was to remind Mama that she couldn't teach an old dog new tricks. She didn't bat an eye before she tossed her angry retort, "Maybe not, Joe, but I can damn well get a new dog."

It seemed if you were married to a drunkard and had a houseful of children, a pragmatic attitude and a sense of humor were good qualities to have. And then one Sunday morning Daddy unexpectedly agreed to accompany us to church. When the pastor called upon those unsaved souls to give their lives to Jesus, Daddy dropped to his knees at the altar and prayed for forgiveness. Mama said it was the power of prayer because she'd prayed for daddy every day.

As a testament to his newfound salvation, Daddy gave up alcohol, smoking, and the occasional affair that had left Mama furious and heartbroken. As an adult I realized she would surely have left him several times over, but she had nowhere to go and couldn't have afforded to support all of us on her own. So she suffered both heartache and humiliation, but her commitment had been "until death do us part." Mama stayed, not necessarily because she was trapped, but because the color of love couldn't be defined. And she forgave. But I don't think she ever forgot.

Due to his atonement I grew up with the daddy who'd never striped my scrawny legs with a hedge switch, as Mama had done several times. I was his baby, and he'd spoiled me. He was a different man from the daddy my older siblings had known.

Before he left my office he gave me a pat on my shoulder, which was the closest Daddy ever got to a hug, and said, "Well, honey, reckon I better get goin'. I can see you're busy, and I need to pick up a few things at Thriftown." He was visibly shaken, and I noticed the glisten of tears as he turned to leave. No doubt the memory of losing Mama only a few months ago was still painful, but it was clear he was hurting for Barry and me. The hand we were dealt caught us all off guard.

Thoughts of yesterdays were interrupted by Barry's apology. "I'm sorry I was short with you this morning."

"It's okay. You're right, I should have remembered to call the refrigerator repairman and reschedule, but it completely slipped my mind. It was only the ice maker."

"But I shouldn't have been upset about something that doesn't even matter."

We both knew the argument hadn't been about the ice maker and my not cancelling the early morning appointment when we were in a hurry to be on our way. Our squabble was because we were both on edge. And it didn't help matters when Mr. Parson, the repairman, shared with us that he'd recently lost his wife to cancer and began to relive his pain in vivid detail. I interrupted him, not because I was being deliberately rude or insensitive, but because neither Barry nor I needed to hear how cancer had taken his wife of thirty-two years. I flat-out refused to believe our outcome could be the same. We had to stay positive.

"I'm about to merge onto the downtown connector. What's the exit number off I-75/85 North?"

I double checked the directions we were given because I was as lost as last year's Easter eggs. "It's Exit #100, Pine Street. The receptionist wrote down that it's around a curve, immediately under the Peachtree Street Bridge. After we exit we need to stay in the middle lane in order to proceed straight at the red light. Parking is on the left, and the doctor's office is on the right."

Years ago I-20 had crawled its way from the Alabama state line. The interstate was an effective time saver as an alternate to Highway 78, with its numerous small towns and red lights. Neither of us liked driving in Atlanta traffic, especially in the rain, but Barry volunteered because as he pointed out, I would most likely have to drive the remaining trips. We merged into the connector's congestion, exited at number one hundred, and made our way up Pine Street where Dr. Miller's office was conveniently located next to the hospital. We found an empty spot in the six tiered parking deck, caught the elevator to the first floor, and crossed busy Pine Street that was right off Peachtree Street in Midtown.

As we reached the steps of the building, I took a moment to reflect on the weathered bricks where ivy climbed the walls like a lost wave. Our destiny lay nestled inside, and I prayed that God had led us to the right doctor. Barry closed the mist covered umbrella and found a couple of chairs while I proceeded to the desk, signed his name, and delivered the test results to the gray haired lady who greeted me with a smile. She handed me a clipboard with the prerequisite paperwork for new patients, and I took a seat next to Barry to begin filling out the forms, retrieving the insurance card from my wallet.

Forms completed, I returned to my seat next to Barry, and he took my hand in his. Within a few minutes we were called back to an exam room where Dr. Miller entered on our heels. He was tall and lanky, older than I expected. Wrinkles encircled blue eyes that sat beneath a thatch of gray hair, and his comfortable face wore a relaxed smile. I immediately felt at ease and cast an encouraging glance at my husband, who also seemed more at ease than he'd been in the last two days.

The doctor extended his hand, first to Barry and then to me, "Hello, I'm Dr. Miller. We each shook his hand, and I tried to stay calm as he began to discuss treatment. He continued as he flipped through the folder, "Yesterday I reviewed your diagnosis with Dr. Seeman. The good news, Mr. — "

"Barry. Barry is fine." He motioned towards me. "This is my wife, Sheila."

"Alright, Barry. As I was saying, the good news is you are young and overall healthy. There is a surgery that has a moderate success rate, one that I developed specifically for this type of cancer. The bad news is the tumor is larger than I would like, and this particular type of cancer is very aggressive. We don't have time to waste making decisions regarding the best course of action."

I interjected, "Dr. Miller, we've been told you're the best surgeon in our area for treating this particular cancer. In fact, an acquaintance of mine who lives in our town called as soon as she heard the news of Barry's cancer and recommended you. Her husband had the exact same type of cancer with a tumor at the gastro junction, the same as my husband's." I glanced at Barry to make sure we were on the same page and knew we were. "Whatever you recommend is what we'll do. We have to trust you to make medical decisions for us."

He removed his glasses and hesitated, choosing his words carefully. "Every patient, every case is different, and I cannot in all fairness guarantee the same outcome as your friend's husband. But let me assure you both that I will do everything I possibly can. As I said, your husband is young and healthy and that's to our advantage."

I immediately appreciated his use of "our." He was an ally in this fight. Dr. Miller pulled a diagram from a filing cabinet behind him, turned his attention to Barry, and proceeded to expound on the treatment plan. "I'll admit you to the hospital today where you'll be given a series of tests, including a stress test to ensure that your heart is strong enough for chemo and, subsequently, the extensive surgery. You will remain in the hospital for a few days in order for your reaction to chemo to be supervised. I don't know the specifics of the chemo treatment, but the oncologist to whom I'm referring you will meet with you at the hospital once you've been admitted. He'll discuss in greater detail the chemo and its side effects."

Barry and I remained speechless and hung onto every word as Dr. Miller moved on to the diagram and surgery. "The surgery, as I said, is extensive, but it's the only way to effectively remove the tumor while allowing the digestive system to function. I won't know for sure until we're in surgery, but from the CT scan I've determined I'll need to remove approximately one-third of the esophagus and half of the stomach to ensure complete removal of the cancerous tumor and any remaining cells." He looked Barry directly in the eye as he continued with a sense of determination. "Recovery time is not going to be swift or easy. You'll be in the Intensive Care Unit for three days, barring complications, and another ten to fourteen in the hospital."

I tried to process what we were told but had questions. "I understand the surgery is complicated, but will his life be normal after removing part of his esophagus and stomach? Will he be able to eat without problems? How big of an adjustment is all of this going to be for him?"

"Let me reiterate that it's not going to be easy, but he will survive the surgery. For the first couple of weeks he will have nothing by mouth—and before you question whether or not he will starve, he won't."

Barry had a question of his on. "How will I live if I can't eat or drink?"

"You'll be fed intravenously with a formula containing all the nourishment your body needs, and you won't be hungry. Food will then be gradually introduced, and it will take several days for your new digestive system to adapt. Thereafter, it will be essential to eat six or more small meals a day, and you won't ever be able to eat more than a few ounces of food at any given time. After a few days your intestines will adjust accordingly, and your bowel movements will return to normal."

He shook our hands and told us hospital personnel were expecting us; he turned on his heels and left. Despite the grim enlightenment of truth and what we could expect, his air of confidence was encouraging. Dr. Miller didn't dress up the prognosis to alleviate our apprehension. And although he made it very clear the road before us was not going to be an easy one to travel, he gave us something we desperately needed: hope.

*Name changed

CHAPTER 9

Welcome to the Fifth Floor

RAYS OF SUNSHINE broke up the clouds as Barry and I crossed the damp, busy street to the parking deck and retrieved our weekend luggage. After checking into the hospital we were directed towards the elevator and the fifth floor by Jennifer from admissions. We held hands as we stepped out of the elevator into a hospitable atmosphere where a portly nurse greeted us with a broad smile. She resembled Aretha Franklin so much that I half expected her to break into a rendition of "Respect." Her name tag introduced her as "Lilli."

"My goodness, y'all are very young. We don't usually have such a young man here on the cancer ward. I'll show you to your room, Mr.—"

He interrupted her, "Barry. No need to call me 'Mr.'" He shifted the small suitcase to his left hand and reached out to shake hers. "I would say it's nice to meet you, but the truth is I'd rather be just about anywhere else right now."

"I understand completely, but we're going take good care of you." She noticed my bag and observed, "I see you brought your bag, Mrs.—"

I held out my hand. "Sheila. Please call me Sheila. And, yes, I'll be staying until we can both go home."

Despite the recent trend toward the more comfortable scrubs many nurses seemed to prefer, Lilli wore the traditional, immaculate white nurse's dress and cap. She exuded an air of both confidence and caring that I interpreted as a no nonsense attitude tempered with compassion. I could understand how she'd chosen nursing as a profession, and I relaxed the grip I held on my bag as she led us down the hallway to room number 520.

The room was large, nondescript green, with windows that offered a view of Mick's restaurant across the street, as well as a couple of "adult" stores to the right. My nostrils momentarily flinched at the pungent smell of bleach combined with the distinct odor of illness indigenous to hospitals, an odor all its own that would become much too familiar.

Lilli verified Barry's patient ID number from his chart with the plastic band fastened on his wrist in admissions. With another glance towards my bag, she assured me she would round up a cot and bedclothes. Thankfully, I wouldn't have to sleep in the one comfortable chair that sat in the corner. Two smaller, straight-backed chairs flanked the windows.

I'd barely unpacked our toiletries when there was a knock, followed by the entrance of a doctor who appeared to be in his mid-thirties. He was a wisp of a man, not much taller than I and skinny as a rail. He had reddish-brown hair, with a matching beard, and glasses that were too big for his undersized face that he repeatedly pushed back into position. Yet he was perfectly at ease in both his stature and his demeanor.

"Hello," he greeted with a smile and a handshake. "I'm Dr. Carson, the oncologist to whom you were referred by Dr. Miller. I'm one of a group at the Georgia Oncology Center. I'm here to discuss the course of action in treating your cancer and answer any questions you may have."

There was no testing the waters; we jumped right into the deep end. Dr. Miller's office hadn't wasted any time in getting the ball rolling. But from that morning's appointment I comprehended that cancer is a disease that feeds on healthy tissue until, like the "Blob," everything in its path is destroyed. Time was our most valuable, and limited, asset; the progression of Barry's cancer had to be confined. Immediately.

My husband replied to the stick man, "I'm Barry, and I'm anxious to do whatever you feel is best. The sooner I start treatment, the sooner all of this will be behind me. What's the first step?"

Dispensing with pleasantries the doctor began his outline. "The next couple of hours will be spent evaluating your overall health in order to determine that you are healthy enough for chemo and surgery. I've rushed the test results because your first chemo infusion is scheduled for early evening. The second and third rounds will follow tomorrow and Friday. We'll keep you in the hospital to monitor your body's reaction to chemotherapy and unless there are complications, you'll be released on Saturday morning. In three weeks the next treatment will be administered at our offices, also on three consecutive days, followed by the third and final round a few weeks before surgery. We've experienced a high percentage of success with this particular regime. The chemo will shrink the tumor as much as possible before Dr. Miller proceeds with a rather complicated surgery, which I assume he has discussed with you?"

Barry seemed slightly dazed, so I nodded in the affirmative and replied, "We've heard chemo in itself is horrific. What side effects should we anticipate?"

"Chemo is unavoidably, to use your term, 'horrific', but it's our best option in treating your husband. To answer your question, while every patient responds differently, hair loss will most certainly occur. During the first week he will experience severe diarrhea, followed by periods of nausea, vomiting, and loss of appetite. Some patients develop blisters inside the mouth and throat, and I'll prescribe a compounded mouthwash to help ease the pain and difficulty in swallowing. If Barry experiences the lesions, he may be able to tolerate only yogurt, ice cream, or buttermilk. Additionally, he may not be able to bear the smell of food, especially as it's being cooked. Let me caution you that should he not make it to the bathroom before vomiting, you must wear disposable rubber gloves when cleaning in order to prevent skin burns."

He momentarily studied Barry to, perhaps, gauge his reaction and returned his attention to me. "Before his next appointment he will need to have a portacath installed here, beneath the skin and right below the clavicle," he explained as he pointed to the left side of Barry's upper chest area. "The catheter connects the port to a large vein and will be used not only for chemo but for any other medications or fluids that need to be administered intravenously for the duration of treatment."

"Will the procedure be done here?" I regretted I didn't have a pen and notebook and made a mental note to remember those items for our next visit.

"No, it's a simple procedure any surgeon can do. It will be more convenient for you to schedule it with a doctor in your area." He waited a moment, possibly for me to ask questions, but I didn't have the presence of mind to ask questions.

Barry remained silent, and Dr. Carson continued to address me. "It will be necessary for you to check his temperature often. Should it reach as high 101.5° he must return to the hospital where antibiotics can be given intravenously. As the chemo will not only attack the cancer cells but the white blood cells as well, he will be more susceptible to germs that inhabit our everyday lives. In some instances the attack on his body can come from within. A compromised immune system means something as common as a bad cold could have serious complications."

He cleared his throat and went on with his litany. "Fortunately, there is a drug, Neupogen, which you will inject for ten days following each chemo cycle. The drug will help his body to replace the healthy white cells more rapidly than normal, but he may experience some muscle and joint pain during the accelerated cell production. It is to be injected subcutaneously, not ever into a vein. One of the nurses will teach you how to give the shot before you leave. We'll need the contact information for your pharmacy in order for the prescription to be faxed tomorrow and allow time for the Neupogen to be ordered. Due to the drug's expense and unambiguous use, it's not regularly stocked and is purchased by most pharmacies only on an as-needed basis."

We were shell-shocked and speechless as he faced us both. "A few weeks after surgery Barry will need a thirty day round of radiation, five consecutive days a week and possibly another round or two of chemo. But we'll cross that bridge when we get to it. The only way to cope with cancer is one day at a time." And then he made the understatement of the year. "I realize the two of you must be overwhelmed right now. But chemo is the proverbial 'necessary evil.'"

My husband and I exchanged glimpses of desperation. Barry smiled and asked me, "Would you like to run away now?"

I laughed nervously because running away was exactly what I wanted to do. Far, far away. I took my husband's hand in mine and smiled, "Yes, where would you like to go?"

Realizing the futility of our desire to bolt, Dr. Carson pointed out that no matter where we ran the cancer would be with us. "I realize that what lies before you is upsetting, but I assure you there is a light at the end of the tunnel. A year from now all of this will be behind you, and you can run away to anywhere you want to go. Keep reminding yourselves that each day will take you closer to the end of cancer, and each hurdle will be a milestone." He excused himself and scurried out the door, with the promise to see us tomorrow.

I continued to unpack our few belongings while Barry sat in stunned silence. I wanted to grab him and run, but Dr. Carson was right. We couldn't outrun cancer. After several minutes Barry asked, "Did you hear what he said about that drug being expensive? It could cost hundreds or *thousands* of dollars for one ten day cycle of injections. At best I'll be able to work part-time and after the surgery, I won't be able to work for weeks, maybe months. The business will have to support itself while I recover, or I won't have anything to go back to when I'm able. How will I provide for us? Cancer has consequences I haven't had time to think through."

Laughter was not appropriate, but the irrationality of his concern made it impossible not to laugh. *"That's* what you heard? Dr. Carson described in vivid detail a course of treatment that sounded like the road from hell, and what you caught was the cost of a drug?" I dragged a chair over to where he sat on the bed and took his hands in mine. "Listen to me. We have state merit insurance and a supplemental, private cancer policy you were smart enough to buy years ago. As for the business, the boys can help out with keeping things up and running and you have dependable employees. Your concern, your *only* concern, is to survive. I don't want to hear another word about money. We have to get through this together and to take Dr. Carson's advice to remember the light at the end of the tunnel."

Our conversation was interrupted by a young lab tech who came to collect blood and to take Barry downstairs for a stress test and additional x-rays. I gave my husband a hug and promised to be waiting for him when he got back to the room. A room that seemed to grow smaller the minute I was alone. The walls enveloped me and threatened to smother me with green. I grabbed my jacket and walked out.

Lilli saw my mad dash to the elevator and followed. "Sheila? Is there something you need? Anything I can get you?"

"No, thank you. The rain has moved on, and I'm going for a walk while Barry is having those tests Dr. Carson ordered. I realize the weather's a little nippy, but I really need some air." Surely, Lilli understood the need to escape confinement.

She looked me over and noted the leggings, comfy leather boots, oversized cabled sweater, and the hooded stadium jacket thrown over my arm. She glanced at her watch before responding, "Well, you'll be warm enough but be careful and get yourself back inside before sundown. The city undergoes a transformation at night, and you shouldn't be out alone after dark. Take my advice and don't walk to the right when you exit through the front doors and don't walk past the Fox Theatre to your left. You're in unfamiliar surroundings, and I'll expect you back on the floor in a couple of hours." She cautioned me, "Stay on Peachtree Street and don't stray too far from the hospital."

"Yes ma'am," was all I could say as I headed for the elevator and pushed the button to the lobby.

I heeded Lilli's advice, turned left, and walked towards the Fox while inhaling deep breaths of crisp air to clear my head. Dr. Carson's words hit my heart like a sledge hammer, but there was nothing I could do to alter our course. As I walked I began to feel calmer and to think of a future without cancer, when Barry would be healed, and our lives could return to some semblance of normalcy.

That thought was encouraging as my steps took me to the corner of Peachtree and Ponce de Leon, and I crossed the street to the

"Fabulous Fox." I stopped to admire its architectural beauty and noted the posters promoting *The Nutcracker* ballet for the holidays. I remembered reading on a playbill years ago that the theatre was a historical landmark that had opened in 1929 and was originally designed as a Shrine Temple, which explained its Moorish design. The structure resembled a sand castle that had emerged from a concrete beach. It was difficult to imagine that a couple of decades ago such a building, with its Islamic like turrets and courtyard reminiscent of Arabian nights, was going to be torn down in the name of progress. But a group deemed it worthy of saving and restoring to its striking, rather unique grandeur. Reluctantly, my distraction slipped away like melting ice as I threw my coat around my shoulders.

I didn't need the jacket because the sunny weather was mild for the end of November. Yet the chill of late afternoon reminded me it was time to go back to our room and keep my promise to be there when Barry returned. Although my brief interval helped restore my equilibrium, my mind still spun with more questions than answers. We could opt out of treatment, throw our luggage in the car, and drive as fast as we could go, but the cancer would be an uninvited traveler. What had Dr. Carson said? Something about a light at the end of the tunnel. With that affirmation planted firmly in my mind, I turned around and backtracked to the hospital well before the sun became one with the horizon.

The elevator delivered me back to the fifth floor, and I was surprised to see a visitor waiting on the other side of the doors. "Marnie, what are you doing here? How did you even know we were here?"

Marnie was one of my colleague's mothers and had lived in Atlanta since her divorce. She came from money and had married into money.

Hence, hers was a life of privilege, a byproduct of wealth. She wore class, beauty, and grace as comfortably as she wore the beige cashmere sweater that perfectly matched tweed slacks. A leather shoulder bag and practical, Aigner flats completed her ensemble. Her impeccably coiffed hair was expertly colored to its original ash blonde and cut in a style that took years off her real age, which I could only estimate. Her flawless complexion was made up but not overdone—no gaudy eye shadow or lipsticks or blushes in the wrong shade that often plagued mature women. Her appearance and demeanor exuded self-assurance.

If a casual observer saw Marnie strolling through the mall or leisurely pushing a grocery cart, the assumption would be that she'd never suffered heartache or that her life hadn't known even a hint of sorrow. Unfortunately, her ivory tower had been made of glass, and Bremen's gossipmongers were quick to dispel her shrewdly crafted mirage. Perhaps that was why she'd returned to Atlanta and established her new residence.

Marnie's daughter, the middle of three girls, and I had been classmates, but not friends as we belonged to different cliques. It wasn't that Cyndie and I disliked each other, it was just that we ran in different circles. Her parents, specifically, her father and his family, owned the clothing manufacturing company where my parents were employed for decades, until retirement. Most of Cyndie's friends had been from other affluent families in the community, but as adults we'd left the drama of high school in the halls of our alma mater. With shared office space, Cyndie, the high school counselor, and I, the registrar, worked well together and became good friends.

Marnie greeted me with a warm hug. "Cyndie called me as soon as you notified her and your boss that you would be spending the next few days at the hospital. I put together a care package to tide you over. I'm only a few miles away and will be glad to help in any way I can. Barry has always been good to take care of my car. You know, I still schedule maintenance with him when I'm going to be in Bremen because I don't trust anyone else. Please call me if there's anything I can do. I've got to run. I have dinner plans and don't want to be late."

With those parting words and a hint of Estee Lauder perfume that wafted in the corridor, she was gone. I thanked the already closed doors and made my way down the hall, past the nurses' station to our room. I was rummaging through the goody bag of magazines, crossword puzzles, assorted candy and gum, and a bottle of hand lotion when I heard the approaching trolley. The orderly chauffeured my husband to the bedside, and I forced myself to sound more cheerful than I felt as I bent to kiss Barry on the forehead. "Well, hello. Did they put you through the wringer?"

He replied with a smile, "Yes, but everything's good. One of the techs told me I'm the healthiest cancer patient he's ever seen. I told him that was great news, except for the fact that I have a fast growing tumor in my stomach."

I didn't bother to mention the irony. "Well, I'm glad you're strong enough for what lies ahead. It's not going to be a walk in the park."

He ignored my reference to the unavoidable. "What's in the bag? Did you find a gift shop in the hospital?"

"No. Marnie, Cyndie's mama, brought it for us. She dropped by while I was out walking, but I ran into her at the elevator as she was leaving. It was thoughtful of her."

"Yes, it was, but why were you out walking alone? You have no sense of direction, so did you leave a line of breadcrumbs? I realize you walk a few miles every day at home, but as what's-her-name said, 'we're not in Kansas anymore.'"

"Dorothy, from the *Wizard of Oz*, which you know very well, is one of my favorite movies, and if I'd left breadcrumbs the pigeons would have scarfed them down. I didn't walk far, and I was careful.

Lilli gave me a few pointers, and I was fine." I changed the subject to distract his worry. "Are you hungry? It's almost supper time, and since we skipped lunch I'm starving. I'm going downstairs to the cafeteria and see if there's anything I want. If not, I'll go across the street and pick up something from Mick's. Your dinner tray should be here soon, but if it's not appetizing I'll get something else for you."

I turned around to find Lilli behind me. "Mick's delivers so you don't need to go out again, and the patient meals are very good, especially since Barry is not on a restricted diet. And you should be able to put together a meal in the cafeteria. It serves a variety of choices that are better than standard cafeteria food. Also, there's a patient and family room adjacent to the nurses' station where you can help yourself to crushed ice, sherbet, assorted juice, ginger ale, Cokes, and crackers in case either of you needs anything in the middle of the night. There's usually a fresh pot of coffee brewing if you want a cup in the morning."

"Thank you, Lilli. That's good to know," I replied.

She continued in her efficient manner, "I'm here to insert the IV and start the chemo infusion, per Dr. Carson's orders and to post Barry's vitals before I leave for the day. Your night nurse will be Tabitha. She's young but dedicated and takes her duties seriously. Her experience over the past couple of years has taught her the specifics of caring for cancer patients, and she will monitor the three hour chemo drip. I'll be back in the morning, and you can start learning how to give the injections your husband will need after chemo. You'll practice on an orange."

Barry was wary at the prospect of me administering shots, but Lilli reassured him, "You'll be amazed at how quickly she'll learn. Most wives have a tendency to rise to the occasion and do whatever necessary. Trust me on that."

I left the room with her and made my way to the hospital's diner where I found I was not as hungry as I'd thought. I picked up a sandwich, chips, and a bottle of water and returned upstairs to have supper with my husband. We finished our meal, and Barry turned on the t.v. and found an old western to occupy his restless time. But I couldn't concentrate on John Wayne. Instead of trying I walked over to the window and was astonished to see the transformation as the sunset painted the sky a deep violent with streaks of muted pink.

Street lights illuminated another side of life in Midtown. Gone was the hustle and bustle of traffic that had scampered around like mice. Most of the people in business attire who had earlier made their way to various destinations with a sense of purpose had disappeared. I glanced up and down the street, but that section of Peachtree Street was now devoid of activity, except for the few customers patronizing Mick's. Evidently, there wasn't a play at the Fox, or the street would have been busy with the hubbub of patrons.

There were a dozen or so homeless persons who, under the cold blanket of nightfall, moved furtively from stoop to stoop where an almost tangible hopelessness waited. Like nomads, everything they owned was carried with them tucked under their arms or on their backs or in a shopping cart most likely stolen from an unobservant parking lot. None of them looked dangerous, but I understood why Lilli insisted on my returning to the hospital before the daylight exodus. I silently thanked God I'd always had a roof over my head and food on my table.

Nurse Tabitha entered, and I turned from the window as she disposed of the empty bag, leaving the IV needle in place for tomorrow's "cocktail." She recorded his stats and insisted the bedside rail be raised. She said she wouldn't disturb us unless necessary and made sure Barry knew how to locate and use the call button. Tabitha was friendly in a competent, professional manner. And she was beautiful, with curly golden-red hair, a heart shaped face that boasted a flawless peaches and cream complexion, and vivid, emerald eyes that displayed compassion. Yet she seemed unaware of her beauty.

Barry turned off the t. v. and asked, "Honey, are you ready for bed? It's been a long day, and I'm very tired. It could be that today's chemo treatment has made me tired, and there's another one tomorrow. And the next day. I hope there won't be any problems, and we can go home Saturday morning."

"Yes. I'm tired, too. I'll make up the cot and change into my pajamas. I've already washed my makeup down the drain and brushed my teeth." Even though we were exhausted, I doubted if either of us would be able to rest.

As I fought with the cot to find a comfortable position, Barry reached through the guardrail on his bed. "I'm not used to sleeping without you next to me. Hold my hand, and maybe I'll be able to fall asleep."

"Okay. Maybe we'll both sleep." I placed my hand in his, and his touch had a calming effect. The subdued lighting combined with the hushed echoes of a hospital at rest to create a surreal atmosphere. In only a couple of days our lives had unraveled.

"Sheila?"

"What?"

"I'm sorry about getting so mad at you when you dented the new minivan all those years ago. It wasn't your fault and was unimportant in the big scheme of things."

"It's okay. You're right, it's not important, and it was a long time ago." His hand slipped from mine as he drifted off. But my restless mind refused to submit to my weary body's will to sleep and instead stumbled back a decade to the minor accident.

It was in late spring of 1985 when Barry decided it was time for me to have a brand new, custom ordered car. Over my objections he proceeded to convince me. "You've driven whatever I bought and not complained about any of the cars or vans, and I've had more than one new truck—and the Jeep. Business is good, and it's time you picked out a car you want. Besides, remember how carsick Brad got riding in the backseat of the Cougar a couple of summers ago? It was the trip to Cocoa Beach to visit your brother Gene and his wife Vern. Gene got us a NASA pass for Sally Ride's first shuttle launch. When we got home you mentioned you would like to have one of those new Dodge minivans, but I'm not a big fan of front wheel drive. Chevrolet has come out with its version that's a rear wheel drive, an Astro minivan. Tomorrow is Saturday, so let's go to the Waffle House for breakfast and then to the Chevrolet dealership."

I protested that I didn't have to have a brand new vehicle, but he was unwavering and reminded me of our planned trip out West in the next two or three summers. A minivan would be much more practical than the two-door Mercury I drove. The owner of the Chevrolet dealership, Norris, was eager to work with us on ordering a new model. I selected the color, maroon, and we both agreed four high-backed chairs and a third bench seat in the rear was the best option for our family. Norris assured us the van would be delivered well before our scheduled summer vacation to the Great Smokey Mountains where hiking and rafting were planned.

As promised, the minivan arrived a few weeks later and it was exactly what our family needed. I was unexpectedly excited to drive the fully-loaded-with-accessories new car. We'd sold my car and transferred the insurance to the minivan. My shiny new chariot was ready to roll.

Three days later I sipped a New Coke, which was not better than the original. Madonna's "Material Girl"—which pretty much summed up the narcissistic eighties—reverberated from the radio.

Cathy and I were driving down Pleasant Ridge Road to Carrollton to do some shopping. We were a few feet from the Hog Liver Road intersection when a dog, a full grown boxer, ran directly in front of the car. Although I blew the horn and slammed on the brakes, I couldn't stop in time to avoid hitting the dog. My only other option to dodge the dog was to swerve into the ditch because there was a car in the oncoming lane. It wasn't feasible to hit the car and miss the dog.

I couldn't bear to look and asked Cathy if the dog was dead. She glanced over her shoulder and mimicked the dog on its back, legs twitchin' in the air. "Oh, he's dead alright."

A man wearing overalls, a plaid shirt, and a large straw hat that shielded his face from the sun waved me over. I struggled with tears of remorse as I pulled into his driveway, got out of the car, and told him how sorry I was to have hit the dog that was without a doubt dead. I braced myself for his reaction, but he wasn't distraught or surprised.

"Don't worry yourself too much, Miss. It was just a matter of time before the fool got himself run over. Tried to break him from chasin' cars, but he'd run every vehicle on the road no matter what I did." The man walked around to the front of the minivan and retrieved a red handkerchief from his pocket. He wiped the sweat from the back of his neck and said, "I'm sure sorry about the dent in your car. Looks like it's a brand new car."

I walked to where he stood and was almost sick to my stomach when I saw the huge dent in the front bumper. "Yes, it is a new car. I picked it up from the dealer a few days ago."

"Well, your insurance ought to pay for the repair. You shouldn't have to meet a deductible seeing how it wasn't your fault. The dang dog ran right out in front of you."

"I'm sure you're right. I'll call our agent when I get home. And again, I'm really sorry about your dog." I left the man with his recently deceased dog, and Cathy and I continued down the road to Carrollton. When I got back home I contacted our insurance company to report the accident and to find out how to proceed with the repairs. Due to my inexperience in filing a claim, I wasn't prepared for the extensive line of questioning that streamed from the other end of the phone.

"Can you explain how you came to run over the dog?" asked the young man.

"Yes, the dog targeted the car at a fast-paced gallop, and there was nothing I could do because he was in the lane directly in front of me, and there was another car in the opposite lane."

"Did you apply your brakes?"

"Of course, but I couldn't stop the car before I hit the dog."

"Was anyone hurt in the accident?"

"Unfortunately, the dog is dead as a doorknob, but neither my passenger nor I were injured."

"Was the dog in the road?"

I considered the absurdity of his question before I answered, "No. The dog was napping under the shade tree, and I had to blow the horn and run him all over the yard before I nailed his ass on the porch." It was a sarcastic answer, but it should have been obvious the dog was in the road. "Is there someone else with whom I can discuss this matter?"

Once the specifics were resolved, I waited for Barry to get home so I could show him the dented bumper. He was going through the mail when I told him about running over the dog and calling the insurance company regarding the dented bumper. I figured he would be aggravated, but he completely overreacted. "I can't believe you've already wrecked the new car! You've had it for less than a week. What is wrong with you that you couldn't miss a damn dog? Did you even consider asking the dog's owner to pay for the damage?"

Upset by his uncalled for anger I lashed out. "No, I didn't because we have insurance." He wasn't the only one mad, and I threw fuel on the flame. "I did this on purpose you know, just to piss you off. I got up this morning and decided to run over a dog and not just any dog, but a big 'ole dog that would be sure to put a large dent in the new car I was told to order."

"Oh, now it's my fault because I twisted your arm to get a new car."

"It's nobody's fault, asshole. It was an accident and falls under the category of 'shit happens', so stop blaming me for something I couldn't avoid."

Although we didn't speak to each other for several days, the angry flare-up passed, and the bumper was replaced at no cost to us.

But until then Barry hadn't apologized for his inexcusable outburst, which was not his nature. I must've dozed at some point because I was awakened by early morning sunlight that found its way to the drab green walls. Lilli stood next to the bed reviewing the notes from the night shift. Her voice roused me, "Good morning, Sheila. I see you got some rest. There's fresh coffee if you'd like a cup. Barry's doing very well. There are no immediate adverse effects to report to Dr. Carson, who should be here in the next half-hour for patient rounds."

She turned with his chart to leave as I said, "That's great news. And coffee sounds heavenly. I'll get dressed and find the snack room. Thank you."

I kissed Barry, who was already awake, on the cheek and hurried to find some clothes to throw on before the doctor arrived. "Good morning, sweetie. Can I bring you a cup of coffee?"

"No, thanks. Breakfast and coffee should be here any minute. Why don't you run down to the cafeteria and find yourself something to eat? You've always been like a baby bird that wakes up hungry."

"Later. After the doctor has come and gone." I dressed in comfortable sweats, brushed my teeth, put my hair in a ponytail, and made a beeline for the miraculous elixir. In my haste I nearly collided with Lilli in the hallway.

"Oops, that was close. There's a message from admissions that they need to see you sometime this morning. Jennifer, I think."

"Okay, but I'm sure I gave her everything yesterday when we were admitted."

With a shrug Lilli stepped aside so I could find the much needed caffeine boost.

As soon as Dr. Carson finished his brief exam, I located my purse, took the elevator to the first floor, and waited outside Jennifer's office until she finished her phone call. She looked to be in her late twenties, very fit in her navy business attire; blonde hair brushed her shoulders. She hung up the phone, retrieved a compact from the desk drawer, and powdered her nose. Based on her love affair with the mirror, it was clear someone had once told her she was pretty, and she hadn't forgotten it. Miss Priss glanced my way and motioned for me, and I entered an office that reeked of efficiency. "Hello, I was told you need to see me."

She forced herself to simulate a smile, and I wondered if somebody had pissed in her Cheerios. "Yes, that's right." She shuffled through a stack of alphabetized folders until she found the one she needed and motioned for me to have a seat. "We admitted several new patients yesterday, and I didn't have time to fully discuss your financial obligations. I need to clear everything up before your husband is released from the hospital. Your estimated balance is four thousand, eight hundred and twelve dollars. But of course that doesn't include doctors' fees. Those charges will be billed separately. I'll also need the information for the Liberty National cancer insurance policy your husband mentioned."

Maybe Jennifer thought I'd just fallen off the turnip truck. Or that I could be easily intimidated. Or she didn't realize I had bigger fish to fry. I didn't bother to hide my annoyance as I dug through my purse.

Visibly relieved, Jennifer, who had no south in her mouth said, "I'll make a copy of the additional insurance card. As for the projected balance, we accept personal checks and credit cards. However, if you need to set up a monthly payment plan I'll give you the forms and run a credit report for both you and your husband."

I salvaged an emery board, touched up a couple of ragged nails, and pushed back a stray hair that escaped the scrunchie before I replied in a syrupy sweet Southern drawl, "Oh, sugah, that's not necessary. I'm not lookin' for my checkbook or a credit card. It seems I'm the one who needs to 'clear everything up' for you. The supplemental cancer policy is a private policy to which you have no claim. Our agent will file the bills, and the checks will be mailed directly to us. That insurance money will be used to pay our living expenses while my husband is unable to work."

Jennifer was put off by my knowledge of how insurance claims are handled but persisted. "I see. Since you've already decided to have those funds paid directly to you, then we need to resolve the unpaid balance before your husband can be discharged."

I retrieved the state merit insurance card, laid it on her desk, and pointed to the toll free contact number for medical personnel.

"If you'll find time in your busy day to call the office at United Healthcare, someone will verify coverage, as well as the fact that this hospital and each of our doctors are 'in-network'. And because we met our out-of-pocket max months ago, this hospital is obligated to accept whatever payment our insurance company deems fair and reasonable. Therefore, there is *no* 'estimated balance'."

Taken aback that anyone would challenge her competence, she lost the fake smile. "I doubt if you're aware of the workings of a hospital and its administrative procedures."

"You're right, I'm not. But what I am aware of is that I have a contract with United Healthcare, and their company's premium is taken out of monthly my paycheck. I also realize Crawford Long has a contract with United Healthcare. So if you have a problem regarding the payment agreement, I suggest you discuss the matter with the insurance company. When Barry is discharged I'm sure there won't be any unexpected problems with our account. Have I cleared things up for you, Jennifer, or do we need to review the facts again?"

"No. You've made yourself perfectly clear. I'll contact United Healthcare today to discuss this claim." She mumbled under her breath, "So much for the gracious 'Southern Belle.' That's obviously a myth."

Word to the wise: Don't ever tangle with a woman raised in the South. Jennifer's condescending contempt jumped on my last nerve, and I was on her like a chicken on a June bug. "Listen, sweetie, anytime your happy ass is tired of the South, 'Delta is ready when you are'. In the meantime, I'm gonna trust you to pull your head out of your ass, contact the insurance company, and resolve the claim because, well, that's your job." I stood to leave and leaned over her desk. "Pay attention so you'll comprehend. I don't have the time or the energy to fight you and the cancer, and I can guaran-damn-tee you fighting cancer is my priority."

I snatched the insurance card from her desk, strode to the door, and as an afterthought—because Mama had taught me to be polite and because I was a grown woman who'd just thrown a hissy fit—turned and added in a voice that dripped honey, "Have a real nice day, ma'am."

I sashayed out of her office without a second thought of insurance matters and sought out the cafeteria.

After a hasty breakfast I returned to our room to wait for my first lesson in administering the shot Barry would need for ten consecutive days after we returned home. True to her word, Lilli entered bearing a small syringe, a cup of water, and an orange and began her instructions as a well-trained, experienced nurse. I, on the other hand, was a nervous wreck. She recognized my anxiety and kept her voice calm and patient, which had a soothing quality. "The first thing you'll need to do is thoroughly wash your hands with a good antibacterial soap. I recommend that you stock up on Dial. The shot is to be given subcutaneously, beneath the fatty layer of skin like an injection of insulin. If at any time you see blood in the syringe, it means you've hit a vein. You'll need to withdraw the needle, replace it with a new one, and try again. The preferred location for Neupogen is in the thigh area, to be alternated each day. I want you to siphon water into the syringe, firmly grasp the orange, and inject the water into it."

Barry winced as I jabbed the needle into the orange. "I wish you would go easy on that orange. In a few days, that will be my leg on the other end of a needle. I hope you get it right the first time because I don't like the idea of pulling the needle out and trying again."

"Don't worry, Barry. Sheila will get the hang of it, and if she's too aggressive, unlike the orange, you can yell out in pain."

With those reassuring words she smiled and breezed out the door, leaving me to practice while Barry watched skeptically. After lunch and his second infusion of chemo that I wasn't convinced wouldn't kill him, he needed a nap; I needed a walk. I kissed him and said, "You rest while I go for a walk. I'll be back soon."

"Be careful and don't get lost," he muttered as his eyes grew heavy from fatigue.

I felt guilty as I made my way to fresh air and sunshine, but to maintain my sanity I needed to get away, even if it was for only a few minutes. I found that away from him, away from his concern for me, was the time for tears. I walked and cried until the tears receded. It was a contradiction that I needed a few minutes of breathing room, but couldn't bear to be gone for long, not when thoughts of Barry occupied every step of those brief diversions.

Saturday morning finally came and brought with it the end of round one of chemo and the release from our first stay at Crawford Long Hospital. Armed with a list of instructions and emergency contact information, I made the short walk across the street to retrieve the car. I would be driving us home and hoped traffic wouldn't be too bad on a Saturday. I drove into the circular patient pick-up area to find Barry in a wheelchair, with Lilli as his motorist, both smiling. Barry climbed into the car and fastened his seat belt.

Lilli stuck her head in to speak to me. "You have the emergency contact numbers; use them if you need to. And don't forget to pick up the Neupogen today because he will need his first injection tomorrow, and your pharmacy may be closed on Sunday. Dr. Carson should have explained the importance of the medication. Don't worry. You'll be fine administering the injections."

"Thanks, Lilli. Yes, he did, and I've already called to make sure the prescription has been filled. I'll stop by and pick it up on our way home."

With a wave good-bye, I exited the driveway and turned towards I-75 and then I-20 West and home. Traffic flowed smoothly under a sun filled sky, and I was grateful when I parked in front of our drugstore. I walked inside and greeted the owner, "Hi, Bill. We just got back into town, and I need to pick up the Neupogen and syringes for Barry." It wasn't necessary to explain that Barry had been diagnosed with cancer or that we'd been at Crawford Long for the past few days. It was Bremen.

"Yes, it's ready. I'll get it from the refrigerator, which is where you need to store it when you get home." He handed me a small carton that contained the ten vials I would be injecting and a white bag. "There are ten syringes in the bag."

"Okay, thanks. Could I please add two or three extra syringes? If I mistakenly hit a vein I'll have to discard the needle and start over."

"Sure. And although we usually don't file the insurance claim until after the customer has picked up and signed for the prescription, I took the liberty of contacting United Healthcare to make sure the drug would be covered and when I could expect reimbursement due to the cost of Neupogen. The cost for the syringes is negligible."

"Oh, that's fine. As long as you get paid. Dr. Carson mentioned the drug is expensive."

"Exorbitant it is more accurate."

"Well, exactly how much does it cost?"

He checked the receipt before answering, "A ten day supply is almost nine thousand dollars."

Holy shit. I almost dropped the box of ampoules until it clicked that I was holding more than the amount we had left in our savings account. I thanked Bill for filing with our insurance company and waiting for payment. As I returned to the car I decided there was no reason to mention the expense to Barry since, thank God, it was covered by our insurance. He didn't bother to ask about the cost, and I didn't volunteer that information. Instead I said, "If you're not too tired, I need to stop by Ingle's and pick up a few things so I won't have to make another trip. I especially want to buy ginger ale, sherbet, Popsicles, yogurt, and maybe a carton of buttermilk—if they have the good kind you like. Almost home."

"Ok. I'm just glad to be out of the hospital and on our way home. The fresh air and sunshine feel great. Funny how I'd taken those simple pleasures for granted. "

CHAPTER 10

Home Sweet Home

WHEN WE ARRIVED home from the drugstore and grocery store, there were several cars parked in the driveway that signified a welcoming committee. Pat, her daughter Kim, and Brad's fiancée Valerie were waiting for us. Valerie and Brad were friends long before they began dating, and Barry and I already loved her. She was petite, with big chocolate brown eyes, long silky, curly hair the color of coffee stirred with a few drops of vanilla creamer. And she wore one of those beautiful, thousand watt smiles I'd longed for in high school. More importantly, she was kind, easygoing, and she loved my son.

Even though Barry and I knew they were perfect for each other, we knew better than to push Brad in Valerie's direction. My friend Emily warned me to lay low when it came to sons and their relationships. She also advised me to be nice to every one of the boys' girlfriends because I never knew which one of them would birth my grandchild. Good advice that I took to heart, although I wished I felt as confident about my younger son's choice. While Brad and Valerie's relationship was a match made in heaven, I worried Chuck's upcoming marriage was doomed for divorce from the words, "I do."

Thankful for Valerie, I dropped our bags and gave her a hug. I peered around and was pleasantly surprised by the work of our "elves." Not only was the house immaculate, but the Christmas tree sat in the living room and proudly displayed its colorful lights and glistening ornaments. The family room was also fully decorated for the holidays, right down to the manger on the mantle. The dining room table held Christmas china that gleamed in afternoon sunlight that danced across the dishes' green and red holly wreath pattern. The women's labor of love brought tears of gratitude to my eyes after the most difficult week of our lives, and I thanked them profusely.

Barry also expressed his gratitude, "I can't thank y'all enough for doing this. You have no idea how much I appreciate it. It was almost worth going through chemo to get out of haulin' all the decorations up from the basement."

He had to be joking. I couldn't believe he loathed dressing the house for Christmas so badly that he preferred chemo. There was no denying he complained every year about how many boxes had to be retrieved from the basement and then packed up and returned to their position downstairs. But to essentially prefer chemo and confinement in a hospital over a few decorations was astounding. On the other hand, there was the year when Brad was a toddler, and I'd made plans to put up the tree one Sunday afternoon while he napped. I anticipated Brad's delight and Barry's help until he'd, literally, shot himself in the foot.

~

Barry didn't want to put up the tree and procrastinated by going with friends Chris and Mitchell out to the country to try out his new .22 pistol, but they all promised to lend a hand when they got back. As I took a chocolate pound cake out of the oven, I received a phone call I thought was a prank the three of them concocted to avoid the task of decorating the tree.

"Hello is this Sheila, Barry's wife?"

"Yes, who's speaking?"

"This is Sandy calling from the ER. Your husband has shot himself in the foot and asked me to notify you. The doctor on call is on his way to review the x-ray, and Barry thought you might want to come over and hear the verdict with him."

They were so funny. "Who is this? Is this Mitchell's sister? You can tell the three stooges they're not going to get out of helping me. For one thing the decorations are in the attic, and the boxes are too heavy for me to bring down by myself. So let them know I'll be waiting for their help when they get themselves back here."

"Sandy" didn't have anything to say, and I assumed they were all having a good laugh at my expense. But as it turned out, Barry actually had shot himself in the foot. The doctor said another quarter inch and there would have been permanent damage instead of the minor wound that would heal in a couple of weeks, thank God. Barry had sworn it was an accident, and Chris and Mitchell were all too willing to corroborate his story. Due to the accident Barry propped his foot up and supervised while our friends grudgingly helped me with the tree. Guess they should've shot themselves in the foot.

~

As I thanked the trio of women for all their hard work, I studied the Christmas tree and the dozens of ornaments that included the angel tree topper. It was beautiful, but it didn't look quite as I remembered. I realized its branches weren't as laden with ornaments; many from my collection were not among the decorations.

Pat watched me for a moment, hands on her hips, and said with her no nonsense attitude. "I know what you're doing. You're trying to find the ornaments that are missing. Well, after two hours of hangin' baubles, I got tired of it and left the rest of 'em packed up. If you want them on the tree, I believe you know where to find them. It's no wonder Barry doesn't want the tiresome chore of helping you every year." She gave Barry a sympathetic hug.

I laughed because I was caught. "Alright. Guilty as charged, but the tree is very pretty, and I'm grateful the decorating is finished. I don't know if the number of ornaments has anything to do with Barry's reluctance or the fact that his mama goes wild with her decorating every year. Maybe he helped her when he was growing up and was burned out by the time we married."

"Hey," Barry interrupted, "Mama's decorating is not that bad. Her parents were sharecroppers, and they didn't have much growing up. She told me Christmases were sparse, especially after her only sister died of leukemia before her tenth birthday. Mama makes up for her childhood poverty by going a little overboard at Christmas."

I was familiar with sparse. When I was a child, we'd had an aluminum tree with an opaque, four color wheel that rotated on a light bulb to change the color of the tree. It was set up in front of the living room's picture window and decorated with red, glass ornaments. My stocking was hung on the mantle, and a few red candles on the piano and a wreath on the door were the finishing touches. Barry and mine's first Christmas tree had been decorated with a few lights, about a dozen ornaments, and lots of cheap foil icicles from the 5&10.

Although we'd added to our decorations through the years, I couldn't understand overdoing it to the point of borderline tacky. I teased, "'A little overboard'?" Oh, c'mon, Barry, if she stuck a 'Joe's Bar and Grill' sign in the front yard, I guarantee she'd draw a crowd on Saturday night. You have to admit her house during the holidays resembles a honkytonk that can be seen from Mars."

He chose not to further discuss his mama and instead used the opportunity to remind me of a Christmas I'd just as soon forget.

"While we're on the subject of Christmases past, what about our last visit to the tree farm a few years ago?"

Pat laughed at the jostled memory. "Oh, I remember that Christmas. Really, Barry, I don't know how you kept from wringin' her neck. Any other man probably would have."

"Let's not rehash that tired tale. Why don't I make us all a cup of hot chocolate or put on a pot of coffee? I have a tin of delicious shortbread cookies on hand."

Barry smacked me on the butt. "I *had* wanted to wring your neck. I had no idea why you had your panties in a wad, but you were hell-bent on ruining our trip to find a Christmas tree."

I couldn't argue with him. I'd attributed my lousy mood to an extreme case of PMS or exhaustion from holiday shopping, a job, meeting the demands of two children and housework, or a combination of all of it. Whatever the reason I was a complete and undeniable bitch the day we went to the tree farm—for the last time.

The boys were at a friend's house and, to my disappointment, didn't want to go with us to cut a fresh tree, a family tradition. It was just Barry and me as I wandered from tree to tree, deciding on one but then finding a flaw that led me to the next section of fragrant firs. Barry's patience was wearing thin and after almost two hours of ramblin' through the field in a cold drizzle and not finding one that was exactly right, Barry made a decision. He began sawing the very next tree from its planted home.

I gripped his arm. "Stop! That's not the tree I want. Why are you cutting that one down? I want to look at some more trees before I pick one. Don't cut that tree because I don't want it!" He continued to saw, and I stomped my foot and continued to yell, "Okay, then you can damn well pay for two trees—that one and the one I choose."

"Too bad it's not the one you want, but I'm not paying for two. I'm tired of looking at trees and not finding one that's 'just right'. It's a tree, Sheila, and as long as the trunk is straight, they're all good ones."

Despite my protests he finished the job. I warned him, "If you get that tree, it's not gonna be put up for Christmas. And you can load it on the truck, but I'm not leaving here until I find the tree I want."

"Then you can walk your ass home." He dragged the felled tree to be secured with mesh and paid for it while I continued to whine. As the youngest of seven I was an excellent whiner, which had usually gotten me what I wanted, more or less to shut me up.

I didn't want to climb in the truck, but it was a cold day. The drizzle had turned to an icy rain, and Barry had sounded dead serious about me walking home. I pouted like the spoiled child I'd been, the one I thought I'd outgrown, and let my stubborn streak replace reasoning. The tree remained in the stand outside where he left it after he'd rinsed off the loose needles because I refused to have it in the house. It was a week before Christmas when I apologized for my childish behavior. I asked Barry to please take the tree inside so we would could decorate it and have a tree for the gifts to be arranged underneath. He indifferently obliged.

The day after Christmas, as usual, the lights and ornaments were removed and boxed up for another year. I expected Barry to take the tree outside to cut it up for firewood, as he always did. However, as I climbed the basement steps the sound of the chainsaw lured me to the living room. I found him sawing the tree apart, limb by limb, right there in the living room like an angry Paul Bunyan. I wanted to shout at him over the harsh jangle of the chainsaw to take the damn tree out in the yard before he ruined the carpet. Though after a brief and wise consideration of the situation, I realized yelling at a man holding a chain saw, a crazed lumberjack on a mission, would not be the best strategy.

I didn't know, and didn't want to know, if his wrath was directed at the tree or me. Either way, it took six months of vacuuming twice a week to remove the last of the sawdust and pine needles from the carpet. On the upside I found out the best time to purchase a very pretty, realistic, artificial tree was during the after-Christmas sales. I saved seventy percent.

Three nights after that amicable homecoming Barry began to suffer from uncontrollable chills, and his fever spiked to 103°. I located the emergency phone number for Dr. Carson's service and left a message regarding my husband's downward spiral. Within five minutes Dr. Carson returned my frantic message and as he was on call, instructed me to wrap Barry in a blanket and to meet him at Crawford Long's ER. I reminded him we were an hour away but that we would be there as quickly as we could. It was almost eleven o'clock, but neither of the boys was home yet.

Hesitant to drive to Atlanta alone late at night with a sick husband, I called my oldest brother Jerry; he lived in the neighborhood. He was adamant I not go alone, and he and his wife Jerline were at my door in less than ten minutes to help load Barry into the large back seat of their Lincoln. I regretted I'd unpacked our bags, but there was no time to collect even the basic necessities as I grabbed the folder with the directions. We wouldn't have time to get lost in downtown Atlanta, with its multiple one-way streets that conspired to direct any driver unfamiliar with the area away from where he wanted to go.

When we arrived Dr. Carson was already there, but it was almost three a.m. before we were taken to the cancer ward where the nurse was waiting for Barry. She aided Barry in getting undressed and into a hospital gown. When she hung the bag of antibiotics, she turned to me and asked, "Why doesn't he have a port?"

"What? Oh, a portacath. We couldn't get a preliminary appointment until next week with one of the surgeons in Carrollton. Neither of us thought it would be a problem since he's not scheduled for his next chemo treatment for another two and a half weeks."

"Okay. I'll have to use a vein in his arm, but make sure you keep that appointment."

"We will. If you have time, I would really appreciate a cot, but if there's not one available, I'll sleep in the chair."

Jerry and Jerline left the hospital, with the promise to pack a few things and return later in the day with our belongings, along with my car. A cot and bedding were located, and I held Barry's hand through the guardrail until his even breathing signaled he slept, although restlessly. It was almost impossible for either the patient or the spouse to sleep in a hospital. In a daze of exhaustion I realized a new day had begun on the demanding fifth floor when Lilli breezed into our room with a smile.

"Well, good morning. Y'all must've missed me to be back so soon." She busied herself with checking Barry's stats and changing the IV bag. Glancing my way she noted my fatigue. "Why don't you find yourself a cup of coffee? You'll feel like a whole new woman after caffeine and a shower."

I stood, stretched with a yawn, and looked over at my husband, who seemed to be much better than he'd been the night before. He, too, was awake.

"Take Lilli's advice and find the coffee. I'm feeling better, and I'm hungry."

Lilli reiterated, "Go. His fever is down, which means the antibiotics are working. You've got about an hour before Dr. Carson will be here to check on him."

I dragged myself to the coffee pot before I showered and redressed in the clothes I'd slept in. I called my boss and told him I would be in as soon as we were home again. I was waiting for Dr. Carson when one of his associates appeared and introduced himself as Dr. Jones. "Good morning. Dr. Carson has brought me up to speed regarding your husband's condition. I don't want either of you to worry as this reaction is perfectly normal and is expected, particularly after the first infusion of chemo. Barry's temperature is almost normal, but we need to keep him another day or two in order to administer the antibiotics intravenously. The nurse will continue the daily Neupogen injections." Satisfied with Barry's improvement, Dr. Jones left the room with a brief farewell and an air of purpose, on to his next patient.

Barry watched me for a moment before he smiled and said, "I don't know how I would get through all of this alone."

"You don't have to go through the tunnel alone. Just remember the light at the end of it." I held his hand in mine. "We'll get through this together. We will."

After lunch his body submitted to the need for sleep, and he napped soundly. Although I craved a much needed nap, I was either too tired or too keyed up to sleep. I stood at the window and regretted I wouldn't be able to flee the hospital for a short walk. A cold rain had set in and pelted irritably against the glass pane. The dreary, dismal weather that held me captive mirrored my mood. I was dog-tired when I didn't have the indulgence of being tired. But I had to help him live through the next few months until cancer was erased from our lives. His survival was, in essence, my own.

The rain was unrelenting. Unable to take my daily walk outside, I roamed the corridors and utilized flights of stairs until my meandering led me to the maternity floor. I loved babies, and in a big family like mine where babies were community property, there was always a new baby to love. I gazed through the transparent partition at the adorable newborns, wrapped securely in their pink or blue blankets, and heard "Brahms' Lullaby" floating throughout the hospital. I'd asked Lilli about the melody last week, and she told me the music was played with each new birth as a joyous announcement of life. I observed the sleeping newborns, lingering over their perfection, and I was completely at peace.

Barry was released a couple of days later, and he seemed to have recovered from whatever infection had attacked his weakened body. As soon as I had him settled in his oversized recliner, I unpacked our bag and immediately repacked it should another unexpected trip to the hospital arise. I returned a few calls, tossed in a load of laundry, and loaded the dishwasher. As I kept thank-you cards on hand, I took a few minutes to send one to Marnie for her thoughtful gestures. She'd left another gift bag in our room while Barry slept, and I'd roamed the hospital in search of solitude.

Although Barry would be staying home, I needed to return to my office and job responsibilities. Dr. Carson said after the ten day cycle of Neupogen, Barry could return to work with limitations and the understanding that when he was tired, he would have to go home and rest. I dreaded having to leave him home alone, but I needed my paycheck and, more importantly, the health insurance. We shared a light breakfast, and I gave him the daily shot. I reminded him I was only a couple of miles away should he need anything and that I would be home for lunch to check on him. With a kiss and a wave I was out the door. Work would, at least for a few hours, provide a slight distraction.

After I prioritized my littered desk that groaned with mail, folders, messages, and a "to do" list compiled before our latest hospital stay, I walked down the hall to find Susan in her classroom. She was one of the first teachers to make use of the computer based learning tool, the Internet, and had even ordered items "online"—putting her credit card and other personal information out there in a place known only as "cyberspace." While I was computer literate and proficient in various software programs relevant to my job, I hadn't yet had the opportunity or inclination to delve into the cache of information via the Internet. As a history major I'd spent hours researching topics for term papers, but that research was limited to my preference for books that beckoned from the college library. However, I didn't have the time to peruse dozens of medical books and sought a shortcut instead.

I knocked, entered, and asked for her assistance in using the newly acquired access. If knowledge was power, then I had much to learn. And the "web" was supposedly a wide-ranging profusion of data.

Susan greeted me warmly, "Oh, hi, Sheila. I'm glad you're back at work. How's Barry?"

"Much better, thanks. I need a favor, if you have time."

"Of course. What can I do?"

"I realize I'm able to use the Internet, but I don't actually know how to begin since I've had no reason to familiarize myself with 'surfing the web'. But due to recent events there's information I would like to have regarding Barry's diagnosis, treatment plan, recovery—anything that will help me help him. And the next time we have an appointment with either the surgeon or the oncologist, I want to be able to understand enough of what they're telling us to ask questions."

"You're a quick study, and it won't take more than fifteen minutes of basic instructions before you'll be able to do all the research you want." She dragged a chair over next to her desk where the computer awaited her command. "The first thing we'll do is create a password so you can login. Here's a pencil and paper. You'll need to write it down."

True to her word, it was not a complicated undertaking. I thanked her for her instruction and stopped by my boss's office to let him know I planned to stay late to catch up and to do some personal work on my own time. I explained that I needed answers for questions not yet formed. Mr. Rogers agreed but with misgivings. "Sheila, I can appreciate your eagerness to find out more about your husband's cancer, but remember the old saying that sometimes ignorance is bliss." I disregarded his warning.

When everyone left for the day, I eagerly began my exploration on the World Wide Web. The overabundance of information was daunting, but I was determined to continue with my quest for facts. I searched the diagnosis and found that Barry's particular cancer was, as Dr. Miller had said, very aggressive. What he hadn't shared was the fact that ninety-eight percent of patients die within the first year of diagnosis. I swept that information into the corners and chose to hold onto the one glimmer of optimism: not a hundred percent die.

An acquaintance, who was diagnosed a few years earlier with the same cancer in the upper GI tract, had survived. His wife had called to offer solace, and we discussed that our husbands' regimen was similar; Dr. Miller had also been his surgeon. I continued to search for recommended treatment plans, including chemo drugs that yielded the best results. Our oncologist referred to the plan as "slash/burn/poison," and my inquiry confirmed the methodology behind surgery/radiation/chemo proved to be most successful among available options. The order of that treatment was based on individual patients. I was reading material that pertained to a portacath and how it worked when the phone rattled me from my "surfing."

It was Barry calling. It was well after five o'clock, and he was worried since my day ended at four. He forgot I planned to work late to catch up. I didn't want to share with him all I discovered regarding his illness, especially the prognosis there was a mere two percent survival rate. Barry hadn't asked to know more, and I understood why my boss cautioned me. Knowledge could be the proverbial two sided coin.

"Hi, babe. I was calling to check on you. Are you coming home soon?"

"Yes, I'm fixin' to lock up and head for home. I want to run by the video store because Larry called and said he had a couple of new movies you might enjoy."

"Okay, thanks. But please make him let you pay this time. He's got a business to run, and he can't afford his overhead if he doesn't charge rental fees."

"I'll try, but according to Brad he stubbornly refused last week when I sent him to pick up a few movies for you. Larry said providing movies for your long days at home was the least he could do."

Barry continued, "That reminds me, one of my long-time customers came by today for a visit and told me not to worry about the grass next spring and summer. He promised to handle the lawn care for as long as necessary since the boys are working at the station in my place, and Brad's taking classes part-time at the college. I told him we wouldn't let him do that unless we pay him, but he wouldn't hear of it."

"That's generous of him." Barry and I were very grateful for the help of family and friends. We'd accepted that we couldn't do everything because we were entwined in the selfish, relentless demands of cancer. Both the advantage and disadvantage of living in a small town was that everybody usually knew everybody else's business. In times of need people were readily available to offer assistance.

And if you ever had a memory lapse all you had to do was ask around, and you could bet some busybody would be able to tell you exactly what was going on in your life. Our town's personality could be surmised by an incident that happened when I was learning the rules of the road. I'd pointed out to Daddy that he'd failed to use his left turn signal when he pulled into our driveway. He'd dismissed my observation with a wave of his hand and, "Aw, sugar, everybody in town knows I live here." Of course they did.

~

We kept our appointment with the surgeon in Carrollton to schedule a date for the portacath implant. Dr. Reid wanted to wait until a few days after the last Neupogen injection in order to reduce the risk of another infection. A date for the following week was scheduled for the outpatient procedure. There were no more trips to the ER, but the first round of treatment had left its vindictive evidence. Not only had Barry suffered an unknown infection that required hospitalization, but the vomiting and diarrhea had been severe—as had his fatigue. Despite those physical symptoms the worst for him seemed to be the afternoon I came home to find him wearing a baseball cap. I understood immediately the significance of the hat and his attempt to hide another heart wrenching symbol of cancer.

I greeted him with a smile, "Hello, my sweet husband. How are you feeling? Can I get you anything?"

He slowly removed the cap, with tears in his eyes, and a voice that cracked. "I couldn't help but notice that this morning's shower washed away more than body odor. I cleaned the drain and tub…I didn't think it would be a big deal, but…"

I glanced at his pathetic, patched head that resembled a dog with mange and was careful with my words. "Hey, we knew hair loss is a side effect of the chemo. I think the best solution is to call Linda and have her shave your head. What do you think?"

"Yeah, I guess that's the only choice unless I want to walk around lookin' like a freak."

"Don't ever say or even think that again! We're in the valley right now, a valley that's temporary. Your hair will grow back, but we do need to dig out a few warm boggins."

"You mean since the heat is going to seep out of my bald head. Guess you can call me 'Mr. Clean.'" He gave me a wry grin at the nickname.

His resilient spirit amazed me. I immediately called our hairdresser who agreed to a late afternoon appointment, after her last customer. Linda firmly refused to charge us for her work. "You don't owe me a dime. As many times as Barry has helped us out with car repairs and charged less for labor than he should have, I'm more than happy to repay his kindness." She patted him on the back and said, "We're just thankful you're here for us."

Linda wasn't the only one who, thankfully, depended on Barry. In a town that had waited patiently for progress, self-service gas pumps at those get 'n go stores became increasingly popular, and many people chose convenience over service. But progress had dramatically changed our town as the economic lifelines, the manufacturing plants, were suffocated by foreign competition and a decreased demand for their merchandises. One by one plant closings and mass lay-offs created a domino effect, and local businesses struggled to survive amid a sea of unemployment. Many were forced to close doors that had been open for generations.

Despite those economic upheavals and an interstate that diverted traffic away from town, the doors to our business remained opened—although some years were leaner than others. Barry had a good business that was dependent upon loyal customers, loyal because he was a good mechanic and an honest man. Linda was another example of not only the advantage of living in a small town, but of how Barry's integrity and the way he conducted his business and treated other people came back to him. He was a good man and didn't deserve to have cancer. But as he'd pointed out to me right after his diagnosis, nobody did.

CHAPTER 11

The Long, Winding Road

OUR DAYS WERE dominated by a single mindset: cancer. We thought our lives were busy, filled with the demands of life. And then cancer entered our lives and clarified the cloudy lens of perspective. While nobody ever said it would be easy, nobody ever told us it would be so damn hard. We became slaves to the chaos of cancer. Doctors' appointments, chemo infusions, and tests became our new normal.

Another consecutive trip to Atlanta was necessary to the Georgia Oncology Center for Barry's last round of his second chemo treatment. The weather was cold and rainy, typical for Georgia winters. It was the Friday before Christmas, the last weekend for those who had not had time to shop or had procrastinated or had forgotten that unlike Thanksgiving and Easter, Christmas was the same day every year.

As we entered the waiting room and hung up our rain coats, we were met with confident smiles and comments regarding the weather. The rain increased traffic headaches, and we were late for the appointment. Nevertheless, we were shown directly into one of several chemo suites. With a grin Barry collapsed into one of three comfortable recliners. "Well, let's get this party started."

His positive attitude and his acceptance of what couldn't be changed were hard to comprehend. Had I been the one diagnosed with cancer, I would have been furious at everybody and everything. And mad as hell at the world in general.

"Good afternoon, Barry," said Jill, a nurse we didn't recognize. "I'm glad to see the portacath has been implanted. It saves time and wear on the veins in your arms." She inserted the IV and began the drip.

"It was put in last week. If possible, we would like to be on our way before four o'clock when the traffic will begin to peak." His concern regarding the traffic seemed disproportionate in comparison to the liquid torture being pushed through his veins.

"We'll do what we can to finish in the required three hours." Jill adjusted the IV and turned to the radio. "Oldies station, right? Or if you prefer, you can watch television."

"No," I said. "Music is fine. Thank you."

"Okay. I'll be back in an hour or so to check on you. Should you need anything before then, push the red button."

"Got it." I'd learned the three hour routine on the first visit two days ago. There were no other patients who shared our supposedly soothing blue room, and I was grateful for the privacy. It was difficult to make conversation with strangers—and the elephant in the room. As the torrential rain poured outside like the tail end of a hurricane, the soft music glided through our provisional shelter. One of my old favorites, The Casinos' version of "Then You Can Tell Me Goodbye," entangled my heart in its nostalgic lyrics.

Barry noticed my misty eyes as I reached for a tissue. "Please don't cry. Please. I may not be here for a million years, but I promise to love you every day for the rest of my life. As our song goes, 'Never My Love.'" He took my hand in his and with the other hand motioned to the IV and the room in general. "You know, the worst part of all of this for me is seeing your tears. We have to stay upbeat, remember?"

"I remember." I kissed his cheek and swore to myself I wouldn't cry again, at least not in his presence.

Love, Life, & Broken Rainbows

With a sigh he said, "Honey, I'm not feeling well. Can you press the call button for Jill?"

His complexion was pasty, with a hint of green, and he reached for the barf can next to his chair as the nurse appeared in the doorway. One glance at Barry was all she needed to realize he was too sick to continue with the treatment. She closed the line from the IV to the port.

"This happens sometimes. We'll stop the chemo until the nausea has passed. I'm going to bring an injection of Zofran that will help ease your symptoms. Don't forget the relaxation and visualization techniques that were reviewed with you on Wednesday. Would you like ginger ale on ice and some crackers? Or a Popsicle?"

Perspiration beaded on his forehead. "Yes, thank you. Ginger ale would be good, and maybe a few saltine crackers."

I assumed the nurse would stop the treatment, and I asked if we could leave and return on Monday to finish when Barry would be feeling better. But I was told that once the infusion had begun, it was necessary it be completed on the same visit. An hour passed before Barry felt better, and Jill began the IV that flushed the remaining chemo, or as I referred to it "liquid hell," through his system. The clock mocked us as it greedily ate the lost minutes we needed in order to dodge the surge of traffic that would come like a salmon run upstream.

At five minutes after six Jill disconnected the IV and instructed me to drive to the back door as the office was closed, and the front entrance was locked. I retrieved our rain coats and dashed through the puddle filled parking lot where our car was the last one in patient parking. Barry was drowsy from the Zofran, so Jill helped me buckle him into the passenger seat.

He took my hand and said in a weak voice, "I'm sorry you have to drive us home in this downpour and at this time of day."

"Don't worry. I do know how to drive, and I'll get us home."

Jill wished us a "Merry Christmas" and thought of something regarding the traffic. "The t.v. was on in the waiting area, and I heard there's a huge traffic jam on I-75 due to an overturned tractor trailer. I don't know an alternate route for you, but I would avoid that interstate if at all possible."

"Okay. Thanks."

Given her warning, the only option was to make our way from Howell Mill Road, down Highway 41 to the I-285 junction which, unfortunately, was just past Cumberland Mall and its invasion of holiday shoppers. The rain continued and darkness covered the multitude of headlights and taillights that resembled a muddled ballet of hyper lightning bugs. There was nothing to do but join the rush hour. I handed Barry the pillow from the back seat and retrieved a bottle of ginger ale from the miniature cooler. I merged into the frenzied scurry of traffic and drove past the OK Café where we'd planned to have an early supper.

"Thanks for the drink. And the pillow. The medicine the nurse gave me for nausea has made me sleepy, but maybe I won't need the barf bag this time. I'll try to stay awake and keep you company until we get out of Atlanta. I know how much you hate driving in this weather at night and with all this traffic, but you did drive us over a portion of the Rocky Mountains."

"I'd almost forgotten you're an acrophobic. Neither of us realized it until your fear of heights became apparent, very apparent, on our trip out West. You were terrified on those curvy, narrow, roads that slithered over the Rocky Mountains like a snake. Your dizziness and the fact that there were no guardrails made it worse. And it hadn't helped that the Coors truckers drove around the curves like maniacs—and tailgated. By the time we found a spot to pull off the road and swap places, your knuckles were white from your strangle hold on the steering wheel. I'd almost needed a hammer to pry your tense grip from the wheel."

"Stop. My palms are sweatin' just thinking about the Colorado Rockies. I was excited about the drive over the parkway from Estes Park to Durango, until I thought I was going to pass out and drive us all over the side of the mountain. Thank goodness for the lunch break in the valley. What was the name of that place with the big lake? Grand Junction? Let's go back one day. I'm glad we included the Grand Canyon on that trip, but on our next trip I'd like to see Yellowstone Park and the Grand Tetons. We'll go without a couple of teenaged boys who found a reason to argue about everything. Brad had wanted nothing but to catch a plane or hop a bus back home. You would have thought we'd tied him to the back bumper and were draggin' him across the country."

"He was sixteen and trapped on a road trip with—dear, Lord—his parents and younger brother. In a minivan. It didn't take you long after that trip to sell the Astro and buy the '88 Mustang convertible. When I'd pointed out the smaller car would accommodate only two comfortably, all you said was 'That's right'. It was obvious that two weeks with our teenagers discouraged you from family vacations. But another trip with just the two of us sounds wonderful. It'll give us something to look forward to when you're healthy again."

As we inched closer to the mall, Barry drifted into the arms of sleep. It was just as well because we weren't getting anywhere. Traffic had all but stopped at the mall entrance, and the I 285 ramp was clogged with cars. I made the decision to stay on Highway 41 to the 120 loop and drive the back roads home, which would probably take longer, but it was better than being stuck in traffic. Without conversation for company, I tuned the radio to a station that played Christmas music nonstop during the holidays and switched the windshield wipers up a notch. The trips were tiresome for both of us, but necessary.

Faye, a local volunteer with the American Cancer Society, had called a few weeks after his diagnosis to offer assistance if we needed it. She said she would be happy to arrange for drivers to transport Barry to his chemo appointments so I wouldn't have to take time off from work. I thanked her for the generous offer but politely declined. I couldn't tell her how embarrassed Barry would be if he had to throw up in a trash bag or if the diarrhea kicked in before he was at home, which could result in an intestinal explosion in the car.

I glanced at my sleeping husband. It was better that I shuttled him to his appointments in the used, four-door Blazer we bought last week because it was more comfortable than the Mustang. Other than the traffic I enjoyed the time we shared, even when Barry slept. It was rainin' like pourin' piss out of a boot, and I settled into what was sure to be a long, tedious ride home.

The following week it was necessary to contact home healthcare, another link in the healthcare chain. Although Barry's temperature remained normal, his blood pressure was dropping. Dr. Carson recommended IV fluids that could be administered at home and provided the phone number. Lynn, the home healthcare nurse, was very thorough and proficient in training me in the necessities involved with caring for him. Once she inserted the IV into the port, she instructed me to scrub my hands with an antibacterial soap and to use disposable gloves.

"I have both items on hand because I've been injecting the Neupogen after his chemo treatments."

"Good." She proceeded to teach me how to change the bag of fluids and how to regulate the flow should Dr. Carson prescribe an adjustment in the rate. Once the last bag was empty it was necessary to flush the port with saline solution before and after in order to keep it sanitized, followed by heparin, an anticoagulant.

The most comfortable place for Barry to rest while hooked up to the IV was in his recliner in the den. The bag had to be changed every four hours, and I slept on the sofa in order to hear the beep that signaled it was time to change or disconnect the bag. His blood pressure stabilized in a couple of days, and I was injecting the heparin into the port when the doorbell rang. I yelled for whoever was on the other side to come on in. It was Pat bringing soup that she left in the kitchen and walked into the den. I appreciated her thoughtfulness because for several days following chemo Barry wasn't able to swallow anything except buttermilk due to the severity of the mouth and throat blisters, painful tracks left by a double edged sword.

"Hi, hope this isn't a bad time. Since Barry can't stand the smell of cooking, I brought homemade chicken noodle soup he can enjoy without the odor. I also picked up a carton of Mayfield Strawberry Cheesecake ice cream that he likes and put it in the freezer. Maybe he can eat a few bites of each." She gave Barry an affectionate pat on the arm and noticed me handling the IV. "What are you doing?"

"I'm doing exactly what the healthcare nurse told me to do, injecting heparin into the port to prevent bleeding. His blood pressure is normal, and he won't need any more fluids, per Dr. Carson."

Barry smiled at me, "I don't know what I would do without her. She's been a regular Florence Nightingale."

"Well," Pat replied, "maybe Sheila should have been a nurse."

I couldn't get the words out fast enough. "No, no, and no. It takes a special, compassionate person to take care of sick strangers. I've learned what I had to from the home healthcare nurse in order to avoid multiple hospital stays and to take care of my husband because I love him. And because he would do the same for me."

Three weeks later, as scheduled, the last of the chemo was dispensed, and tests were ordered to gage the success of the vile treatments. Dr. Miller allowed Dr. Seeman to perform a second GI endoscopy because he'd initially diagnosed the cancer, and the hospital was closer. Dr. Seeman was very pleased with the latest results and showed us the film from both procedures. The first revealed an ugly, black mass while the second exposed clean, pink tissue. The second CT failed to show an image of the tumor. Our next appointment was a pre-op with Dr. Miller.

He walked into the exam room all smiles and slapped Barry jovially on the back. "Everything looks great. The chemo has done exactly what was hoped for and shrunk the tumor. We're ready to schedule your surgery."

"Well, guess it's time to get it over with," answered Barry. I'm sure you've noticed I've gained almost thirty pounds despite the side effects of chemo."

Dr. Miller reviewed Barry's chart. "Twenty-eight pounds to be exact. You've gained weight because the tumor has shrunk, which created more space in your stomach and allowed you to eat more. But it's good you've bulked up because you'll lose weight after the surgery."

I thought of something I needed clarified, even if it was grasping at straws. "Dr. Miller, according to the last endoscopy, the tumor is gone. Is surgery still necessary?"

He rubbed his chin thoughtfully before he answered, "I realize test results can be misleading, but I don't want to give you false hope. The cancer is still there, and without surgery to remove the deadly cells it will return with a vengeance. Cancer is programmed to survive, and if it survived chemo it's just a matter of time before it would consume your husband. Consequently, to answer your question, yes, the surgery is necessary. Now let's look at the calendar together."

He pushed the call button, and his office manager immediately appeared with a master datebook in hand.

She opened the calendar, pen in hand. "Dr. Miller, you'll be in England for the next two weeks at the medical convention." An explanation wasn't required, but she continued with an undertone of pride and self-importance. "He will be training a team of doctors in London on the very surgical technique that will be used on your husband. You do realize that Dr. Miller developed the surgical procedure."

"Yes, I'm aware." I perused the calendar she flipped to February.

She and Dr. Miller reviewed the dates before he spoke, "We can schedule him for the last week of February. We'll notify the hospital and take care of the details. Barry will need to check in a day early for last minute tests and bloodwork."

Tests. Always more tests. A brief calculation revealed that surgery would not take place until five weeks after Barry's last round of chemo. "Dr. Miller, you explained to us at our first appointment the surgery would take place approximately three weeks after his last chemo treatment, which would be enough time for his body to recover before major surgery."

"Yes, that's the usual time lapse, but I'll be out of the country for the first two weeks of the month, and my schedule is filled my first week back. Therefore, Barry's surgery will have to be pushed into late February. It will give him an extra two weeks to rest and put on some more weight."

"I don't mean to be argumentative, but that date will be five weeks after his last chemo. He hasn't gone that long between treatments since the onset. Surely you understand my concern, given that not five minutes ago you made clear the importance of the surgery and how the cancer would 'consume' my husband if it's not removed."

"I do understand, Sheila, but my trip has been scheduled for months, and it's too late to cancel or to reschedule other patients. You're going to have to trust my decision."

It was Barry's turn to speak, "Dr. Miller, I do trust you, and I'll take your advice to get plenty of rest. And I may even pack on a few more pounds." He laughed and took my hand as we stood to leave the office. "I feel better than I have in the last year, and it'll be nice to have a break from all of this."

We left the office and agreed to stop at The Varsity a few blocks away. I wasn't hungry, but a luscious frosted orange shake would be a treat. It was a good idea to know in advance what you wanted to order at the popular eatery or else encounter their famous slogan, "what'll ya have" chorus in rapid succession while impatient patrons stood in line for cheeseburgers, chili dogs, and hand cut fries or homemade onion rings.

While Barry had gained weight, I'd lost several pounds and really should have something for lunch. But as we made our way to the parking deck, I couldn't quell an uneasy feeling that pervaded my gut, although I trusted Dr. Miller. I brushed the sensation aside as nothing but nervousness over the surgery. It could have been that I'd spent too much time researching his particular cancer and was paranoid. At least his surgery was scheduled, and we could plan accordingly.

Finally, the day of his surgery arrived. Barry and I had spent the day before and night in the hospital, as always, together. In addition to the pre-op procedures, two members of the pain management team visited us to explain they would be responsible for controlling his post-operative pain. They, as had Dr. Miller, warned the pain would be intense, but Dr. Byrd assured us they would control that pain.

Barry would be in the ICU for the first three nights following the surgery, and I would not be allowed to spend the night on a cot next to him. I promised him that I would sleep in the waiting room to be close to him, but he insisted I get some rest. The Renaissance Hotel was located a block from the hospital, and a security guard escorted those alone to the hotel lobby. The hotel gave discounts to patients' family members because many patients and their families traveled from neighboring states. There were no accommodations for the time frame I required, and I needed to make other arrangements.

One of my cousins, Aunt Reba's son Butch, lived only a few miles from the hospital and resolved the matter. He had a guest room and agreed to pick me up at the hospital each night at eight o'clock, when ICU visiting hours ended. He would drive me back to the hospital each morning, and I could sit with Barry for one hour every four. Although our car was parked in the allocated space across the street, Butch saw no reason for me to make the drive to his home, especially at night. I was appreciative of Butch's hospitality. I couldn't have coped without the love and support of our family. They all pitched in to do their part.

On the morning of his surgery Jerry and Jerline arrived early, predawn. We wanted to have prayer time before Barry was wheeled into the operating room, where he would be held in unconscious restraint for eight hours. My siblings and I had grown up in the same small, country Baptist church where our mama had attended all of her life. As a child she rode to church in a mule drawn, buckboard wagon every Sunday with Grandma Pearl at the reigns. I was grateful my brother and his wife had come to pray with us.

As we held hands and bowed our heads, the first pale fingers of a new day crept over the window sill and brought life to the room's dim, artificial lighting. The minute our collective "amen" was spoken, there was a knock on the door followed by the entrance of an orderly assigned to transport Barry to the operating room.

The young man with a mop of dark hair and glasses introduced himself as Kevin. "I was standing in the hallway and didn't want to interrupt your prayers. Not everybody here prays for their loved ones, but it's good to know some folks do."

Barry was already groggy from his pre-surgery "happy shot," but managed to tell Kevin prayer was important. As I bent to kiss him he whispered, "I'll be right back."

"And I'll be right here. I love you."

Barry slipped into unconsciousness as Kevin raised the bed rails and deftly carted my husband out of the room and down the corridor to the service elevator. I followed beside the trolley and held tightly to Barry's hand until I had to release my grip. The service elevator doors hissed shut with a soft swoosh, and tears ebbed silently down my cheeks. My big brother put his arm around me and let me cry on his shoulder as we made our way to the surgical waiting room. Within the hour several of our family members commandeered a quarter of the large waiting room and set up camp, complete with snacks and magazines. They had come for the duration, and I loved them for it.

They were there to help me through one of the longest days of my life. Pat encouraged me to eat something, but I couldn't and declined her offer to go to the cafeteria and get something for me. Instead I drank watery, lukewarm cappuccino from the vending machine and either sat impatiently fidgeting or pacing like a caged lion. The huge wall clock taunted me as it dragged the hours in leisurely revolutions. When I was certain I couldn't stand the wait one minute more, our corner was approached by a surgical nurse.

I jumped from my chair to greet her, "Are you looking for me? My husband's name is Barry." I glanced at the sardonic face of the clock. It was hard to accept that only four hours had passed, and I was alarmed something had gone wrong during surgery.

"You're Sheila?"

"Yes. How is he? Is everything alright?"

She gave me an encouraging smile. "Dr. Miller asked me to let you know the surgery is going well, but it will take approximately another three hours to complete the procedure. As soon as he's out of surgery, Dr. Miller will discuss everything with you."

"Thank you. Thank you very much for the update."

She recognized my anxiety and took my hand. "Try not to worry. Dr. Miller is one of our best surgeons. Your husband is in very capable hands."

She hurried out, leaving me with the positive comments of my family. Melba hugged me tightly. "Well, the news that all is going as expected is good. My son is strong, and he will get through this."

Carl nodded in optimistic agreement. I wasn't sure if his parents were trying to convince me or them, but their confidence was reassuring. However, time seemed to stand still.

Waiting was the hardest part, and in an effort to pass the time and to distract me, Pat asked above the chatter, "Sheila, do you remember the time Daddy left you, Brad, and me on our trip to Florida? What were you, eight months pregnant? I don't know what in the hell we were thinkin'."

I leaned back in my chair and let my worried mind travel to a happier time and place as Pat coaxed me into retelling the story of being left by Daddy.

It was springtime when Daddy and Mama, both retired, decided to take a road trip to Panama City Beach. Pat and I loved the beach and saw no reason not to take Brad and tag along, even though I was very pregnant. We were close to our destination when Daddy decided to fill up the car, although it had almost half a tank. He asked if anybody needed anything before he went inside to pay for the gas. Brad was almost three and needed another potty break and at eight months pregnant, I could always go to the bathroom. Pat desperately needed a cigarette; Daddy wouldn't let her smoke in the car.

The three of us climbed out of the large back seat, leaving Mama behind. We finished our business and walked towards where the car had been, but it was gone. We looked around the parking lot and asked the attendant if he knew where the man and woman in the white Cadillac had parked. He scratched his head, confused. "They're gone, got their gas and left."

"'Left'? What do you mean left?" asked Pat, who reached for another cigarette.

"Exactly that. They got back on the road. The tall man wearing a hat said they had to hurry on down to the beach."

Daddy had always enjoyed the trip more than the destination. With nothing to do but get out of the hot sun, we found a spot in the shade of the building and waited. Surely Daddy would miss us soon or Mama would tell him, and he'd come right back. But after half an hour, we were beginning to wonder if we'd been abandoned. Pat was especially concerned. She'd also been left at a gas station when Daddy, Mama, and six kids were on a trip to Texas—wrapped in July heat and an old Chevrolet.

She knew from that childhood experience Daddy would eventually come back and get us. While we waited I entertained Brad with a game of "I Spy." Pat paced, smoked, and cussed. Brad was the first to see Papa Joe coming toward us, motioning us towards the road. "You girls get the boy and come on. We've wasted enough time."

I yelled, "Where's the car?"

Daddy was as agitated as a worm in hot ashes. "Down the road a piece. I forgot where I filled up and left y'all. Now come on!"

We did as we were told and hurried along behind him to a nearby gas station where he'd parked the car. Daddy stormed inside to buy Rolaids and ignored Mama, who was in the front seat with the door opened, doubled over with laughter. I think she'd peed her pants a little, although Pat and I didn't see what was so funny. I couldn't believe her hysterical laughter over her daughters and grandson being left behind and asked, "Mama, what is wrong with you? Why didn't you tell Daddy he'd left us at the service station?"

Between wiping tears and gasping for breath she explained what had transpired. When Daddy cranked the car and pulled into traffic, she asked him where he was going. Daddy abruptly told her, "You just sit right there and keep your mouth closed, and I'll show you where I'm going—to the beach if you won't sidetrack me."

Mama was a stubborn woman, and Daddy had pissed her off with that remark about keeping her mouth shut. They rode along in silence, and Mama waited for Sherlock Holmes to figure out we weren't in the car.

About twenty minutes down the road, Daddy remarked, "You girls sure are quiet back there. Brad must be asleep if he's not chattering away like a little monkey."

His comment was met with silence. After several more miles he adjusted the rearview mirror and looked in the backseat. Mama said when he realized the seat was empty he slammed on the brakes, turned around in his seat with eyes that popped out of his head like they had springs on 'em. "Good goshamighty! Where in the hell are 'em kids?"

Mama took a few minutes to enjoy Daddy's panic before she answered, "I reckon they're back at the gas station where you left 'em."

Daddy sputtered, "Well, why in God's name didn't you tell me they got outta the car?"

"If you remember, Joe, I was told to keep my mouth closed. So I did."

⁓

Although the story was well-known, my family thought it was hilarious and laughed every time they heard it. Their amusement snapped me back to the waiting room, and I nervously glanced again at the clock. It was almost two-thirty, and everybody decided some fresh air and a meal were needed. They agreed to walk across the street to Mick's for sandwiches. They gathered their jackets and tried to coax me into leaving for a respite from the deserted waiting room, but each of them knew I wasn't going to budge.

I was alone for almost an hour with nerves that squealed through every inch of my weary body when I saw Dr. Miller approaching me, still wearing his surgical scrubs. I hastily rose from the armchair and sprinted across the gray tiled floor. "How is he? When can I see him? It took longer than we expected. Did you get the cancer? Is he going to be alright?"

With a soothing hand on my shoulder he replied, "Let's take this one question at a time, shall we?" He motioned to a sofa and skimmed the area with tired eyes. "Why don't we sit down? Are you here by yourself?"

I took a seat, and he folded his tall frame into the chair beside me. "No, several of my family members are here. Our sons, Barry's parents, my brother, and—"

Right on cue the elevator opened. Laughter and lively conversation tumbled out, which were very much out of place in the somber setting. I held my finger to my lips to shush the boisterous gang. My family immediately grew silent as they gathered close enough to hear the conversation between Dr. Miller and me.

With a nod of acknowledgement to concerned relatives, Dr. Miller addressed the group. "To answer your questions, Barry is doing very well, but he won't be out of recovery for another couple of hours and then you can see him. The surgery lasted longer than I anticipated because until the patient is in the operating room, it's hard to pinpoint exactly how long any given procedure will take."

As calmly as possible I asked, "But were you able to remove all of the cancer?"

With a worn out sigh and a slight shrug, he scanned the concerned faces that hovered around us and returned his attention to me. "Yes, but it was necessary to remove slightly more of his stomach and esophagus than I'd estimated. The first pathologist's report indicated the lingering presence of cancerous cells and without clean margins, all that Barry has endured would have been in vain. The second report was completely clean, free of any persistent cells. Had the deadly cells invaded even a fraction beyond the healthy parameters, I wouldn't have been able to effectively remove the cancer."

I thanked God as Dr. Miller stood to depart, and I thanked him with a hug. I hadn't considered how fatigued he must've been after almost eight hours performing a complex surgery. He assured me I would be allowed to see Barry in the ICU, but only for a few minutes. I gratefully accepted whatever scraps I was thrown.

~

At last, long after darkness collected the day, I was permitted to enter the protective domain of the ICU. Despite the fact that I thought I was fully prepared to see Barry, I gasped at the sight of the numerous tubes, machines, and bandages that swaddled my dear husband.

He was sleeping but stirred when I picked up his hand and held it in mine.

His brown eyes struggled to focus, and he smiled at me. "I knew it was you, here by my side."

"Where else would I be?" My eyes glistened, but I held the tears in check.

He attempted to shift in the bed. "I feel like I've been hit by a train."

"What a coincidence. You look like you've been hit by a train."

"Have you seen Dr. Miller? How did things go?"

"Yes, I've spoken with him, and the surgery was successful. He assured me the pathologist's report revealed nothing but healthy tissue. No more cancer." There was no point in telling him he was left with less of a stomach than originally planned. Dr. Miller could elaborate in the morning when he made his rounds.

"That's good news, really good news." He turned his attention to me. "You're tired. Have you rested at all today? Have you eaten anything?"

His concern should have been for himself instead of me. "Not yet, but I will. And I promise I'll get a good night's sleep at Butch's house. I have to rest so I can spend the day here with you tomorrow."

"Okay. Has everyone else gone?"

"Most of them. Your parents, Brad and Valerie, and Chuck are waiting their turns to see you before they leave. Everybody else left only because the head nurse told them in no uncertain terms they wouldn't be allowed in the unit—immediate family only. Their plans are to coordinate visits to see you over the next week or so."

His voice was hoarse from the breathing tube that had been down his throat all day, but he managed to say, "Sounds good to me."

I sacrificed a few precious moments with him to allow Carl, Melba, Valerie and our sons to have a couple of minutes each to speak to him. As soon as they gathered at the elevator, I hurried back to his side for another brief visit. However, the minute my butt touched the seat of the straight-backed chair the curtain was yanked open. The night nurse, who introduced herself as Doris, stood before me in a huff, hands on her hips. "You have to go now. He's had enough visitors and needs to rest. Now. You can see him again in the morning, but not before nine a.m. Not a minute before." The unit was positively her turf, and she wasn't going to bend the rules an inch.

I was pretty sure Doris had been a former drill sergeant. She continued to stand at the opened curtain and waited for me to go, certain I wouldn't challenge her authority. I would like to have had a few more minutes with him, but accepted that she was doing her job and what I wanted was not on her agenda.

I kissed Barry's hand and whispered, "I love you. I'll see you in the morning." He'd already floated backwards into peaceful oblivion.

I asked Doris to take good care of him, claimed my suitcase from the waiting area, and caught the elevator to the lobby. I exited the main doors and found Butch, true to his word, waiting in the circular drive with a box of fresh, hot Krispy Kreme donuts. Although it was barely past nine o'clock, other than a brief review of the surgery, I was too beat to carry on a conversation. Butch offered me a donut, and I ate the sugary sawdust out of politeness for his thoughtfulness.

I was relieved when we turned into his driveway. Butch's wife Brenda met us at the door and offered to make a sandwich for me, but I wasn't hungry and preferred sleep over food. My demeanor must have revealed that I was worn to a frazzle. She picked up my bag, showed me immediately to the guest room, and told me to make myself at home. With a promise to wake me no later than seven a. m., she closed the door behind her, and I was alone. Alone with my relief, gratitude, and exhaustion.

CHAPTER 12

Family Ties

MORNING BROUGHT A February frost and the delicious aroma of fresh coffee and sizzlin' bacon. I stretched myself awake and was momentarily disoriented in the tastefully decorated, although unfamiliar, blue and beige setting. The clock on the night stand informed me it was almost seven; I'd slept for over eight uninterrupted hours. I pushed the floral comforter to the side and hurried to get ready for breakfast and my ride back to the hospital. I had to be there for the nine a. m. visiting hours, or I would have to wait until one o'clock before I could see Barry.

Determined not to be late, I went into the hallway, leaned over the stair rail and called downstairs to Brenda that I was awake and would be down in half an hour. She answered for me to take my time because she was just fixin' to pop the biscuits in the oven. I'd barely eaten the day before, and I was famished. I showered, brushed my teeth, and put on a bare minimum of makeup before I made the bed and organized my belongings. My suitcase would remain in the guest room until Thursday, when Barry would be moved to a room, and I could stay with him day and night.

I hurried downstairs where hot coffee and a scrumptious breakfast were waiting. As soon as we finished eating I put my dishes in the sink and thanked Brenda for her hospitality. With a hug goodbye I was out the door, anxious to see Barry.

Butch drove expertly through familiar morning traffic and dropped me off in the same curved drive designated for patient pick up. I thanked him and hurried to the ICU; it was ten minutes before nine. At the hour I pressed the button and was admitted to the shushed, sterile setting with its atmosphere of seriousness. I hurried to his cubicle and was shocked when I saw the pain sketched across his face. My entrance startled him, but he reached for my hand when he recognized me. His voice was weak and raspy. "Good morning. I'm really glad to see you."

I was cautious not to overreact. "I'm not sure it's a good morning. Did you sleep at all? How are you?"

"The pain medication isn't working. Every inch of my body aches, the kind of pain I can't even begin to describe. It hurts to move, to breathe. Hell, it even hurts to blink. Doris gave me a bath this morning around three, and I thought I was going to die from the pain. She's not exactly gentle with her bed bath technique and didn't seem to mind that I was in agony. Do you remember when I had kidney stones and was in so much pain that I had to crawl to the bathroom to throw up in the toilet?"

My heart was screaming with anger. Fortified with a good night's rest and a hearty breakfast, I was ready to kick somebody's ass and didn't give a damn whose. I tried to remain calm and answered, "Yes. We were both relieved when the stones passed, but why did you ask?"

"Because that pain makes what I'm going through now seem like a day at the beach." Each word was labored, and his breathing was heavy with suffering.

"I'm sorry. I'll talk to someone about your medication." I took a few deep breaths and changed the subject. "Aren't you hungry?" I noticed the bag of milk colored fluid that dripped through his IV.

"No, not at all." He nodded toward the white sustenance. "Guess Dr. Miller was right when he said the concoction would keep me from being hungry."

I sat there as long as I could, but it was time to get off my ass and find somebody from pain management. I stood and said, "I need to speak with one of the nurses. I'll be back in a few minutes."

"Okay." His face was as white as the sheets.

I hated to miss even a minute of my visitation hour, but his weak smile was an attempt to hide the fact he could barely breathe without pain. I made my way to the nurses' station and asked to speak to the head nurse.

"She's with a patient. Can I help you?" asked a nurse.

In as composed a voice as I could manage, I introduced myself. "I really hope you can. I'm Sheila, and my husband is Barry, in unit three. He had major surgery yesterday, and his pain medication is not preventing his pain. Either you or I need to contact the department responsible for controlling his pain."

"Your husband is on the standard dosage of Demerol prescribed for most of the post-op patients. He must be exaggerating his discomfort."

I'd tried the polite, calm approach, but that hadn't yielded results. I slammed my hand down on the counter and in a frustrated voice repeated my request. "No, my husband is NOT 'exaggerating' when it comes to how much pain he's in, and he is not going to endure his pain anymore. Find the head nurse—*now!*"

She was flustered but scuttled away to find the person in charge. I spent the next fifteen minutes arguing with Lauren, a woman who seemed unaccustomed to the tirade of an angry spouse. "I'm not leaving this ICU until you contact pain management and resolve this matter. If you want to call security and have me escorted out, then do it. But let me assure you that would not be your smartest move."

"Are you threatening me?"

"Absolutely not. I'm simply making it very clear to you that my husband has had massively invasive surgery. There's absolutely no reason for him to suffer the aftereffects of that surgery. As a medical professional you must realize that his pain is unnecessary."

Lauren wavered momentarily before reaching for the phone. She explained the situation to whoever was dangling on the other end of the line, made some notes on his chart, and replaced the receiver. "I've been authorized to increase the Demerol for your husband. The dosage prescribed should alleviate any lingering pain."

"Then do it. Increase his dosage before you do anything else." The idiom about catching more flies with honey than vinegar came to mind, and I placed my hand on her forearm and implored her, "Please."

With the additional Demerol his pain was lessened, and he felt like visitors. Although only ten minutes per hour were allocated for visitors and limited to two at any one time. I was reluctant to sacrifice any of my precious minutes with him, but I understood other family members were anxious to see him. Barry's brother Phil and his wife Janice arrived for the one o'clock hour. I warned them that Barry looked rough and to try not to be too shaken by his appearance and all the paraphernalia involved in his care.

Janice put her arms around me and said, "Sheila, I can't believe you're preparing us for the worst when the two of you have been through so much. We'll handle this visit and be strong for him."

But I wanted them to be aware of Barry's condition. "Well, it was a jolt the first time I saw him, and I thought I was prepared. I don't want either of you to be alarmed by his current state; y'all need to know what to expect. On Thursday some of the medical apparatuses will be disconnected before he's moved to a room on the fifth floor, but for now he does bring to mind a train wreck."

Phil and Janice stayed the allotted ten minutes and promised to stay in touch. They were two of only a handful of visitors, and I was grateful his need for rest was respected. With only snatches of time with Barry, it was a long day. Contradictory to the concept that waiting in a hospital is not tiring, it's wearisome. Tired or not, Nurse Doris and I were going to have a come to Jesus meetin' regarding her three a.m. bath routine and her lack of concern for Barry's well-being. But I was informed that she was off for the next few days, and that confrontation was avoided. By the time Doris returned, Barry had been relocated to the more empathetic care provided on the cancer ward.

Thursday arrived and, as indicated, we were moved to a room where we were happy to find that Lilli was on duty, vigilant and compassionate in meeting the demands of her patients. She made Barry comfortable, reviewed his chart, and noted he was still experiencing some pain. She also confirmed that my cot would be delivered well before bedtime and hurried on her way. Barry encouraged me to find myself some lunch, but I felt guilty about eating when he couldn't. He motioned to the milky liquid that coursed through his veins. "Don't be stubborn. You're not being fed by an intravenous meal, and you have to eat. I don't think Lilli will bring a bag of this stuff for you. Go have lunch and take your walk. It's been a busy morning, and I'm beat. I'll sleep while you get some fresh air."

I was torn between hunger and the need to breakout of the room's boundaries or staying with him. But Barry was right. I had to eat something, and a walk would be good for me. "Okay. I'm going. I'll be back in a little while."

Even though it was the tail end of February it was not very cold, and the sun was shining brightly. I inhaled the refreshing air and decided to walk before eating as a midafternoon meal would get me through until tomorrow's breakfast. I walked the familiar maze so as not to stray too far, a trek that would lead me back to the hospital before the whisper of dusk. As I walked I made a mental note to call my boss and discuss upcoming deadlines and my work schedule over the next week. He knew I wouldn't leave the hospital until Barry and I could leave together. Mr. Rogers and I didn't always see eye-to-eye, but under the circumstances he was understanding and supportive. He'd traveled the road himself and, therefore, knew all too well the demands and complexities of having a spouse with cancer.

―

The day's visitors had come and gone, and Barry and I settled down for the night. Jason, our first male nurse, gave Barry his injection of Demerol, charted his stats, and left us to ourselves. I fought with the cot for a comfortable position, but despite my long walk and perpetual state of weariness, sleep proved to be as elusive to capture as an early morning fog. I reached for Barry's hand through the bed rail and knew when he squeezed my hand sleep had not yet found him either. Although we'd become accustomed to the room's dimmed lights and the hospital's hushed sighs that came with late evening, it was still hard to sleep.

"Are you awake?" he asked.

"Yes, why? Are you okay?"

"I was thinking about the blizzard of '93. You haven't forgotten those few days when we were snowed in, have you?"

I smiled into the semi-glow that enveloped us. "No, I haven't."

March of 1993 had, indeed, come in like a lion. The blizzard gave us about an inch of solid ice, covered with ten or more inches of snow and drifts up to three feet. The storm had plunged most of the state into a deep freeze that knocked out power and brought travel to a standstill. Interstates were closed, and side streets were impassable. Fortunately, we were prepared with plenty of firewood and groceries. Our sons were snowed in at friends' houses, which left Barry and me with four days wrapped in the warmth of a fire and the afterglow of our passion—a passion that hadn't diminished with the years.

Our snowbound lovemaking was a wonderful memory made almost three years ago, a memory from another life. His grip loosened, and my hand slipped from his. We eventually slept, but not for long. In less than three hours Barry was awake, in a fit of pain. I vaulted from the cot and hit the call button for the nurse who entered our room immediately and evaluated Barry's discomfort. "Are you in pain? On a scale of one to ten, what is the level of your pain?"

"A ten plus and I'm sorry I'm still hurtin' like hell. The Demerol has been increased twice, but I can't stand this pain much longer."

Wide awake and alert I demanded information from our night nurse. "Why is he suffering like this? His pain medication has been adjusted to relieve his pain, but he's still in pain. Can he have another injection?"

Jason checked his watch and seemed conflicted when he answered. "He's not due another shot for an hour, at three-thirty. I'll get in touch with someone from pain management." He paused before he hesitantly continued, "Demerol if a very effective pain killer, but—"

"But what?" I questioned harshly.

Jason was reluctant but answered, "It's not effective for one hundred percent of our post-op patients, especially for someone who has undergone the extensive surgery your husband has. I'll make the call now and try to contact someone who can adjust his medication. If not, I'll leave a message with the service to get in touch with the head nurse first thing in the morning."

"That's it? That's the best you can do—take two aspirins and call me in the morning?"

"I'm sorry, but without explicit orders from the doctors responsible for monitoring his pain, I can't do anything except contact their answering service and wait. I'll be back at three-thirty on the dot with his next dosage."

Although I understood the nurse's position in following doctors' orders, it was agony to see Barry writhe in pain. It was unacceptable for my husband to suffer the consequences of decisions made by the ineptness of a vital link in the caretaking chain. While helpless to do anything to alleviate his pain at two-thirty in the morning, I would be ready and waiting in the morning to take control of this situation.

At daybreak Lilli came in to greet us with her usual cheerful smile. "Good morning, Barry. I understand from Jason that you had a long night."

Groggy from the few hours of sleep he'd managed to catch, he replied, "Yes, even though I'm glad to be out of ICU, and Sheila spent the night next to me, the pain is much more than I bargained for after meeting with the pain specialists. They gave me the impression I wouldn't be in pain, but the pain I've had since the surgery has been almost more than I can handle. In general I'm not a complainer, and I don't mean to inconvenience anyone, but I hurt so much that I've forgotten what it's like not to hurt."

Lilli proceeded to competently check his blood pressure and temperature, made a few notations on his chart, and patted his hand. "You're not inconveniencing anybody. Our sole responsibility is to take care of you, and as soon as someone from the pain clinic returns the messages Jason left with their service, I'll discuss your case with them in detail."

At that point I was awake, and although I felt like I'd been hit by a truck, I sat on the side of the cot and made it clear to Lilli that I wanted to speak with whoever got back to her. And in a softer tone added, "I appreciate that Barry is your patient, Lilli, but please let me know when to expect someone. I'll be here, ready to resolve this matter once and for all. My husband has spent his last night in pain."

She was quick to comprehend that I was not in the mood to argue. "I'll relay that information, Sheila, but their office doesn't open until eight-thirty. Why don't you get a shower and find yourself some breakfast?"

"Thanks. Good idea." Breakfast was usually a cup of cappuccino and, some mornings, a muffin or a bowl of grits. I needed to eat something before I confronted the SOBs who weren't doing their jobs. By nine o'clock I was a ticking bomb ready to explode.

At nine-fifteen a well-dressed and relaxed Dr. Byrd, with whom we'd met before the surgery regarding pain management, knocked on our partially opened door and strolled in. I sprang to my feet as he greeted Barry.

He shook my husband's hand and spoke in a congenial manner, as if we were all friends. "Well, good morning, Barry. I've been informed that although we've increased your Demerol dosage twice, you're still experiencing some pain. That's unfortunate."

I didn't wait for Barry to reply, nor did I bother with pleasantries. "You can bet your ass he's in pain, and 'unfortunate' doesn't begin to describe his suffering. Look at him. No, no, don't glance out the window or stare down at your freshly shined wingtips. LOOK. AT. HIM!" I walked over to the bedside and gently lowered the hospital gown to Barry's waist in order to reveal the incision that stretched from front to back. The gastric drain tube dangled like an octopus tentacle from inside the surgical wound. "He's been shucked like an oyster."

Dr. Byrd did look at Barry but spoke to me. "I realize you're upset. Wives, especially ones who opt to stay at the hospital day and night, have a tendency to become overwrought due to fatigue and stress, not to mention the spousal bond under difficult circumstances. Wouldn't you agree, Sheila?"

Agree? I visualized myself rippin' his head off and slammin' it against the wall like a discarded Halloween pumpkin. But I refrained from a physical assault and remained as calm as possible as I responded to his indifference, "I'm going to ignore your asinine assumption that I'm exaggerating his level of pain because I'm 'overwrought'. But don't mistake this southern drawl and my small town upbringing for ignorance. You can drop the patronizing attitude, and don't even for a minute try to pull that emotional woman crap. You're not blind. Even without noting Dr. Miller's capable handiwork, anybody can see that my husband has been in agony since the anesthesia wore off days ago. Look at his pain wracked body, the dark circles under his eyes against the stark whiteness, and listen to his labored breathing. As difficult as it may be for you, try to find one ounce of empathy somewhere behind that designer suit."

Dr. Byrd appeared embarrassed as he approached the bed to examine Barry. "We might be able to increase his Demerol, but not by much."

While Barry remained complacent, I wasn't finished. "He's been given enough Demerol to bring down a horse, and I doubt if you or anyone else took the time to consider that the drug is not working." I ran my fingers through my hair and took a moment to compose myself before I persisted. "I realize you think highly of yourself, but step out of your arrogance and accept that what you're prescribing has not been effective."

Barry spoke up for himself. "The Demerol hasn't helped much at all. Is there anything else you can prescribe?"

Dr. Byrd stood there without comment, and I continued, "Your responsibility, your *only* responsibility was to keep him comfortable and his pain to a minimum. Despite your assurances, you have failed miserably to meet your obligation. So let me clarify this, to use your word, 'unfortunate' situation. I'm going to the cafeteria for another cup of caffeine, and when I get back it would be in your best interest for my husband to be pain-free. If not, I'll be on the phone with United Healthcare faster than you can say 'malpractice'. I'll advise them to disregard any medical claims from your office and that you are not to be paid one dime because you haven't controlled his pain and, therefore, haven't earned a penny. Do you understand, Dr. Byrd?"

"Yes. I'll examine Barry in your absence and reassess his needs."

"Good. I'll be back in about an hour." I kissed Barry's pale cheek and left the room in a huff.

When I returned to the fifth floor, Lilli was all smiles. "You're going to be much happier when you see Barry. He's sleeping as peacefully as a baby."

"Oh, Lilli, that's wonderful. Did Dr. Byrd adjust his pain meds?"

"He certainly did. He authorized a morphine pump, and Barry can self-administer the drug to control his pain. There is, of course, a limit to the contents in the bag, but morphine is ninety-nine percent effective. Dr. Byrd said he will stop by later this afternoon to verify that Barry's pain is under control."

"Thank you. Thank you very much."

I noiselessly entered our room and noticed the closed blinds. I stood next to his bed and thanked God that Barry's breathing was normal, and the ravages of his pain were no longer visible. The dark circles and dreadful grimace had been erased by a wondrous drug. I dropped into the recliner and held his hand in mine. I didn't realize I'd fallen asleep until Lilli came in to unlock the plastic box that held the morphine filled bag.

"Pleased to see you both had a nice morning nap."

She busied herself with the key, and I couldn't help but question why the lock and key were necessary. "Why is the box locked? Would anybody want to steal the hospital's equipment?"

Lilli crossed her arms over her chest and enlightened me. "I realize you're from a small town and this is your first encounter with a serious illness, which makes your confusion reasonable." She expertly replaced the empty bag with a new one, locked the box, checked his port, and wrote down the time and contents of the bag. After jotting down her initials she explained, "If the morphine is not locked and the dosage controlled, a junkie would drain the contents within an hour. Even with the safeguards the more experienced addicts can find a way to dispense the drug in one dose in order to feed their life consuming addictions. While most of our patients, like Barry, are not drug addicts, the same guidelines must be followed to the letter."

Noting my concerned expression as she checked the bag filled with whatever substance was feeding Barry, she must've read my mind. "Don't worry, Sheila. Barry won't be on morphine long enough to become addicted, and his dosage is controlled. I'll be back later." She picked up his chart and left the room.

⁓

Butch stopped by around lunch time. "I was in this neck of the woods and thought I'd check on you two." After shaking Barry's hand and asking how he was doing, he turned to me. "If you haven't eaten lunch yet, I know just the place." He coerced me, with Barry's insistence, into going with him to Mary Mac's Tea Room for a "home cooked" meal. "It won't be nearly as good as your mama's cookin', but it's the closest you'll find here in Atlanta. C'mon, it'll give you a break from the hospital cafeteria and Mick's."

He was right in that the meal couldn't compare to Mama's cooking, but it was better than I'd had in the last few weeks. A change of scenery was welcomed, and the dining room was charming with its country styled wooden tables and chairs and blue gingham checked tablecloths and curtains. I enjoyed reminiscing over our childhood and dessert, banana pudding, but the beckoning urge to return to the hospital lured me from the temporary diversion—as it always did when I was away from Barry for more than a couple of hours. I glanced at my watch and laid my napkin on the plate. "Thank you for the delicious meal and the company. I don't want to seem ungrateful, but I really do need to get back to the hospital, and you must have to get back to work."

"I'm ready when you are." He picked up the check and left a generous tip. "I'm sure you haven't forgotten that Brenda and I married when we were teenagers, too. I can't imagine walking in your shoes right now. As for me having to rush back to work, you know I own the construction company. The boss won't mind if I have a long lunch with one of my favorite cousins."

We walked to the car in companionable silence. No, I hadn't forgotten Butch owned his construction company, Oak Street Developments. It was named for the street in Bremen where his paternal Grandma had lived and where he'd made many happy childhood memories during summers spent in her two-story, framed house, with its white picket fence. Butch and his younger sister were Aunt Reba's kids and lived in Atlanta, where I seldom visited. However, the two of them spent summers with their Grandma and enjoyed the freedom I and other cousins and friends took for granted. We roamed the town on bicycles and went to the show and the city pool, when we had fifty cents, or waded in a nearby creek—all without adult supervision.

But we couldn't be anywhere in town when the five o'clock whistle blew. Its shriek signaled the end of the day at the factories and traffic was hectic with hundreds of tired workers anxious to get home to their families. However, we hadn't thought twice about walking home from the movies, even on Friday nights, even after seeing horror movies that sent us running through the night as if the devil himself were chasing us. Our parents didn't bother to wait up for us because the doors were unlocked; they were always unlocked. I'd been sad for my city cousins, that they hadn't had anything fun to do in Atlanta. We grew up miles apart but were, nonetheless, family and could call on each other when necessary.

Memories of our shared childhoods dissipated when Butch left me at the hospital's front entrance. I thanked him again for the outing before I hurried through the revolving doors to the elevator. When I slipped into our room I found Barry resting comfortably but felt guilty that I could eat, and he couldn't. Rather than take a meal to the room, I ate in the cafeteria or at the sandwich shop a block up the street. Although Barry assured me he wasn't hungry, it was hard to believe he didn't want a drink of water or a few bites of something to eat.

Two days later, when there were no visitors, Cathy and Bill appeared after work, around five-thirty. I appreciated that they took time to drive into the city during rush hour. Their visit made the end of a long day brighter.

Cathy all but demanded I go with Bill to eat while she stayed with Barry. I wasn't hungry, but Bill was, so I agreed to go with him to the IHOP a few blocks away where we enjoyed breakfast for supper on a bitterly cold winter evening. Their visit was brief as they had to make the trip back to Bremen and their two little girls, my goddaughters, Meri and Susan. After some of my experiences with boys, Cathy felt fortunate to have the girls she wanted.

───※───

Family visitors continued to come and see us during our hospital confinement, and the next day ushered in the youngest of my three older brothers, Donnie, and my sister-in-law Shelby. She readily agreed to sit with Barry while Donnie and I went out for lunch and a walk. Out of habit I began to stroll towards the Fox, but Donnie opted for another route. His steps led us to an area several blocks away and one that was completely unfamiliar to me. But he knew exactly where we were going. "I don't work in Atlanta on a regular basis, but about a year ago Southern Bell sent me to a jobsite at Rio Mall, just a few blocks from here on the corner of North and Piedmont. Are you hungry?" he asked.

I'd lost only a few pounds, but everybody who came to visit wanted to feed me. Maybe it was because in the South we loved with food and were used to big Sunday dinners and holiday spreads that would feed an army. "I could eat something, but I'm not starving if you want to keep walking."

"No, we're almost there, and there's a very good diner that makes hand patted cheeseburgers and fries from fresh cut potatoes. You've lost too much weight and need to eat more than whatever you've been living on. And you'll love the fountain."

"Fountain? What kind of fountain?"

We rounded the next corner, and he said, "Look over there." He pointed to the center of a courtyard where there was a large fountain that in itself wouldn't have been anything special. But in the pool beneath the fountain dozens of gleaming, gilded frogs were assembled under the rainbow created by the fountain's spray. The smiling amphibians were perfectly at home as they seemed to jump in the watery sunshine.

"Oh, it's beautiful! Thanks for bringing me on this city hike. I wouldn't have walked this far or in this direction on my own and would've missed the golden frog pond."

"I thought you would like a break from your routine. Ready for lunch?"

"Yes." I didn't realize how hungry I was as we enjoyed our burgers and hand-dipped milkshakes. By the time we finished the calorie laden meal, I was more than eager to return to the hospital. I was as stuffed as a Thanksgiving turkey and couldn't help but worry how Barry's surgically altered digestive system would react to the first thing he swallowed. We would find out in four more days, when he would be able to eat and drink again.

~

Day ten, or as Dr. Miller referred to the tenth day after surgery: "D-Day." The "D," as we quickly discovered, stood for "Dump"—and with good reason. Per both doctor and nurse recommendations, I notified family and friends that visitors wouldn't be allowed on D-Day, although our visitors had reduced themselves to a few stragglers. Barry and I understood everybody was busy, and it was a hassle to drive to Atlanta during the work week. Besides, he needed to rest as much as possible.

Breakfast tray before him, bedside potty next to him, and with an audience of three—Dr. Miller, Lilli, and me—Barry slowly chewed and swallowed a bite of soft scrambled eggs. He washed them down with a sip of coffee and immediately had that deer in the headlights look. Lilli was ready to hastily assist him onto the toilet chair. He was mortified, but Dr. Miller laughed and assured him his dump was expected.

"I'm releasing you day after tomorrow, when your body will be more tolerable of its new gastric structure. But it will be a few more days before you can return to a normal diet, and as previously discussed, you'll need to eat several undersized meals a day. Lilli will see that you have a list of the most nutritious choices. You can't afford to waste your limited caloric intake on anything that's not healthy. No junk food."

With a smile and a fatherly pat on my shoulder, he reminded me to schedule an appointment with him for one day next week and to contact Dr. Carson's office. "He and I have concurred that another round of chemo in conjunction with a month of daily radiation treatments, as we initially discussed, are essential precautions. Dr. Carson mentioned the radiation facility in Carrollton, which I understand will be a much easier commute for the two of you."

"Yes, it will be more convenient than driving to Atlanta five days a week. Thank you, Dr. Miller, for all you've done for my husband."

He reached to shake Barry's hand. "The worst is behind you." With a smile and glance in my direction, "For both of you. Take care of him, Sheila."

I returned his smile and replied, "Of course I will."

Part Three

"True love stories never have endings."

RICHARD BACH

CHAPTER 13

The Calm Before the Storm

MARCH DIDN'T COME in like a lion, but it was going out like a lamb; the winter of 1995-96 as a whole was very accommodating. It was a crystal, blue filled Saturday sky, three weeks after surgery. Though I'd returned to work, Barry was limited to no more than a few of hours a day to sit at a desk and supervise his business. He wouldn't be able to drive for another three weeks, so either Daddy or I drove him to and from the service station. Barry lost more than the extra pounds gained before surgery and adapted to reduced portions at mealtime. Kids' menu items became his best option, or he could easily make three meals from an adult entrée. For the workplace we'd purchased a mini fridge and stocked it with assorted juices; one desk drawer was allocated for healthy snacks. Barry was slowly adjusting to his new digestive system.

Although he was recovering, Barry grew restless as his healing gradually progressed. He was tired of sitting like an invalid while the auto mechanic work was done by employees, and he was bored with television, magazines, and VCR movies. When the weather permitted he passed many hours in one of the front porch rockers. Visitors were infrequent and rarely had more than half an hour to spare from their busy lives, and we both accepted that their time was valuable.

So it was understandable Barry wanted to get out of the house on weekends. After he finished his petite sized breakfast, he asked me to take him for a drive—anywhere to get him out of the house. "I can't drive yet, and I know you have a lot to do on Saturdays, but I'm going stir crazy in this house day after day."

"I have an idea. Let's go window shopping."

"I'm tired of being tired and of being stuck at home, but a mall would be worse. It's too nice a day to waste strolling around inside. Besides, we don't need to spend any money right now, not until I can get back to work full-time. Let's take a ride through the country."

"As any woman will tell you, it doesn't cost anything to browse and, besides, we're not going to the mall. You'll like this road trip." Our destination was an old favorite of his when we were out knockin' around on the weekend.

"And as any man will tell you, that's bullshit because no woman ever just 'browses'. But I'm going to take your word that I'll like whatever it is you have in mind."

He found his shoes, and I dressed in Levi's, a pullover cotton sweater, and loafers before I packed a small cooler with juice, water, yogurt, nuts, fruit, and granola bars in case we found ourselves stranded in a snail trail of traffic. With him settled in the passenger seat I headed east, towards the interstate, and was pleased with myself for remembering to stop by the station and have the Blazer filled up with gas yesterday. I was notorious for running on fumes. We both enjoyed the Mustang, but it was not yet warm enough to drop the rag top. Spring was fickle in the South. Today's forecast was sunshine and sixty degrees, but next week we could be hit with another cold snap. And blackberry winter was a chilly reminder not to put away our coats too soon.

"Okay, where are we going? Aren't you tired of I-20? Hell, we've traveled this route enough in the past few months."

I smiled and told him to be patient. Out of necessity I'd left my dread of driving to Atlanta behind and merged competently into the morning's traffic, which ran smoothly as it was the weekend. I retrieved the pillow from the backseat. "Why don't you relax and let me drive? I'll be careful, and I won't get lost because I know the way." I was also notorious for getting lost.

He lobbed the pillow back to its resting place. "The way where?"

"You'll see when we get there. It's not very far. I promise you'll enjoy yourself."

When I took the Austell exit and turned right onto Maxham road and proceeded to South Cobb Drive in Marietta, Barry sat up straighter and smiled. "Are we going to Earl Small's Harley Davidson?"

"As a matter of fact we are. I told you would like this road trip."

"What man doesn't enjoy lookin' at Harleys? And you're right, it won't cost a dime to look." He took my hand in his. "Thanks."

At least he could enjoy the distraction from monotony. We'd sold his last motorcycle a few years ago to recover some of the loss when one of his long standing customers, who owned a local construction company, filed for bankruptcy. Frank, the owner, was working on a big project in the nearby city of Douglasville. Regrettably, he'd accumulated a large amount of debt with more than one hometown business that extended credit to a handful of reliable patrons. When the contractor for the job was unable to convince enough of the investors to cover the escalating costs, the project fell through. Frank didn't have the funds to pay his debts. As a result of the trickledown effect, we and a few other businesses were out thousands of dollars. I pushed those insignificant thoughts aside as we arrived at our destination.

I turned into the parking lot of Earl Small's where the early springtime weather had evidently induced motorcycle fever.

I made several loops through the parking lot before I secured a spot. As we looked at both new and used Harley Davidsons, I remembered something from our past, a remark Barry had made about owning a Harley one day before he died. I shook off the cold hand of trepidation and followed Barry to where a red, chromed out Road King was parked. He resembled a five year old in a toy store.

A go-getter salesman wearing a leather Harley vest, compensatory ponytail, and a moustache that flowed into a goatee approached us almost the moment we paused to look at the bike. "Good morning, I'm Dave. We got this bike less than an hour ago. The owner wanted to trade her in for a new model, even though, as you can see, this dressed out beauty is in excellent condition. Only three years old and low mileage. Don't know why the owner wasn't happy, but my job's to sell the bikes, not question the motive of the buyer. Check out the accessories, especially the air filter cover and its chrome and gold colored eagle with the "Live to Ride, Ride to Live" motto. Now, as I was sayin'—"

Barry interrupted the salesman. "I agree it's a nice bike, but we're only browsing today. Thanks."

Slightly deflated but not deterred the salesman persisted. "Now before you make a hasty decision, one you're sure to regret, take the bike for a test drive and see how it runs. It's hard to appreciate a Harley until you've had one on the road."

"Sorry, buddy, but I can't even drive a car right now. I'm pretty sure a motorcycle is out of the question. I had surgery three weeks ago, and my doctor hasn't released me to drive. You wouldn't want me to total one of your bikes and find out your insurance won't pay. Again, we're just lookin'."

The salesman was genuinely confused and momentarily lost his sales pitch poise. He wrestled with indecision but found a solution.

Love, Life, & Broken Rainbows

"Barry, that's your name, right? How 'bout if I grab a couple of helmets and take us for a ride? It won't be the same as you driving, but you'll get a feel for the bike all the same."

Barry was about to tell Dave for the third time we weren't in the market for a Harley when I put my hand on his shoulder. "Dave seems competent. And why not? He's not going to charge you for a ride."

That was all the encouragement the eager beaver needed and in a flash was firing up the bike. "Smart woman. I'm sorry, but I didn't get your name."

I took his proffered hand. "Sheila."

"Good to meet you. Climb on, Barry. You're gonna love how smooth she runs and handles. Really have no idea why the owner traded this bike."

Barry waved goodbye, and I prayed they would make it safely back to the dealership. I needn't have worried as Dave, indeed, was a capable cyclist. Within fifteen minutes they roared into the entrance, bringing with them the distinctive "potato-potato-potato-potato" sound made exclusively by a "Hog." If nothing else Barry had enjoyed the ride through fresh air and a sun doused morning.

As he climbed off, helmet in hand, he thanked Dave for his time. "I appreciate the ride, and when I'm in a position to afford a Harley, I'll be back. Do you have a card?" Although he was disappointed he was resigned to the fact that we couldn't afford a "toy" at the time. The Jeep, the last of Barry's motorized splurges, was sold three years ago when we'd underestimated our quarterly taxes and were hit with a six thousand dollar tax bill. The Internal Revenue Service stipulations were to pay in full or face additional penalties and late fees. The only logical solution was to sell the Jeep, and as Barry had said, "It's just a car."

The salesman was like a dog with a bone. "Of course, but I wish you would reconsider. We both know this bike won't be here long. At thirteen thousand it's a steal. Unfortunately, that price is nonnegotiable because, as I said, we just got it this morning, and it'll easily bring that amount."

"I realize it's a good deal, but you're not listening to me. I've already told you we didn't come to buy, we're—"

"We'll take it." Nobody was more surprised than I when those words jumped right out of my mouth, seemingly of their own accord.

Dave immediately turned his attention to me. "Well, alright, Sheila. Let's go inside and fill out the paperwork. We do offer financing, but the interest rate is high. If you have the down payment and can borrow the remainder from your bank, you'll probably get a lower rate." He held the door opened and motioned us inside.

Barry grabbed my arm before I stepped across the threshold and pulled me aside. "Have you lost your mind? We can't afford that motorcycle. The price is more than we have left in our dwindling savings account. I'll have a Harley one day when we can actually afford one."

"We're buying this one." With a stubborn sense of purpose I yanked my arm free and strode into Dave's office. Although I wasn't exactly sure where I was going to come up with the money, I wrote a check for the entire amount and postdated it for Monday. And then I recollected that Mama had said good credit was the next best thing to cash. Therefore, I would contact my credit card company and have a deposit made first thing Monday morning to cover the check—and to hell with the interest rate for cash advances and the additional debt.

The bike wasn't serviced and cleaned, and Barry couldn't drive it home anyway, so we made arrangements to pick it up the following week. When Barry protested he wouldn't be able to drive then either, I assured him we would ask Brad or his youngest brother, who had been riding for years, to go with us and drive the bike home. My husband's annoyance at my impulsive determination to buy a motorcycle we didn't need with money we didn't have went from bad to worse. We argued all the way home, but in the end I had my way. And, by damn, Barry had his Harley.

Chemo and radiation were behind us, and Barry resumed a close proximity to his pre-cancer life. He was working full-time, felt better than he had in months, and we were both enjoying the smooth ride of the Harley. An added bonus was that his hair had grown back, the same black but curly. We had one last appointment with his surgeon, and when I scheduled it I avoided any date between July 19 and August 4. Although my work routine was flexible during the summer months, Atlanta was host to the 1996 Summer Olympics. While I had adapted to chauffeuring us to and from various appointments, I didn't want the headache of additional traffic created by tourists who were sure to be confused in an unfamiliar city—especially one with multiple "Peachtree" streets.

Dr. Miller was optimistic and pleased with Barry's recovery. Other than Barry's large scar that served as a lasting reminder of life's uncertainty, the implanted portacath was the only physical evidence that he was a cancer survivor. Dr. Carson told us if there were no unforeseen problems the portacath could be removed after one more CT scan and bloodwork. He laughingly told us of one patient who'd slipped her device on a chain and wore it around her neck as a reminder to not ever take life for granted. A memento was something neither of us wanted or needed. But we were planning to celebrate by running away to the beach in September when the weather was cooler and accommodations were cheaper than during peak summer months.

The last CT scan proved somewhat of a challenge in that there was no physical way Barry could drink the required pint of contrast fluid prior to the scan. It took all morning before the technician was satisfied he could get the scan ordered by Dr. Carson, who failed to consider the limitations of Barry's smaller stomach. When he called to tell us the scan and bloodwork were clean, we thanked God our lives were finally cancer free.

The portacath was removed, but not by the same surgeon who'd embedded the device. At our appointment Dr. Ingram strongly opposed Dr. Carson's decision to have the catheter removed and was very verbal in expressing his disagreement. With a sardonic laugh that was more of a smirk, he stated that to remove a cancer patient's portacath less than a year after diagnosis was irresponsible. I was furious at his negativity and refused to discuss the matter further. Since the first day we were told of the diagnosis, I'd ensured that Barry was not subjected to discouraging comments. We hastily left his office, and a surgeon in Bremen performed the minor procedure. Two weeks later we packed our bags for a welcomed getaway to the beach.

⁓

It was the third week of September, ten months after the cancer diagnosis and almost seven months after surgery. The weather fully cooperated with our seaside vacation, and Mother Nature supplied incredible orange sunsets that drifted into pink and purple hues as the sun merged with the liquid horizon. Twilight made the ocean and sky indistinguishable as they melted into one. Barry and I held hands, walked on the beach, and chased the surf like five year olds. I fed the seagulls, ignoring the "Do Not Feed the Seagulls" signs.

We were relaxed, happy, and willing when our sun kissed bodies reintroduced us to passion. We'd had sex during his recovery, but it was cautious, tepid sex that vanished in a predictable routine. But with cancer and its stress removed, our sex life was better than ever before. Bathed in the softness of tranquility we fell into satiated slumber, and I was disoriented when Barry awakened and roused me well after midnight. "Are we going to have to listen to that noise all night?"

I drowsily brushed away the cobwebs of interrupted dreams as I sat up and listened to the sounds of a darkened hotel suite: the steady hum of the mini-fridge, the whirr of the ceiling fan, the drone of the air conditioning. But there was nothing out of the ordinary that would have disturbed him. "What noise? I don't hear anything."

He threw back the covers and swung his feet over the edge of the bed. "The waves. The waves crashing onto the shore are keeping me awake."

Remembering the ocean slapping the sand usually lulled us into a sound sleep, I was even more confused. "Well...the surf has rushed to greet the shore since the beginning of time, and I'm almost certain it's not going to stop for you." I perched on my knees and put my arms around his shoulders as he sat on the side of the bed. Although I didn't want an answer there was an unavoidable question that hung heavily between us. "What's wrong, Barry?"

He stood up and switched on the bedside lamp, which cast his eerie shadow on the wall behind him. Both he and the Bigfoot shadow paced. I repeated the question, and he ran his fingers through his regrown black, newly curly hair. The pacing stopped as he reached the sliding glass door, opened it, and stepped onto the balcony—with me right behind him. "I'm not sure what's wrong, but I've had a pain on my right side for the past couple of weeks. I've been taking ibuprofen, but it hasn't helped. The last time I ignored my pain, well, it wasn't a good thing."

I wrapped my arms around him and buried my face in his chest because I couldn't let him see the anxiety that was chasing my heart. We held each other close and watched the moonlit whitecaps roll onto the shore only to recede and repeat. I deeply inhaled the saltwater air as the cool hand of the ocean breeze calmed my borderline panic. With feigned confidence I attempted to reassure us both. "I'm sure it's nothing serious. I bet you over did things at work too soon and pulled a muscle. We're leaving tomorrow, and as soon as we get home I'll call Dr. Gordon's office and schedule the first available appointment. Let's not borrow trouble."

"No, let's not turn into your mama and look for a reason to worry. I must be paranoid. Everything that hurts can't be cancer. Right?"

"Right. Now let's get some sleep. We need to be on the road first thing in the morning." With a kiss and another reassuring hug, we climbed back into bed. Barry slept, and I snuggled close to him, pulled the covers up to my chin, and fought to keep fear confined to the shadows.

CHAPTER 14

The Storm

I SCHEDULED AN appointment with our general practitioner two days later. Barry would be a work-in, but it didn't matter. Dr. Gordon had been our family GP for several years, and we trusted his medical opinion. He entered the exam room, chart in hand, and smiled at us. "Well, how are you two holding up? I've made a point of staying updated over the past few months, and I realize you've had a rough time."

I wanted to tell him "rough time" didn't begin to summarize the road upon which we'd traveled, but decided it would be a waste of time. Instead I answered, "We're okay. Granted, cancer has taken a toll on Barry, but we're on the other side now."

"Great news." He switched gears into medical professionalism and directed his attention to Barry. "So what brings you in today?"

I waited for Barry to answer, "I don't know what's wrong, but for the past two weeks I've had a constant ache in my right side. I may have strained a muscle at work. Hopefully, it's something minor."

"Ok. Take off your shirt and let's have a look."

Barry complied, and Dr. Gordon proceeded to probe and prod, ignoring the massive scar, concentrating his exam in the area where Barry had complained as the source of his pain. I sensed an imperceptible shift in the doctor's manner and asked, "Any idea what's wrong, Dr. Gordon?"

I was holding my breath, and his hesitation did nothing to alleviate the anxiety that was almost palpable—anxiety that had followed us into the exam room. He handed Barry's shirt to him and made a few notes on the chart before he replied in a remorseful voice, "I'm referring you back to your oncologist."

I gasped and felt the rope of stability slipping from my grip. "What? No, no. We're here to see you, Dr. Gordon. Whatever is bothering my husband has nothing to do with cancer, and we don't need an appointment with Dr. Carson. Our next appointment with him is not until the first of the year, and that's for a follow-up visit only. We need for you to tell us what's wrong and treat him accordingly."

Barry wore the frightened expression of an abused animal. Agonizing acceptance was reflected in his brown eyes, but he managed to ask, "Can you tell me why you're sending me back to my oncologist?"

With a heavy sigh Dr. Gordon laid the chart on the small table. "Because your liver is enlarged."

It was my turn to intercede. "What are the implications of an enlarged liver? Can't you give him a prescription or send him to a specialist? Maybe Dr. Seeman?"

"Sheila, if Barry was an ordinary patient I would set up a series of tests to confirm a diagnosis. But given his history, I strongly urge you to see your oncologist as soon as possible. I'm sorry."

We were dismissed with nothing more than "I'm sorry." I fought to maintain control tears filled with fear. Barry hopped off the exam table and thanked Dr. Gordon for his time as he slipped his shirt over thin shoulders.

The next morning we sat with uncertainty in the exam room and waited with for the dreaded appointment with Dr. Carson. Barry and I anxiously watched the door as footsteps approached, steps that paused on the other side of the door. Hesitancy resolved, Dr. Carson entered the exam room and for the first time since our initial meeting, his confidence waned. That observation did nothing to appease the raw fear that had threatened to consume me for the past ten months.

"Good morning, Barry. I understand from Dr. Gordon we have reason for concern." He cleared his throat before he continued, "If you'll remove your shirt, I'll examine you."

Tension crouched in every corner of the room as I sat next to the exam table, my hand on Barry's thigh. After a few minutes, minutes that seemed much longer, Dr. Carson cleared his throat again, nervously adjusted his glasses, and spoke to Barry, "I'm afraid the cancer has metastasized to the liver. I could order a biopsy and a CT, but there's no need to put you through unnecessary tests when I, regrettably, have no doubt as to why your liver is enlarged or why you've been experiencing discomfort in that area."

"Wait, that can't be right, Dr. Carson." I all but screamed at the man who stood uneasily before me. "Dr. Miller assured us he removed *all* of the cancer and the margins were clean before he closed after surgery. Call him. He will confirm there is no more cancer."

Dr. Carson removed his glasses and rubbed his eyes, but I couldn't tell if it was from fatigue or if he was combatting tears. He regained his composure and sat down on the wheeled stool to speak to us both. "You have to realize that cancer is a multifaceted disease, one that's hard to confine. All it took was for one cancerous cell to survive everything that we've done, to imbed itself into the liver and wait until radiation treatments and chemo were over to replicate."

I was beside myself with anger as I paced the confinement of the room. "Then why wasn't his liver targeted with radiation instead of frying what was left of his stomach, where the cancer was completely removed? My husband can't possibly be your first patient to be diagnosed with this type of cancer. Why—"

Dr. Carson interrupted my rant. "Sheila, none of us, including myself, can foresee the outcome of any given cancer diagnosis. Cancer is unpredictable, and therefore, impossible to treat when the variables are unknown. I'm sorry. I truly am."

If one more doctor told me how sorry he was, I was going to rip out his throat. That vicious, albeit imagined, scenario was cut short by Barry's soft-spoken question as he stared down at feet that dangled from the edge of the exam table. "How much time do you think I have left?"

And there it was. That fear, that murky, scary, horrible creature I'd held deep inside me since the day we were told of Barry's cancer. The "thing" surfaced with the force of a physical assault, a fist to my stomach and my senses. The unnamed monster devoured the last remaining crumbs of our hope. The room spun and breathing was crushingly painful as I held onto Barry's arm and struggled to keep the unnamed thing from dragging me into the endless darkness where it lived—and waited to swallow me whole. I held up my hand in the "stop" position and cautioned Dr. Carson loudly, "No, do *not* answer that question. I won't give up because I can't. I can't live without him. There has to be another treatment, one we haven't tried. You have to make some calls, do some research, whatever it takes to find a cure."

The room's silence waited for a response to my denial of the facts. Dr. Carson stood and patrolled the parameters; he seemed to be having an internal debate. I seized on his delay. "What? What can you offer in the way of treatment?"

He rubbed the bristle of his beard. "There's a procedure, chemoembolization, in which chemo is dumped directly onto the liver. We've had some moderate success, but in this case it would be a longshot as the cancer has grown at a remarkable pace. It may be too little, too late."

"I don't care what the odds are. If there's any chance the technique will work, then we have to try. Please don't give up yet."

The doctor asked Barry, "What do you want to do? This has been your fight from day one, and this final decision should be yours."

Barry gaged my level of panic as he stared into my pleading, tear filled eyes. With a sigh of submission he agreed to the chemoembolization. He took my hands in his. "Sheila, I'll do this for you. Not for me because I know I'm beaten and despite all we've been through, the cancer has won. And I'm tired. But for you I'll agree to the chemoembo whatever."

I threw my arms around him and cried. Dr. Carson mentioned something about contacting Dr. Sheffield to schedule the procedure at the earliest date available. He slipped out the door, leaving us alone with our misery.

With assurance from the receptionist to call as soon as the procedure was scheduled, we made our way through the waiting area where I noticed a phone for patients' use. I'd promised to call Pat as soon as we finished the appointment and give her an update. I thought I was all cried out, but when I heard my sister's concerned voice, the tears returned. "I'm beyond angry, Pat. The cancer we were told was gone wasn't gone at all. It was hiding in his liver like a thief, waiting until we had our lives back only to steal them again. Dr. Carson said there was only one possible treatment and at best, it would offer a very slim chance of success." My tears couldn't be stemmed as I reached for a tissue and continued my tirade. "They told us he was out of the woods, but that was a lie. Barry asked how much time he had left, but I wouldn't let the doctor answer him. I know life is not fair, but this is *so* not fair!"

There was a hand on my shoulder, and I turned to the receptionist's whisper, "Sheila, you need to continue this discussion when you get home, please."

I took note of the apprehensive faces of cancer, awaiting appointments to learn of their own destinies. They were all warriors, all weary from their untold battles with a dreadful disease. I realized the significance our news had on those patients—patients who were still fighting the fight, still clinging to flimsy straws of hope. That was not the place to expose our own gut-wrenching hopelessness. I hung up the phone, and Barry wrapped his arms lovingly around my shoulders and led me out the door. Despair and heartache followed.

The procedure was scheduled for the following week, on his forty-sixth birthday. In the meantime Barry went about the business of dying. The day after we left Dr. Carson's office, Barry insisted we see our lawyer to update our will, over my objections. "There's no need in doing anything right now. You're going to beat the cancer. The new technique is going to once and for all kill the damn disease."

As calmly as any man who had come to terms with his doomed fate could be, he persisted. "We haven't reviewed our will since the boys were young, and we'd needed to provide guardianship in case we died together. I'm going to leave the business to them, and they'll either make it or they won't. All I can do is give them the opportunity. They're grown men and able to take care of themselves. But you, you've always been taken care of, first by your parents and then by me. You went from your daddy's house to ours. Both of our sons are engaged and, once they're married, you'll to be living alone for the first time in your life. I have to know that after I'm gone, you'll be alright."

I held back tears that threatened like a monsoon but said nothing. "Sheila, I'm not discussing this with you anymore. Now let's go; Mike's expecting us at four." He held the door open for me. "By the way, I want you to use the funeral home in town for the arrangements since they've been good customers of mine for years. But don't let Bill screw you over on funeral expenses. It'll just my dead body, so don't waste money on a fancy coffin. As for music, choose whatever you want." He paused a moment and said, "But I've always liked 'Amazing Grace'."

I stumbled out the door but stopped on the carport. "I can't. This means you've given up, that you're providing for me when you're gone. Don't you understand without *you*, without *us*, there is no *me*?" I bit into my lower lip and swallowed a sob that caught in my throat.

"Yes, there will be a 'you'. Not you with me, but you. And I have to make sure you have a roof over your head and that you use the insurance money to pay off the mortgage and the car and invest what, if any, is left. You won't need the expense of two cars, so decide if you want to keep the Mustang or the Blazer and sell the other one. You should be able to sell the Harley for almost what we paid and pay off that damn credit card debt." He noticed the sorrow on my face and lost some of his bravado. "I love that you wanted me to have the bike, and we had some great rides, but you have to be practical and sell it." He held me tightly in his arms, kissed the top of my head, and said, "I can't die in peace if I'm worried about you livin' in the street." He opened the car door with eyes that begged compliance.

"Alright." With a heavy heart I realized his love would extend beyond the grave, a grave I wasn't ready to concede. And so I continued to pray.

~

The morning of the chemoembolization was shared by only Jerry, Jerline, and me—no big family gathering this time. But well-meaning Cathy sent "Happy Birthday" balloons without considering the paradox of the Mylar foil message. Dr. Sheffield, surgical cap in hand, found us in the waiting room and greeted our collective concern with a distinct air of frustration. He explained that he'd encountered a degree of difficulty he hadn't expected due to Barry's surgically altered organ structure, which was unfamiliar terrain. The doctor's six foot plus frame slouched in disappointment, although he attempted to reassure me that he'd done the best he possibly could have under the circumstances. There was nothing to do but wait.

We waited in vain for the high fever and the nausea, symptoms Dr. Carson told us to expect. Symptoms that failed to occur. We were sent home the following day, and by the weekend Barry became bloated as his urine output was at a minimum. Dr. Carson was not on call, but one of his partners recommended more fluids and advised me to contact Dr. Carson on Monday. By Monday, the fluid retention had worsened because his urine output was no more than an occasional trickle, and his blood pressure was dropping. I left a message with Dr. Carson's answering service, but it was late afternoon before my call was returned. I grabbed the phone on the first ring and walked the cordless phone out of Barry's earshot.

After listening to my description of Barry's symptoms, Dr. Carson opted to send home healthcare out to evaluate the severity of my husband's condition and to begin a saline drip to elevate his blood pressure. I gripped the phone tightly and stifled a frustrated scream. "Are you out of your mind? The last thing he needs is more fluids. He's swollen to the point that he resembles a blowfish, and your solution is to administer more fluids? He's not passing urine, and home healthcare cannot help him. You're the one who needs to examine him, but it's after office hours. Can you meet us at the ER?"

He evidently heard the desperation that screeched its way through the phone. He answered immediately, "Yes, how long will it take for you to drive into the city?"

"Usually about an hour, but with the rain and the rush hour traffic, it could take an hour and a half. I'm really not sure, but I'll have him there as soon as I can."

"I'll see you both at the ER."

The minute I dropped the phone into its slot, it rang again. In my haste gathering our bag and raincoats, I ignored the phone, but the caller was insistent. I snatched the phone up with an abrupt, "Hello. I don't have time to talk right now. I'm in a hurry—"

Brad's voice interrupted my terse excuse. "What's wrong? What's happened?"

"I have to take Daddy to the ER. He's not able to urinate at all, and his blood pressure is 75/50. Dr. Carson is meeting us there."

"Wait for me. I'll help you put him in the car and drive. You don't need to go by yourself, especially in this weather and this late in the day. Traffic will be hell." He was there in a matter of minutes.

Stormy skies wept sympathetic tears on our desperate ride to the hospital. We arrived in little more than an hour and bypassed the impatience of others as we explained the situation to the harried admissions clerk. After a brief exam Dr. Carson ordered bloodwork, and we waited in an undersized, makeshift exam room as he reviewed the tests results. Without a word to any of us he stepped into the congested hallway and summoned a nurse.

"I want these tests run again. Stat. There has apparently been a mistake in the lab." He strode down the hall.

Brad, Barry, and I were caught in a storm that raged both outside and in as we waited for Dr. Carson to return. After what felt like hours he pushed back the curtain and quietly entered our circle. "I've run the bloodwork twice, but there's no error in the markers used to indicate the seriousness of his cancer."

Dr. Carson was evidently caught off guard by whatever information was concealed in Barry's chart, information I demanded he clarify. "What are you saying—or not saying—Dr. Carson?"

He ran his fingers through his hair and faced Brad. "If you need to contact other family members, now is the time to make those calls." Barry was either sleeping or feigning sleep, so Dr. Carson faced me to deliver the sentence. "I'm afraid Barry may not make it through the night. I'm very sorry the chemoembolization was not successful."

I fell into the straight-backed chair and reached for Barry's hand, not fully comprehending what I was told. He might not outlive the night? Had we shared our last day? The report couldn't be right. Before I could request that the bloodwork be run a third time, Brad was beside me, his voice hinged with pain. "Oh, Mama, we knew but didn't want to know. I'll call Pat and tell her what's going on and ask her to call Granddaddy and Grandmother. They need to know tonight may be their last chance to see their son. And I'll call Chuck and Valerie."

Dr. Carson interrupted, "We'll have him sent to the ICU as soon as possible and ensure he's comfortable." With nothing left to say, he was gone. There was nothing left to be said.

By one a.m. our family was there, once again camped out in the larger of the two ICU waiting rooms. They hovered over me in hushed tones and threw a pillow and blanket onto one of the sofas so I could sleep, but sleep was impossible. Barry was restless and disoriented, and his ICU nurse made an exception and allowed me to sit by his bed. She was the same nurse who was livid because Dr. Carson had allowed us to have the portacath removed too soon, which made accessing a vein for the IV much more difficult.

Despite whatever she mumbled under her breath about doctors, she let me stay in the competent sanctuary of intensive care. The only chair in the cubicle was designed to discourage visitors to the unit and failed to yield to my fatigued body. There was an accommodating space on the bed next to Barry's side where I rested my head and clasped his hand. My presence seemed to soothe him but not to the point of sleep.

"Sheila?"

"Yes, I'm here. I'm right here." I stood and gently stroked his forehead.

"I don't want to die in here, not in the ICU. It's too cold, too much death."

Even though I didn't think there was any chance of getting him out of the Intensive Care Unit, I assured him I would request the first available room. "I'll tell the head nurse to call Dr. Carson and have us moved." At best, he wouldn't be moved until morning at the earliest—a morning that in all likelihood we wouldn't see together.

"The pain has gone. Morphine is a wonder drug. I don't want to die in pain."

"Yes, yes it is a wonder drug. And under no circumstances would I ever let you die in pain." I half sat, half hunched over the edge of the bed in the semi-darkness. Various medical equipment hummed a mocking lullaby.

Still fighting sleep, Barry had another request. "Sheila, don't let me die alone."

I leaned over the bed and kissed his cheek as tears slid down my own. "You won't die alone. I promise I won't leave you. I'm here. Always."

CHAPTER 15

Love Is Forever

As softly as a kitten's first steps, sunrise tiptoed over the Atlanta skyline to claim another day. Death, however, had not yet come to claim my soulmate. I slipped my hand from his and stood to stretch my contorted body when the nurse, Glenda, came in to record his vitals. When she finished with her notes I asked if we could be moved to a room on the fifth floor, not bothering with rationalization because there was none. Although her professionalism was intact her tone held a hint of sympathy as she informed me that she would contact Dr. Carson. She also told me there were no rooms currently available. Nonetheless, she promised to notify the cancer ward of my request.

Glenda convinced me Barry was at last resting comfortably, and I went to the waiting room to update our family. They were all anxious for news and wanted to see Barry. Each one was allowed to enter the ICU for five minutes per person, precious little time to say goodbye to a loved one. Melba and Carl fell apart as they realized that would be the last time they saw their oldest son. Our sons and Valerie stayed for a while longer, after everyone else went home to rest, but I was alone with him when a nun unobtrusively entered the curtained cubicle early in the afternoon.

She spoke in a gentle voice. "Hello. I'm Sister Mary, and I've come to pray with you. What do you need?"

In my weariness I thought I'd misunderstood the question. "I'm sorry, Sister Mary, but what was it you wanted to know?"

She placed her hand on my shoulder and with a luminous smile repeated the question, "What do you need?"

What did I need??? I needed for my husband not to be dying. I needed for the cancer to be taken from him. I needed for him to live and grow old with me. In short, I needed a miracle. Sister Mary couldn't give me a miracle, but her tranquil sincerity let me know she was serious in her inquiry. So I said the first thing that popped into my head, "A room. He doesn't want to die in ICU, but there are no available rooms on the cancer floor, which means he can't be moved until one becomes vacant."

She reached for the hand that wasn't holding his and took Barry's hand in her other one. "Very well, then. We will bow our heads and ask our Father to provide a room."

My prayers had been intense, incessant, and I'd almost forgotten that even simple prayers would suffice. I wasn't Catholic, but I believed God heard the prayers of all of His children. Although I was beginning to realize that whether or not those prayers were answered was another matter. So I didn't know if it was Divine intervention or a coincidence when a room became available for us within the hour. As I gathered his clothes, our jackets, and my purse I noticed that Glenda was placing a bright orange "DNR" strip on Barry's wrist.

"Excuse me, but is that band a 'Do Not Resuscitate' instruction?" My pulse raced as I waited for the answer I already knew.

"Yes. Once he leaves the ICU, they won't be able to resuscitate him on the floor." She continued the business of detaching machines and preparing him to be transferred out of her care.

I was frantic as I considered the consequences of our request to be moved from the unit into a regular room. "But I'm not sure if that's what I want, not sure—"

Barry laid his hand on my forearm. "Sheila, I'm dying. And you have to let me."

I stared into his exhausted, imploring brown eyes and knew he'd accepted what I couldn't and had thrown in the white flag of surrender. With the knife of resignation in my heart, I signed the form that indicated I understood there would be no attempt made to save my husband from the cold grip of death. The nurse buzzed for an orderly, and we were carted to the cancer floor where Lilli waited for us with open arms. Her usual congenial manner and big smile were gone. Death had not been a stranger on her watch, and she knew Barry was there to die.

It was almost dusk when our sons, along with Valerie, came in to say their goodbyes. I was surprised to see Cyndie with them as she greeted me with a warm embrace. "I'm sorry I didn't make it over last night, but I came today as soon as I could get out of the office."

"Thank you," was all I could say. We had prayer and shared hugs before they left me with my anguish—and with a husband tormented by a phenomenon known as "sundown dementia." It was the same occurrence as the night before, only worse. Glenda had told me of the label given due to the typical time of day when critically ill patients descended into a hell of their own making. It was a place where they lost all sense of whom and where they were, a hell where even I couldn't reach him. I pressed the red call button as Barry fought to get out of bed and to jerk the IV from his arm with a strength I didn't know he possessed.

Jason, our well-known night nurse, entered immediately and assisted me in restraining Barry. As suddenly as it had begun, the disorientation passed. It was a frightening experience, and I was relieved when Barry fell into a deep sleep thanks, again, to morphine. Jason assured me, "His agony has passed, and he's resting now." He quietly left the room.

I walked to the window as the street lights came to life in the twilight and watched the homeless. They slowly made their way to roosts that had long been marked as procured property. I closed my eyes in an attempt to hold back tears of sorrow and bitterness, sorrow that Barry would die and resentment that those vagrants lived. If God has a plan for our lives, then what was His plan for society's castoffs? I asked God to spare my husband, the father of my sons, and to take one or two of those useless beggars instead. I bargained and reasoned with Him that nobody would even notice if any of them were gone and that I needed Barry more than He did.

Barry's voice intruded on my prayers. "No tears. Remember?"

I swiped at the persistent tears and reached for a tissue as I crossed the room to his bedside. "Sorry. Guess I forgot."

He threw back the bedcovers and invited me to crawl into bed with him. Despite his fluid retention our combined weight loss allowed us both to fit into the single hospital bed. With the IV free arm he pulled me close to him and tenderly kissed my forehead. "I just want to hold you, to smell you."

"I need to feel you close to me, too." I rearranged myself comfortably in the nook of his arm and rested my head on his shoulder. My love for him had never been stronger, but it wasn't strong enough to take away cancer.

"I love you, Sheila, and I don't want to die. I don't want to leave you and our life. But I've done everything possible to live, and I don't have a choice in this matter. Neither do you."

Despite his acceptance, I couldn't contain myself. "But why would God take you from me? We haven't finished living. We had plans for growing old together."

"Nobody can answer 'why'. As for growing old together, that was not in our wedding vows. The Justice of the Peace who married us didn't mention growing old in those wedding vows, only 'till death do us part.'" He raised my hand to point out the band of diamonds that gleamed in the nightlight. "This ring, the eternity ring I gave you for our twentieth anniversary, is your reminder I will keep my promise to love you longer than forever."

I held him closer and sobbed into his chest. "I will love you every day for the rest of my life. Oh, Barry, I can't do this. I cannot live without you."

"Yes, you can. Sheila, you're the first and the only woman I've ever loved, but you're only forty-three years old. It's just a matter of time before you meet a good man and fall in love again. And that's okay, but don't forget me."

Meet someone else? Forget him? The dementia must've surely returned because in his right mind he wouldn't have said, or even considered, such a thing. Through sobs that threatened to suffocate me, "No, Barry, you're wrong that I'll fall in love again. And to think I would—or even could—ever forget you has to be the morphine talking."

"No, it's not the morphine. I'm being practical and levelheaded. You have to listen to me, Sheila. Your daddy spoiled you and I took over, and you can't do anything practical. While I've loved every day of your quirkiness, 'Lucy,' some days your ramblin' thoughts were as scattered as ping pong balls in the wind. You're book smart, and I expect you to finish college and get that degree you've been working on for years. But, Sheila, you don't even know how to pump your own gas." He stroked my hair and continued, "Our vows were until death do us part and when you meet another man, don't feel guilty. I want you to be happy again. You have a million more memories to make."

How could he be such a calm, kind, and loving man in the face of death? None of us knows how we'll react in any given situation, but I was pretty sure I wouldn't have told my husband to go out and find himself a new wife after my death. "I can't talk about these things anymore. I can't"

"Well, then listen because I don't know how much time I have left, and there are things that have to be said before I'm gone. For one thing, you need to keep fresh water in the birdbath because there were a lot of days when the birds were my only company. Moving on to something more important…I wish I could be at our sons' weddings, but I won't be there. They both seem too young, but they're older than we were, and one day there will be grandchildren. I want you to tell them how sorry I am I couldn't be there to meet them, but I would have loved them very much. Can you do that for me? You'll have to love them enough for both of us."

There was no stopping the flood of tears as I murmured, "Yes, I'll tell them. And I'll love our grandbabies more than enough."

Satisfied that he'd told me all that was important to him, he loosened his hold on me and fell into the sweet serenity of sleep. I wept soundless tears of grief, but there were other tears gushing from the hallway. I thought one of the nurses might have been eavesdropping and had lost all sense of decorum as the crying grew louder. I carefully removed myself from Barry's arms and walked into the corridor to find Cyndie, bawling her eyes out.

When she glanced up at me I was startled by the traces of black mascara that ran down her face and left rings around her eyes as she dabbed at them with an overused tissue. She resembled a raccoon or an amateur wannabe member of the rock band Kiss. I reached into my pocket for a fresh tissue and asked, "Cyndie, what in the world are you doing here at this time of night? I thought you went home when Brad and Valerie left."

Between sniffles she explained her presence. "I went to the hospital's cafeteria with them to have supper. They decided to eat and let the rush hour traffic clear out before heading home. Brad mentioned he didn't want to leave you over here by yourself, but he was too tired to spend another night at the hospital. And in his rush to get Barry to the ER last night, he hadn't packed an overnight bag. I agreed you didn't need to be alone, so I volunteered to stay." I was about to express my gratitude but before I could say anything, she began to blubber again. "Oh, Sheila, if love could cure him we would all be leaving tonight."

I sat down on the bench beside her, hunched over, and buried my face in my hands. I deeply regretted that love was not enough to heal him. "Cyndie, it's got to be close to two a.m. I'm fine. We're fine right now. You should go to one of the waiting rooms and find a place to rest for a while. I'll have one of the nurses find you if I need you."

She hesitantly retreated to the waiting room to catch a few winks, and I returned to Barry's bed where he slept. But for me sleep was impossible. The conversation I hadn't wanted to have left me confused. I couldn't grasp his complacent acceptance of the inescapable fact that he was dying. His concern over something as trivial as water for the birds and his apologetic regret he wouldn't see our sons get married or be there for the yet-to-be grandchildren—and his blessing in the event I should meet another man—amazed me.

He honestly believed that my life would go on without him. I closed my eyes and prayed to God if it was His will that Barry die, then I wanted Him to take me, too. I clung to my husband and whispered, "Please, God, don't separate us. Don't leave me here without him."

Morning delivered Cyndie to our room with a freshly washed face and her replacements, Pat and my other sister, Joyce. Cyndie gave me a warm hug as she was leaving. The compassion in her eyes was a reminder that the next time we saw each other, I would be a widow. She left me with that thought as I turned to face my sisters.

Pat handed me a fragrant caramel cappuccino from the cafeteria and offered me a warm biscuit with bacon. "I asked for extra crispy bacon, the way you like it. You have to eat something, Sheila. Nobody can live on flavored coffee." I declined the biscuit and carefully reached for the hot cappuccino, to Pat's aggravation. She had taken care of me when I was a child and was delighted by my birth. She'd taken the role of mothering me seriously and had been my surrogate mama since our own mama's death.

However, Joyce's position as the baby of the family for almost eight years was displaced by my arrival. I was told her only question had been, "So how long is that baby stayin' here?" She'd reluctantly accepted that the baby wasn't leaving. Despite our lack of closeness we were sisters, and she'd come to be with me. She sat at Barry's bedside, and I looked her over and noted that her teased, poufy hair, too much mascara, and thick eyeliner were the same she'd worn for years, a throwback imitated from Connie Francis, her idol from the early sixties.

I stood and stretched weary bones. Barry was in a deep, morphine induced sleep, and I ached for a much needed, overdue shower. All I'd managed over the past two days was an airplane bath—nose, wings, and tail. "Thanks for making the trip over to the hospital. Would y'all mind staying by his side while I take a shower?"

Pat answered, "We'll be here all day, so take your time. We came to stay until Cindy and Kim get off work. They'll be coming over to stay the night with you. Go. Maybe a hot shower will make you feel better." Her sorrow was evident as she handed me a towel from the stack next to the sink. Pat was a "fixer," but this situation was beyond her control. Regardless of that fact, she'd been there for us for the duration and had done what she could. She'd enlisted her daughters for the night because none of my family wanted me to be alone.

Cindy was her older daughter, a gentle soul with a kind heart. My niece had been in my life since the day she was born, and I'd never seen her fling a fit or display even a hint of an angry outburst. Kim was a good person, too, but more high-spirited than her sister. The sisters were opposites, much like my two boys. Cindy was the sugar and Kim was the spice. While not necessary, I appreciated that they would be my companions during another long night.

The warm shower ran over my tired body, and tears mingled with the reviving spray. I had repeatedly promised Barry there would be no crying, and I hadn't left the hospital since our arrival; the pent up tears poured freely. But the swish of the shower wasn't enough to subdue the sound of my painful weeping. When I dressed and exited the bathroom my sisters were wiping tears from their eyes. It hadn't occurred to them that I, as the youngest, would be the first to lose her husband.

Except for sniffles Pat remained silent, but Joyce spoke to me. "I can tell you one damn thing. I don't *ever* want to love a man as much as you love Barry. Not if it's gonna hurt like you're hurting to lose him." She shook her head in the negative as nervous hands searched her purse. "I gotta have a cigarette. I think I saw the designated smoking area on our way in."

Both of my sisters smoked, and I was thankful neither Barry nor I had picked up that habit. I watched Joyce as she dug through her purse for a lighter and a cigarette, "cancer sticks" as our daddy called them. She found her stash and hurriedly left the room.

The probability of Joyce ever loving a man with the intensity I loved Barry was unlikely. Her first husband was an alcoholic, a mean drunk who occasionally abused her. Despite our pleas she'd refused to leave him. She had two daughters who had to be supported, and he'd had a good paying job at the Ford plant. Finally, after the girls were grown, Joyce had enough and found the courage to divorce him. Although she was the only one of us whose marriage had failed, we were all relieved when the divorce was final.

Unfortunately, Joyce was one of those women who either didn't know how or didn't want to be alone and had, as Mama declared, "jumped out of the frying pan right into the fire." But Joyce pointed out that her second husband hadn't ever beaten her, seldom drank, and went to work every day. It didn't seem to matter that he was a hateful, stingy man who rarely, if ever, had a kind word for my sister. Sadly, Joyce had no real basis of comparison. It bothered me that she expected so very little of a man and settled for what passed as happiness—something she must've felt she didn't deserve. Then again, it was possible that any snippets of happiness she had experienced were fleeting and, therefore, had been lost in the rubble.

Contemplations of my sister were interrupted as Barry woke up when Dr. Simmons entered our room and introduced himself as an urologist. He noted the IV drip and Barry's extremely swollen body. I shook his hand and waited for whatever pointless news he'd come to deliver. Last week I'd picked the internet like a vine-ripened tomato, searching for hope where there was none. But I still had questions. "Why can't my husband urinate? He hasn't used the bathroom on his own since Saturday, and the catheter hasn't been effective in relieving the fluid. You can see from the bag there are only a few drops of urine."

He wasn't there to waste time and got to the point. "He can't urinate because his kidneys have shut down. I've conferred with Dr. Carson, and he is in agreement that the fluids will be stopped immediately. There's no reason to continue giving him fluids when his body can't expel them, and I've already left orders for the nurse to disconnect the IV. The morphine pump will remain in place."

"And why have my kidneys shut down?" Barry wanted to know.

Without hesitation Dr. Simmons explained, "There is a fine line of demarcation when the liver sends a message to the kidneys, 'you don't have to function anymore because I'm dying'. I truly am sorry that nothing else can be done."

Barry extended his hand and thanked Dr. Simmons for his honesty. "It's not your fault. Cancer happens to a lot of people, and I'm one of them." Barry smiled as he said, "But I would recommend using WD-40 on the catheter before it's inserted. Sure would make it easier for the next guy." Dr. Simmons smiled at Barry's attempt at humor and excused himself.

Half an hour later it was Dr. Miller who came by while Lilli and I were using every ounce of strength to turn Barry onto his side. We needed to replace the sheets and bed pad in order to keep him comfortable, which was the least we could do. Dr. Miller, whom we hadn't seen since Barry was released on his last surgical follow-up appointment in August, summed up the scenario and asked, "Is there anything I can do?"

I met the dejection in his eyes that emulated my own. My answer was brief, "Pray." He made no response as he turned and left us to the chore at hand.

News of impending death had evidently found its way through the corridors of Crawford Long; I wasn't surprised when Dr. Sheffield appeared at Barry's bedside. His tone was remorseful and apologetic. "I'm genuinely sorry, Barry. I did everything I could, but more often than not chemoembolization is not effective, and in your case we knew it was a long-shot."

Barry shook Dr. Sheffield's hand with sincerity. "I'll tell you the same thing I told the urologist. It's not your fault, so don't blame yourself. Everything medically possible was done by you and every other doctor who tried to help me beat this cancer. And despite my and the many prayers of family and friends, I've accepted that this time, for whatever reason, God said no."

Barry's humbleness in the wake of his imminent death was remarkable. He thanked Dr. Sheffield for taking the time to stop by and see him. The doctor's head dropped in defeat as he left the room.

When Barry and I were alone again I napped briefly during my sisters' trip to the cafeteria for lunch and one of several outdoor smoke breaks necessitated by their nicotine addictions. They remained quiet as the day dragged on, and their caring concern had been unobtrusive. But I got their attention when our pastor came in to pray with us, and I mentioned something unusual. "Curtis, I've noticed since we've been here that Barry occasionally reaches upward, towards something or someone I can't see. Can you enlighten me?"

Before he responded I noticed my sisters, seated on straight-backed chairs in the corner, eyes as big as saucers, were interested in what the preacher had to say. He took my hands in his and offered what words of comfort he could find. "I can only surmise it is one of God's messengers who has come to take Barry home. Remember Psalm 23 assures God's children that even as we walk through the shadow of the valley of death, we are not alone. And whatever, or whomever, Barry sees is not meant for you to see. You cannot walk this path with him. While I have faith that his life will continue, it won't be here, in the way you think—or in the way you want. God has heard your prayers, but sometimes our will is not His will. Your journey with Barry will end, but only temporarily. Sheila, you have to trust that God has a plan for all of us and that one day you will be reunited with Barry for time without end."

I wanted to scream and kick and curse and question God's plan. Why had He turned his back on me when I needed Him the most? I wanted to demand that my pastor explain to me why God had ignored my prayers and my trust that those prayers would be answered. But my misdirected anger would have been met with further patience and biblical references that God is always in control of our lives and He had not abandoned me. I was simply too tired and heartbroken to listen to those words of devotion.

Sensing I was not receptive to whatever scripture he had in his repertoire and as it would be dark soon, he and my sisters left together. Pat and Joyce were unaccustomed to driving in Atlanta traffic and were anxious to leave before rush hour. Or maybe they were anxious to leave the cancer ward and the precariousness of life it represented. I reassured them that I would be fine and encouraged them to go.

Kim called to let me know she and Cindy were on their way to spend the night but planned to get a bite to eat first. I was relieved they'd stopped for dinner before making their way to the hospital and, therefore, wouldn't arrive on the coattail of dusk, a dusk that brought with it the dreaded sundown dementia. They'd missed Barry's unexplainable manic state, missed the struggle to soothe my dying husband.

An hour later Barry was resting peacefully, with no recollection of his temporary lunacy, when my nieces entered our room with pillows, blankets, and an overnight bag in tow. They were both wearing sweat pants and sweatshirts that would double as comfortable pajamas. Kim gave me a hug. "We're here for the night, and we've already worked out two hour shifts. One of us will be at his side while the other catnaps in the waiting room. No arguing. Tonight you're going to sleep. Mama said you look like a zombie." She took a few steps back and looked me over. "She was right. Actually, you look worse than I expected. You look like hell."

I returned her hug and accepted one from Cindy. "I'm thankful you're both here, but sleep for me is brief, if at all. It will be good to have some company because as long as the days are, the nights are longer."

Kim dropped her shoulder bag onto the dinner tray and searched through the clutter until she retrieved a prescription bottle. "Not tonight. I have a mild sedative for you, and you're going to sleep like a baby. Trust me."

"Are you crazy? I don't have a prescription for anything like that, and I can't take a drug that's not mine. It's okay if I don't sleep. I've learned to make it on a few hours of rest."

"Oh, this prescription is for you." She pushed the amber bottle towards me. "Read the label. It's your name on the prescription. I took the liberty of calling your new gynecologist and told her that I'm your daughter. Once I explained what's going on in your life, she was more than obliging when it came to a prescription of Xanax for you. She sends you her sympathy and said to remind you that you're late for your annual Pap smear."

Only Kim would use minor deception to obtain a tranquilizer, but I realized she'd meant no harm and that it was out of love and concern. She'd gotten away with it because I was a new patient of Dr. Jennings. My former, long-time gynecologist, and his nurse, would have known very well my children were boys. While I appreciated Kim's efforts, I wasn't sure I wanted to be knocked out by Xanax. What if Barry…

Cindy interrupted my indecision. "As for the dishonesty to get the Xanax, I had nothing to with it. But, Sheila, you've got to rest, or you'll be the next one admitted to the hospital for sheer exhaustion—or malnutrition. I won't try to force feed you, but you need to sleep. We're here to sit with him, and I'll wake you if necessary. I promise."

Tabitha, our assigned night nurse, came into the room and overheard Cindy's encouragement for me to rest. "She's right, Sheila, your body needs the restorative benefits of sleep. Your nieces and I will stand watch over your husband."

I swallowed the pill and saw the empathy in Tabitha's eyes that spoke volumes. On one of our earlier hospital stays, she and I had shared our stories of marrying our first loves as teenagers, our high school sweethearts. I sensed there was a piece of her heart that feared we could also share the same fate, the same devastating ending to our love stories. As she checked the morphine supply and charted his stats, Cindy asked subtly, "How long do you think…" She hesitated to finish her question because I was stretched out on the cot, already feeling the lethargic effect of the sedative. But I listened for what I didn't want to hear, what no wife wanted to hear.

Tabitha murmured, "Not tonight, but within the next twenty-four to thirty hours. It won't be any longer than that."

Understandably relieved that Barry would not die on her watch, Cindy settled herself into the one comfortable recliner in the corner, and Kim kissed my forehead. She and her bedding made the way down the hall to find a resting place of her own. Although I fell asleep to the whispers exchanged between Cindy and Tabitha, it was Kim who shook me awake. She shoved the cot next to the bed and tugged my arm out from under the covers. In a fog of tranquilized confusion, it was a challenge to ask from a mouth as dry as cotton, "What's wrong? Is he…?"

"No, he's okay, but he has to touch you. Give me your hand."

Befuddled, I groggily asked, "What are you saying? What?"

"He woke up and wanted to know where you were. I pointed to the cot and told him you were sleeping right beside him. A few minutes later he said he needed to touch you, to hold your hand. Instead of waking you from your out-like-a-drunk sleep, I slipped my hand in his. I thought with all the morphine he's on to control his pain, he wouldn't know the difference—and I wouldn't have to disturb you. But I was wrong, and when he asked, 'Kim, when are you gonna let me touch her?' there was no way in hell I wasn't gonna push the cot closer. Now, give me your hand so I can put it in his."

In slow motion I lifted my heavy arm, and Kim put my hand through the bed railing and whispered, "As much as I hated to wake you up, his smile and the bliss on his face were worth it. He knows that it's your hand he's holding and not mine." She wiped away tears and apologized again for disrupting my sleep.

"It's alright, Kim. We've fallen asleep holding each other's hand for months, every time we've had to stay in the hospital." With the warmth of his hand clinging to mine, I fell back into an oblivious, drug-induced sleep in a matter of minutes. It was a slumber so deep that not even dreams could intrude.

CHAPTER 16

Sometimes Love Hurts

WITH MORNING CAME momentary panic as the sun announced it was well past my usual, early awakening. One glimpse at the clock confirmed it was almost eight o'clock. I jumped up from the cot, which had been pushed against the wall, and rushed to Barry's bedside. He was paler and weaker, but he was breathing. I kissed his hand and barely heard his whispered, "Good morning, sleepyhead. I love you."

"I love you, too."

Lilli, the typically effervescent Lilli, cautiously entered our room as if walking on broken glass. "Well, Sheila, you certainly look better than yesterday. Your nieces have already gone because they were going to work. One of your brothers called, Jerry, and left a message that he and his wife will be here shortly after lunch to stay through the night. Why don't you get yourself some coffee and a shower before they get here? I'll be here, recording his stats."

I couldn't believe I'd slept for more than ten hours, thanks to a prescription obtained by less than honest means. I showered and dressed before the first of many, many visitors began to arrive—as if the Pied Piper had summoned them all on the same day. What had brought these "concerned friends" to the hospital where the Grim Reaper was lurking in the hallway among them? But I knew the answer: news in a small town traveled fast, bad news faster.

Like sharks aware of blood in the water, they swarmed in and out of our room, telling Barry how much he'd meant to them and how sorry they were. I wanted each of them to explain that if he was a true friend of theirs, then where had they been for the past ten months? Why hadn't they taken time to sit on our porch with him and tell him how he'd affected their lives? The futility of my frustration stirred the pot of agitation, a pot that was about to explode like a faulty pressure cooker. I didn't come undone because their intentions were good, although their timing was not. But my patience had a limit.

∽

By the time my brother and his wife arrived, even my docile husband had become agitated. I called Lilli into our room and asked her to post a "No Visitors" sign on our door and to tell any stragglers waiting to see Barry that they should go home. Lilli was one step ahead of me and more than willing to oblige; her primary concern was the wellbeing of her patient. Barry was dying, and I would not allow him to die in the middle of a circus of well-meaning acquaintances. He, along with everyone else, deserved to die in peace.

We weren't disturbed again, and I began to pace in the confined space. Jerline interrupted my stride. "Sheila, you need to go outside and get some fresh air. A walk will be good for you. I'm sure you haven't left his side since he was admitted on Monday night, and we'll be right here with him. One of us will come and find you if…"

It was just a matter of time, and I didn't know how much longer I could hang onto the edge of the cliff before I let go and fell into the abyss of despair. I stepped over to Barry's bedside where he was sleeping, kissed his forehead, and replied to my sister-in-law's reasoning, "I'll go outside, but not for a walk. I can get some air on the steps in front of the hospital, the Peachtree entrance, if you need me. I'll be back in ten minutes."

With one final moment's hesitation, I grabbed my jacket and fled the foreseeable outcome of my marriage and the tragic loss of a kind and gentle man. I wanted to snatch my husband from death's grip and run, but there was nowhere for us to run.

Once outside I collapsed onto the cold concrete stoop, dropped my head into my hands, and began to cry. I felt like I was caught in a rip tide and the harder I fought to keep my head above water, the further I was towed out to sea—further from the shore of a truth I couldn't change. I brushed tears aside and felt a hand on my shoulder, a lifeline that rescued me from the dangerous undertow. I gazed upward and shielded red, swollen eyes from the sun. Marnie stood before me and, to my surprise, proceeded to make herself comfortable on the stoop beside me.

She reached into her stylish Louis Vuitton purse and handed me a lavender scented handkerchief. "Hello, Sheila. I was in the area and decided to stop by the hospital and check on you. You don't seem to be coping with this situation very well. Not well at all."

Well, no, as a matter of fact, I wasn't. I wiped my tear stained face with the lace trimmed handkerchief and involuntarily shivered in the late afternoon coolness of October. I inhaled fresh air that was as crisp as a North Georgia apple and exhaled slowly. "Thanks, Marnie. No, I'm not handling this 'situation' by any means. I'm afraid. I can barely remember my life before Barry, and I'm not sure I can live without him. Or if I want to."

Before the next tear could fall Marnie firmly grasped my shoulders, forcing me to face her. "You can and you will survive what you think you can't. You are young and stronger than you believe you are."

I shook my head to deny her optimism. "I appreciate the vote of confidence, but you really have no idea how much pain I'm in. It's like something alive that threatens to destroy me."

"And it will if you let it! Your pain will eat you up from the inside out. As for not understanding your pain, you can't begin to imagine the hurt and humiliation I've endured at the hands of an unfaithful husband. Do you think I didn't love my husband or that I didn't grieve the end of a thirty-seven year marriage—a marriage I worked to save? I believe his death would have been easier than divorce and his betrayal of our marriage, his betrayal of our family. My husband chose to leave me for another woman, but I survived. And you will survive Barry's death. That's not to say there won't be incredibly bad days ahead, but you'll make it if you want to. Sheila, you'll have to want to go on without him."

I turned my attention to the woman who sat beside me. She'd carefully constructed a façade of aloofness that had crumbled around her. Her pain had lain dormant after years of anguished acceptance until that chilly afternoon when the wound reopened, right there on the steps of Crawford Long Hospital—raw and exposed for all to see. Mama and Marnie, a "high society" woman, seemingly had nothing in common. But I recognized the same anger, the same suffering provided by an unfaithful husband. It was an invisible connection between women who had been good wives and who had deserved better husbands. I momentarily put my own despair on hold. "I'm sorry, Marnie. I've never considered the heartbreak that comes with the death of a marriage."

Without a word of response to my sympathy, she regained her poise. It was as if she hadn't lost her composure and had revealed her hidden pain to me or to any of the curious passersby. The wall of pretense was back in place, her dignity restored.

One glance at my watch hauled me to my feet; I'd been gone for more than half an hour. "I appreciate your words of support, Marnie, but I have to get back to the room. I've been gone much longer than I intended."

She placed her hand on my shoulder. "Of course, I understand. Go to your husband's bedside, hold his hand, and take solace in knowing that Barry has not chosen to leave you or to stop loving you. I have no doubt that he would do anything within his power to stay and grow old with you." Her smile was one of regret. "Be grateful in that knowledge."

She gathered her leather clutch, slipped perfectly manicured hands into matching gloves, and wrapped her herringbone cape closer against the cold. Without another word she turned and hurried towards the red light on the corner and proceeded to the parking lot across the street. I called out a farewell that was lost in the traffic and took the steps two at time. I made a dash to catch the elevator that would return me to the fifth floor where my beloved husband lay dying. It was the last place I wanted to be. But it was the only place I could be.

It was dark thirty, that brief interlude right before dawn when I was aware of whispers. The forthcoming daybreak and I were still in the early stage of awakening. "They look like children taking a nap, so sweet," Jerline observed as she tucked the blanket around us.

I'd slept in the hospital bed snug in the nook of Barry's arm, encircled in the warmth of his love. I listened to the whispered conversation between my brother and his wife as they debated whether or not they should call our sons and maybe Barry's parents. I stirred enough to answer, "Don't call them. They've already said their goodbyes. No need waking them this early with news they don't want to hear."

Jerry spoke, "I guess you're right. Sorry we disturbed you. We went to the cafeteria to wait for them to open and ate breakfast. We brought you a cup of cappuccino and a fresh-baked blueberry muffin."

He offered the steaming cup of my limited source of nourishment, and I disentangled myself from Barry and sat up. I pushed the hair away from my face, rubbed sleep from my eyes, and reached for the coffee. As I carefully sipped the hot beverage, darkness was replaced by the rosy blush of sunrise that bled through the closed blinds. And then I felt his last heartbeat—before the loud, panicked beep of the monitor alerted the nurse.

Supposedly, our lives flashed before us during the last moments before death. Although I was not the one dying, our lives were as one that became a sequence of fragmented colors and patterns, like the view through a kaleidoscope. There were slivers of our first kiss under the stars, wedding vows made in an uncaring courtroom, our first home we'd filled with used furniture and love, the births of our sons and the happy days of their childhoods. When twisted into focus those bits of love, laughter, tears, joy, and disappointments created a lifetime. I sat motionless as the pieces of our lives swirled across my heart.

But I was aware of the tears of my brother and sister-in-law, and I heard Jerline when she said, "God always knows to put us where we need to be."

Her words forced me from my trance as I sat the cup on the bed tray and asked in a flat, monotone voice, "And where is God now?"

Jerry tried to console me. "Sheila, He's here. He's with us always, in every moment of our lives. That is His promise."

I ignored his response. "It's my fault, you know. I shouldn't have sat up and left the security of his arms. Death waited for me to release my hold on him so he could steal him away from me. I should have stayed in his arms and kept Death in the corner, and Barry would still be here with me for a little while longer."

My brother pleaded with me to be rational. "Sheila, you're not making any sense. You know his death is not your fault. His blood pressure has been dropping all night, and Tabitha told us it was only a matter of hours. You sitting up in bed had absolutely no bearing on the timing of his death. You know that."

Logically, of course, but it was hard to be logical in the midst of death, the death of a part of me that could never be replaced. On some level I realized I'd believed what I wanted to believe, that Barry would beat the odds and fall into the two percent who actually survived stomach cancer. But that realization didn't prevent an emotional meltdown.

The barricade, the lie I'd built to protect myself collapsed, and I heard wails from somewhere deep within, wails wrenched from the depths of my soul. I threw myself back into his arms to hold him close one more time. I continued to weep as I held him and whispered words of love I hoped he heard. I drew him closer and willed my heart to stop beating.

I'm not sure how much time passed, but the blinds were open, and the sun was shining, reflecting from the pallid green wall behind the bed. Dr. Carson stood before me; dusty beams of sunlight brushed through his copper hair. His presence brought biting sarcasm. "It's nice of you to drop by during your morning rounds, especially since you've obviously heard of Barry's death." My anger grew louder, but Dr. Carson didn't flinch. "I wish you could have saved him, or have had the decency to have told us the chances were very slim that he would survive. Then we could have spent the last ten months living instead of dying."

He stood at the foot of the bed, accepting my abuse, until he was careless enough to open his mouth. "I am—"

"If you tell me you're sorry, I swear I'll throw the first thing I can grab at your head. I don't think you had any idea how prophetic you were being when you assured us there would be 'a light at the end of the tunnel'. You gave us false hope and to what end? So Barry could make the excruciating trip to hell and back fighting to live?" Sobs choked the harsh words that were spat out in anger.

Jerline pilfered through my bag to retrieve a medicine bottle and handed me a pill with a glass of water. "Here, Sheila, you're going to have a nervous breakdown if you don't get hold of yourself. It's not Dr. Carson's fault Barry died."

"She's right, honey. There was nothing else that could have been done," agreed Lilli who'd entered the room, unnoticed, with Dr. Carson.

"What is that? What kind of pill are you giving her?" Why Dr. Carson assumed that was any of his business was beyond my confused comprehension.

Jerline hastily replied, "It's a Xanax, and it was prescribed by her doctor."

With one last parting glance at Barry and me, the doctor left the room. Evidently, death and irrational widows were not new to him. Widows. With the stroke of his pen on a death certificate my status as a woman would be reclassified from "married" to "widow." The word and all it implied hit me like a ton of bricks, and the sorrowful weeping returned until the Xanax kicked in and brought an eerie tranquility to my demeanor.

A nurse entered to inform Jerry that the funeral home had been contacted, and they were sending an ambulance to transport the body. The body? Was that all Barry was to her—a body? I felt like a detached spectator observing events taking place in someone else's life. I refused to leave the bed until the men from Hightower's arrived. I was relieved Jimmy, a longtime friend who had helped out at the station during Barry's illness, came with the driver. He gently coaxed, "Sheila, it's okay to leave him now. I'll take care of him."

I managed a barely audible "thank you" and released my hold on a husband who was no longer there, a husband who'd told me last night he was ready to go home. Lilli offered a cool bath cloth to wash my face while Jerline found my shoes, and Jerry gathered our belongings. I was led to the back seat of Jerry's car, where I slept until we got home—grateful for the Xanax that had dulled my pain.

Our sons met me in the driveway with tear tracks and swollen eyes that painted a picture of their own grief. Pat was waiting with sympathetic arms, very sorry she hadn't been able to fix this for me. But she was there to love me. "Honey, I'm so very sorry. We all loved him, and we're all hurting right now." She hugged me tightly and, ever practical, added, "You need to get a shower. You and the boys have an appointment at the funeral home at one o'clock. And there's a stack of mail on the trunk in the den. I separated the bills from the cards and threw away the junk."

Mechanically, I showered and dressed for the "final arrangements" meeting with the funeral director. Forgetting Barry's advice not to waste money on an expensive coffin, I told Brad and Chuck to choose whatever they wanted for their dad. I asked that the florist use multicolored fall flowers for the coffin spray. We selected the music together, old Christian songs composed to offer peace, with one exception. I requested Celine Dion's "Because You Loved Me" to be played at the end of the service. I also instructed our pastor to focus the eulogy on love and life, not death. Because love was stronger than death…and because Barry's life was what had mattered.

I was awakened by a clatter that sounded from the kitchen and reverberated through the house, followed by "damn it." Sunlight fought with closed blinds to find its way into the bedroom as I reached for Barry. But his side of the bed was empty except for his favorite faded blue t-shirt. It was the only item of clothing I had that held his distinct aroma in its softness. When I wasn't able to fall asleep in our bed by myself, I remembered he'd worn the t-shirt to the ER on Monday and that it was in my bag. I salvaged it from our unpacked suitcase and placed it on my pillow. The smell of him had eventually lulled me to sleep.

I wrapped myself closer to the t-shirt, but the t-shirt was little consolation as I realized that somehow I had to get through the funeral. The voices continued in the kitchen, and I lay unmoving. The day I would bury my husband had begun, and the sharp pain of his death stabbed at my heart. I wondered how I'd coped with the customary visitation.

The surreal details of last night were like a silent movie that flipped through the fog of grief. Instead of black and white the frames were in color, dominated by blue and white. Last night was Bremen's Homecoming, and many of the visitors wore our school's colors because they were on their way to the big football game. They came to offer sincere condolences, but I could sense they were anxious to be on their ways as they held a restrained excitement in check. I didn't think badly of them because, after all, it was my life that was devastatingly altered, not theirs. They'd taken time from their plans to pay their respects, and each one of them was genuinely sympathetic.

As the hours ticked by, the viewing room became thick with the fragrance of flowers and was filled to capacity with an eclectic crowd that merged in sympathy. Some visitors wore dress clothes, some wore jeans. The older widows were decked out in Sunday clothes and bunched together like a cluster of grapes wearing pillbox hats.

They'd been customers for years because Barry took care of their old cars and charged the minimum since he knew they lived on paltry incomes.

The women had meant no harm when several of them told me I was young and pretty and even though the first year, with its holidays, anniversaries, and birthdays, would be the hardest, I shouldn't have any trouble in finding another man to marry. Remarry? To suggest such a thing at a very inappropriate time and place was an indication of what was most likely elderly senility. But I understood that to many women of their generation, a hasty second marriage was the only thing that separated them from poverty. I'd, therefore, contained my impulse to lash out at them for being insensitive.

Others were more than kind. One friend sent a flowering cherry tree to the house with a note that read, "Plant this tree in his memory and when it blooms every spring, may you be reminded that he, too, still lives." Many friends and family sent flowers that combined with the warmth of the room until the smell of mums, carnations, chrysanthemums, and roses became nauseating. I needed a few minutes of fresh air and solitude, but I had remained and accepted the condolences of our friends and family members.

Carl held tears in place, but Melba was pitiful as she wept over the loss of her son. She whispered into a crumpled tissue, "If only I could have held him one more time."

I wrapped my arms around her in an attempt to console her, but didn't tell her "one more time" wouldn't have been enough. A thousand more times wouldn't have been enough for either of us.

I didn't remember much because pain had numbed my senses. What I was able to recall was interrupted by a knock on the bedroom door. "Sheila, are you awake?" It was Pat. "Sue is here. She brought angel biscuits and ham for breakfast. Sweetie, can you hear me? She would like to see you for a few minutes before we have to leave for the service."

"Yes, I'm awake and I hear you. I'll get a shower. Please ask her to wait, and I'll have a cup of coffee with her." Sue and I'd been friends for the past twenty years, and I needed to drag myself to the kitchen and thank her for her thoughtfulness in providing breakfast.

Pat opened the door and persisted. "Ok, honey. Just throw on your robe after you shower and come on to the kitchen. You have several hours before we have to be at the funeral home to receive visitors. Kim will be here to do your hair and makeup, and we'll find something suitable for you to wear. People have already started bringing food, and Martha has volunteered to be in charge of keeping a list of who brought what. She's agreed to oversee serving and clean up."

Martha was an older second cousin, and while we weren't particularly close, she was family and I appreciated her for pitching in to help. Despite that everything was being done to carry me through the day, I didn't know how I would ever get through it—not when it hurt to breathe without Barry.

⸎

Although I was emotionally anesthetized to surrounding proceedings, the funeral was a beautiful service. Reverend Curtis' eulogy began with 1 Corinthians 13: 4-8, "Love is patient; Love is kind and is not jealous…" He then proceeded to elaborate on the love of Christ, the love between a husband and wife, the love a father has for his children. He included personal anecdotes regarding Barry's life and how he'd lived it.

The music was as planned. Because all Barry had wanted was to go home, I asked Cyndie to sing the evocative, "Sounds Like

Home to Me." Valerie sang "Amazing Grace" a cappella, and as her soulful voice wafted through the country chapel, I lost the raveled strand by which I was hanging. It was several minutes before I realized the wailing sound of a wounded animal was coming from me, as if a part of me had been physically and brutally ripped away. It had been.

To the lyrics of Celine Dion's passionately charged "Because You Loved Me," I was led by my sons up the aisle, thankful they were supporting me on either side. Barry's favorite time of year was fall, and he would have savored the sunny afternoon filled with the beauty of the season. We were cloaked in color as we stepped outside to form a greeting line for our companions in sorrow.

I barely remembered those in attendance or the ride to the cemetery where my family's plot was located, where generations were buried. The pungent mound of red Georgia dirt left by the gravediggers assailed my nostrils as I sat through the graveside ceremony, unaware of the words that dropped over the casket. Afterwards, I was again led to the limo and was grateful to have been spared watching my husband lowered into the ground and covered with dirt, shovel by shovel.

We returned to a home overflowing with noisy friends, neighbors, family—a cacophony that held me hostage among well-meaning visitors and a sea of sympathy. I made obligatory small talk and thanked people for their condolences until I was suffocating from the weight of the day. I had to escape the burden, and my instinct was to flee to the peace and isolation of the cemetery. I needed to go to the gravesite for one final goodbye. I excused myself, found my purse, and headed out the door.

Brad and Valerie followed on my heels and insisted on driving me. They respected my need for privacy and kept their distance as I knelt beside the flower covered mound. I was surrounded by wreaths that dissolved in a multicolored blur of hot tears that streamed down my cold cheeks. Sunset cast an aura of pale golden light that encircled the cemetery. I cried until the chill of a radiant blue twilight forced me to stand, to leave him. And to begin the grueling process of letting go.

CHAPTER 17

Set Adrift

WITH THE HELP of Xanax I slept soundly, but it was hard to rouse myself when morning ushered in Pat, Cindy, and Kim. Pat put on a pot of coffee, and Kim forced me to pull myself from the warm covers of a sedative hangover. But there were thank you cards, customized with Sue's help because I didn't like the mass produced ones provided by the funeral home, to get ready for tomorrow's mail. And there were dozens of fresh cut flowers that had to be dealt with before they wilted. While we shared coffee and Cindy's warm cinnamon rolls, the four of us divided the huge pile of florist cards and the lists of those who had supplied food. With their help, the project was completed in a less than two hours. Cindy offered to drop the cards by the post office when she and Kim left to return home to their families. Pat stayed to help me sort out the flowers.

I walked through the flower garden on the carport. The dozens of beautiful bouquets of fresh flowers wouldn't last more than a few days. Although still in a daze, I made the decision to distribute their beauty among those who had very little beauty left in their lives. Pat and I dropped the back seat of the Blazer, loaded the flowers, and delivered them to the local nursing home.

There were enough vibrant vases for each resident's room, the foyer, and the dining hall. The elderly, whose limited domain was held inside the drab walls of the nursing home where Death was a frequent and familiar—and on most days the only—visitor, were thrilled with the flowers. The women couldn't remember the last time anyone had given them flowers and were especially grateful. Their tears of joy traced the crevices of time and brought another round of tears from me. Those who had generously sent the flowers would never know how much sharing their kindness meant to the lonely recipients and me.

As we made our way through the parking lot, Pat speculated aloud, "I wonder how many of those women will go to their graves without ever having been loved the way you were loved, Sheila." She put her arm around my shoulders. "You were cherished, and not many women can say that."

Her voice was tinged with envy but the insinuation was like a butterfly that floated in and out of my grief, and the comment flitted away. I knew better than anyone how blessed I was to have had such a wonderful husband and to have known true love. It made losing him that much harder. Why hadn't God taken a man who abused his wife or was too lazy to keep a job and support his family? Why had He taken a good man away from his wife and sons? Why hadn't He intervened? Those questions plagued me, haunted my fitful nights, and challenged my faith.

My sons got up early the next morning and left to open the doors of what had become their auto shop business. I didn't bother getting out of bed and tugged the comforter over my head like a turtle who wanted nothing more than to be left alone. Last night's sedative tugged me back to peaceful sleep until the phone on the nightstand intruded. I reached clumsily for the receiver.

A cheerful voice on the other end poked me awake. "Good morning. This is Ashley calling in reference to the oncology center's 'Celebration of Life' reception on Saturday night for all of our cancer survivors. The invitations were mailed two weeks ago, but we haven't received your RSVP. We really need a head count for the catered dinner. Will you and your husband be joining us in the annual festivities?"

Ashley's voice was as irritating as the birds that chirped happily outside the bedroom window; I wanted to reach through the line and wring her neck. But since that wasn't possible I forced myself to reply, "I realize your job is to organize this shindig, Ashley, but you really should spend more time updating your roster of actual survivors before you call to confirm reservations. Let me clarify. My husband died four days ago. So, no, we won't be able to attend the 'Celebration of Life' party."

Her apologies streamed from the mouthpiece as I slammed the phone back onto its base. I was wide awake and angry at the inconsiderate phone call that rudely shoved me into another day without Barry. I yanked on sweat pants and a t-shirt, staggered to the kitchen and put on a pot of coffee. I planned to spend the day wrapped in misery and reading sympathy cards that waited to be opened, but that proved impossible. The day was filled with concerned visitors who wanted to advise or console me. There was an assorted mix of unsolicited interlopers.

First there was Daddy, who stood ringing the doorbell repeatedly. Had the door been unlocked he would have walked right in without bothering to knock, as he usually did. I opened the door, and he made his way to the den and took a seat on the couch. "Morning, Sugar. Decided I'd come by to check on you. Anything you need? I gotta stop by the store and pick up a carton of buttermilk, so if there's —"

I interrupted, "No, Daddy, I don't need anything. But thanks for asking."

He gathered his thoughts and got right to the point of his visit. "Sugar, you're forty-three years old, and none of us expected you'd be the first to bury your husband. 'Em boys plan on marrying next summer, and you'll be livin' by yourself. No sense in both of us having houses with more room than we need. I want you to think about sellin' this place and movin' in with me. You don't have to decide today. There's no hurry, but it does seem like it would be better for you not to live by yourself, and I could use the company."

It was true my household would go from four to one in less than a year, but selling our home was not a solution. "Daddy, I know you've been lonely since Mama died, and we all miss her, but I can't move in with you. As you pointed out I'm forty-three years old, and although I've never before lived alone, it's time for me to learn how to do that."

There was no need in hurting his feelings by telling him that he and I wouldn't last a week under the same roof. I loved him, but loving him and living with him were entirely different. He messed and strewed and didn't bother to pick up after himself. Mama blamed the fact the house was always a mess on a houseful of kids, but as we each married and moved out, she realized Daddy was the mess.

She'd died and left him for us to deal with, but he was managing to live on his own. My sisters and I rotated our schedules to take care of meals, cleaning, and doing his laundry. We had gotten him one of those medical alert medallions for emergencies. I'd to explain to him that he absolutely could *not* use the emergency device to have the ambulance driver pick him up a pack of tobacco from the convenience store—even if he couldn't get one of us "girls" on the phone to run an errand for him. He was capable of making the short trip to the People Pleaser, and the next time he cried "wolf" there would be a fine.

Daddy noted the cup of coffee in my hands and, as evidenced by the faraway look in his aging eyes, he was in another place and time. He abruptly pulled himself back to the present moment. "Well, if you've already made up your mind, I reckon I may as well go." He stood with his cane and awkwardly patted my shoulder, but faltered before he reached the door. He turned towards me and said, "I'm twice your age, and if you live to be eighty-six, well, that's a lot of mornings to have breakfast by yourself." Without elaborating he made his way out the door and climbed into his car.

I didn't bother to close the door or latch the screened one. I took my coffee to the sun-washed screened porch where the spectacular fall day belied my sorrow. I pondered Daddy's comment about breakfast. With different schedules, my family had rarely eaten breakfast together. And then a memory from childhood, long forgotten, surfaced. I had lain in bed in the first light of morning and dreaded Mama's call, "Get up, time for breakfast. C'mon, you'll be late for school if you miss the bus." I recalled their subdued voices and the occasional clink of cups and spoons accompanied by the smell of sausage and biscuits.

It suddenly dawned on me that as working parents with a houseful of kids, those few moments alone together over breakfasts were valued. Daddy wanted to warn me of innumerable years of lonely breakfasts, and my heart ached at the very thought of growing old without Barry. I sipped coffee and watched fallen leaves that blew aimlessly in the breeze; they imitated my dismal feeling of lifelessness. Barry had been my anchor, and without him my equilibrium, my sense of direction were thrown off kilter. I was lost in the wreckage of his death.

My reflections, and porch haven, were disrupted when I recognized Cyndie's approaching voice. "Sheila, are you home? The door's open. The screened one isn't hooked, and both cars are in the carport. Hello?"

To ignore her would have been impolite. I forced myself to leave my refuge and greet her anxious inquiry as I entered the den where she stood perplexed. "Hi, Cyndie."

"Oh, hi, I don't want to meddle, but I'm worried about you. I left the office for a few minutes to come and check on you. How are you? I brought a small token for you, and I hope it will help you get through your loss."

I reached for the gift wrapped box but couldn't answer her inquiry as to how I was. Nobody wanted to hear that pain and emptiness consumed every waking moment and tormented my sleep. "Thanks, but it's not necessary. You've really helped out enough, and the mums you sent were beautiful. I have several I'm going to plant in the front yard when I'm up to it. Pat and the boys volunteered to help me."

"Please open the box."

To placate her I untied the ribbon and removed the cover to find a charming necklace, a gold chain and setting for a pearl mustard seed enclosed in glass. I was confused at her choice of that particular piece of jewelry, but she didn't hesitate to offer an explanation.

"I know you're struggling with your faith right now and you're upset with God for not answering your prayers to heal Barry. But you have to trust Him and to remember your Christian beliefs. The necklace is to remind you that faith the size of that tiny mustard seed has the power to move mountains. And it's faith that will see you through the dark valley of your grief."

Faith was a gift, but my faith had been brought into question. I hadn't grasped that concept because my belief was unwavering until Barry's death planted doubt in my heart. Yes, I was angry with God and yet I continued to pray that He would help me through each hour, each day because I needed His strength—even though I was conflicted. But was prayer without faith nothing more than words?

I bit my tongue but found my manners. "Thank you, Cyndie. It's a very thoughtful gift, and I appreciate it. I'll think of you when I wear it."

People drift in and out of our lives, and God had sent Cyndie into my life when He knew I would need her the most. She gave me a hug and promised to keep me in her prayers as she made her way out the door, back to her uninterrupted life—back to her loving husband. I didn't resent her, but I did wonder how she would handle it if she had to bury that loving husband. Would her faith sustain her?

Cyndie had barely gotten out of the driveway when my friend Joann* parked her car and got out carrying a huge, oblong pillow. "Hello. How are you today?"

Was that a rhetorical question, or did she really want to know how I was? Surely she didn't want to risk being brought into my dark cave of depression. I ignored the question and asked one of my own as I held the screened door for her. "Do you plan to sleep on the porch with that pillow?"

"The pillow is for you. It's a body pillow, and when Dad died Mama said it helped to have it next to her. It kept the bed from being empty, and it might help you adjust to sleeping without Barry."

Really? A pillow for a husband? "Well, uh, thank you," was all I could stammer as I tossed the pillow onto the sofa.

Joann changed the subject. "I'll make a fresh pot of coffee and we can visit on the porch." She rinsed out the coffee pot and set about brewing another one. "By the way, when's the last time you had anything to eat? Those jeans are hanging onto bones and losing the battle."

We carried the aromatic coffee through the den and settled ourselves on the sunny porch. Neither of us said anything, but I sensed there was something on Joann's mind. Oh, dear Lord, what was her advice for me going to be? It seemed everybody had an answer, although most had not walked in my shoes. I was surprised when she began the conversation otherwise.

"I want to tell you something I haven't discussed with anyone other than my husband and our marriage counselor. Of course, Bremen being Bremen, it'll be all over town soon enough. But I want you to hear it from me." She carefully sipped hot coffee and exhaled slowly. "A year ago Keith* had an affair with a coworker. I'm not telling you this because I expect sympathy—you couldn't possibly relate to a lyin', cheatin' husband. There, it's out. I told you only because I want you to appreciate what you had; yours was a marriage I coveted. Despite outward appearances, we don't all have faithful husbands and happy marriages. Actually, very few of us do."

She reached for a tissue, dabbed at her tears as I processed what she'd shared with me. Joann and Keith had children together, owned a very nice home in a rather expensive neighborhood, and both had great jobs in education. They seemed happy, as happy as any of the other couples I knew. And if they were seeking advice from a marriage counselor, then maybe they weren't planning to divorce.

"But, Joann, he didn't leave you. The two of you are still married and living together as husband and wife, seeking counseling to work things out as best you can."

She blew her nose and stared at me like I was a child who didn't comprehend what I'd been told and patiently enlightened me. "Hells bells, Sheila. The sonofabitch left me the minute he climbed into bed with that homewreckin' slut. Our marriage may endure, but it won't be the same. No matter what he promises I won't ever be able to trust him again. But according to our lawyer, at our age and with accumulated, combined assets it's less complicated if we stay married. And you know when it comes to money, Keith is tighter than bark on a tree. You won't understand what I'm going to say, but I envy you your freedom. Your sons are grown, engaged to be married and to begin lives of their own. You were a good wife, but now that door is closed, and you're free from any commitments or responsibilities other than for yourself. You're like a bird out of a cage with options of your choosing. Please don't hate me for saying what was on my mind, but I'm trapped in a loveless marriage for the sake of financial investments and three teenagers who need two parents." Joann sipped her coffee and tilted her head expectantly, waiting for me to say something.

Apparently, mine was not the only fairy tale that didn't end with "happily ever after." The freedom she envied was not by choice—God had not given me a choice. I didn't have the heart to tell her that to stay in a marriage for convenience's sake was almost, if not more so than, as sad as losing a husband to cancer. Perhaps that was her point in confiding in me. I didn't mean to sound trite, but all I could say was, "I'm sorry, Joann. I don't know what to say except that I truly am sorry."

"Thank you for listening and for caring, especially when…. I've got to run, but please call me if there's anything you need, anything either Keith or I can do. And for goodness sake, eat something!"

My stomach grumbled its complaint as I waved goodbye to my friend. To appease my growling gut I made a grilled cheese sandwich, poured myself a glass of tea, and returned to the porch. I left the unfinished sandwich on the plate as tears slid down my cheeks until I drifted off in the warmth of the afternoon.

I was awakened by the insistent ring of the doorbell, and I left the reprieve of sleep to answer the door. Carl stood waiting for me to invite him in; I stepped aside and motioned for him to come inside. "I'm sorry if I've come at a bad time. Did I interrupt your nap?"

"It's okay, Carl. I dozed off in the chaise on the porch. Please have a seat."

I settled myself into Barry's oversized recliner and waited for whatever his daddy had to say. Carl was the personification of the narrow-minded, outspoken "Archie Bunker" character from the seventies t.v. show *All In the Family*. Barry was an optimist, a happy-go-lucky man as different from his daddy as the three brothers were from each other. It was hard to believe they all belonged to the same family. Carl always had an opinion and thought his was always right—and the only one that mattered. I knew he hadn't dropped by just to see how I was doing because that would have been much too considerate and out of character.

He didn't waste any time letting me know why he was there. "When the boys move out you ought to sell this house. It's too much maintenance, and the yard is more than you're gonna be able to manage on your own. I've talked it over with Phil, and when you're ready we'll help you clean out the basement and find an apartment or a two bedroom house with a smaller lot in another good neighborhood. No need in you paying more property taxes than you have to or worrying about taking care of this big yard. Hell, keeping the straw raked from all 'em pine trees is a full-time job."

I sat quietly and let him finish his spiel before I responded to his plan for my life without his son. I wanted to tell him that my finances and where I chose to live were none of his damn business and to stop meddling. But I reminded myself that while I'd buried a husband, he and Melba had buried their eldest son. Carl undoubtedly had demons of regret to contend with in his own way, and I softened my words. "We buried Barry two days ago, and I can barely function—shower, brush my teeth, and get dressed are all I've been able to accomplish. I appreciate your concern, but this is our home, the place where Barry and I finished raising our sons. The three of us have fond memories of living here, but again, thank you for your suggestion."

Carl grumbled a protest, but I made it very clear I was not going to discuss the matter with him any further. Carl being Carl stubbornly intended to interject his protest, but my resolute face must've left even him speechless, a first. My uncompromising attitude had dismissed him and I walked him out, hoping he was the last of the day's intruders. I needed solitude and time to grieve.

I reached for the shoe box filled with numerous sympathy cards Pat had organized and left on the coffee table. I returned to the cushioning of the recliner where I began to open the cards of consolation. They each contained words of inspiration and compassion, words of encouragement, words of devotion that fell from the envelopes. But they were empty words that did little to assuage my pain. Though many of the cards contained offers from our family and friends to help out if there was anything they could do for us.

Several of our business customers had taken the time to write about incidences of Barry's kindness, how he'd let them charge a set of tires so they could get to work, extending credit to customers who could repay only a few dollars a week, charging less or nothing for repair work he knew they couldn't afford, patching together a car to get another few months out of a worn-out vehicle. Although he'd not once discussed those acts of kindness with me, his willingness to help others was not surprising. Neither of us had forgotten our early years of struggle. I placed the cards back in the box, covered myself with the cotton throw from the armrest, and submitted to the intense ache of loss.

It wasn't the doorbell that infringed on my grief, but another phone call that was the trespasser. "Hello? Hello, Sheila? This is Dr. Mitcham from the university. Are you there? Can you hear me?"

I held my tears in check before I replied, "Yes, Dr. Mitcham. This is Sheila."

"I read of your husband's death in the paper's obituary column and wanted to call and tell you how sorry I am for your loss. It's tragic when one dies so young. How are you?"

Sobs invaded her concern but I managed to say, "Thank you for calling Professor Mitcham, but I can't, I really can't talk right now. I'm afraid I'm not coping with his death very well."

She didn't hesitate to cut through the sobbing. "Sheila, I want you to realize you need grief counseling to help you through this nightmare. I have a friend who is a very good Christian counselor and specializes in guiding those who've lost a loved one through the maze of pain and recovery. I'm going to call her right now and give her your phone number. Her name is Patty James*, and if she's with a patient it may take an hour or two before she contacts you. Please make an appointment with her."

How could therapy possibly help me? But I thanked my former professor for calling and promised her that I would consider her recommendation to seek counseling. I curled into the fetal position and covered myself head to toe with the throw, but within minutes the phone demanded to be answered again. "Hello."

"Hello, is this Sheila?"

"Yes. Who's calling?"

"This is Dr. James. My friend Jane Mitcham left an urgent message that I should contact you immediately. I understand you very recently lost your husband."

"Yes. He died of cancer only a few days ago, after almost a year of hell."

"I know how raw your pain is, and I've counseled many widows and widowers. Please let me schedule an appointment for you. I can see you tomorrow—"

I didn't want to be rude, but I interrupted the perusal of her calendar. "Thank you for calling and for your concern, but I don't believe a therapist is the answer."

Dr. James didn't dispute me, but she insisted that I write down her name and phone number. She solicited a vow that I would consider grief counseling either from her or another counselor. I made a false promise so I could get off the phone with her persistence and jotted down her phone number. She may have been a grief counselor, but she couldn't possibly relate to the depth of my pain.

I placed the phone back in its cradle and wrapped myself in grief. The heartfelt lyrics of Jim Croce's "Time in a Bottle" ran through my head as I contemplated our past—and my future. Why had we been so careless with our days? Why had I taken for granted that Barry and I would spend the rest of our lives together? And how could I move forward when I was paralyzed with the fear of facing life without him?

*Name changed

CHAPTER 18

After The Rain

THE PAST SIX months have been the most difficult of my life, and I've survived what I thought I would not. The regular visits to the cemetery, where I sat at Barry's graveside for hours, became less frequent. I was at last able to breathe without the physical ache of having lost a part of myself. And despite Pat and Jerline's conclusion that I was "the worst widow ever," I learned to do some things for myself. I could change the vacuum cleaner filter, turn off the water main, and crank up the leaf blower. I recognized the difference between a flat head screwdriver and a Phillips head and was handy with a hammer. I was a work in progress and learned on an as-needed basis.

For example, when vandals demolished several mailboxes in the neighborhood, I bought a new one and wrangled with it for a while before I figured out how to attach the box securely to the post. The task wasn't without anger, anger that Barry had died and left me with such chores. Ricky, my next door neighbor, had offered to help, but I declined. I couldn't spend the rest of my life depending on other women's husbands. The last thing I wanted was to transfer my dependence from Barry to another man, and that included my grown sons.

Both of them would be getting married in the summer and didn't need their mama calling them every other day because she was afraid of the dark. They encouraged me to have a home security system installed as I would be living alone. Brad also convinced me to buy a pistol that he taught me how to load and shoot, for protection only—although Treetop was a safe neighborhood. Having my family separated and living by myself would be an adjustment, another change in my life. Change was, indeed, the only constant. The transition from wife to widow was not without pain, problems, and decisions that had to be made without Barry.

I sold both the Harley and the Chevrolet Blazer and opted to keep the Mustang, even though it was the least practical of the two cars. It was the car Barry and I'd custom ordered, the last thing he gave me before cancer took him from me. It was a decision that only I understood, but it was mine to make.

It was not without guilt that I dropped the rag top and drove under a blue, cloudless sky. It wasn't fair that I should have even a hint of joy in my life again. Simple pleasures filled me with remorse. Why had he died instead of me? That was but one question I grappled with. Although I hadn't intended to seek professional grief counseling, I called Patty James and booked an appointment. I requested her unsolicited offer to help the morning after a depressed state had almost led me to a rash decision.

It was about a month after his death when I locked the doors and crawled into a bed too big for one person, despite the body pillow that lay lifeless next to me. I tugged his t-shirt from under the pillow and tried to sleep, but insomnia was a familiar companion and had again climbed into bed with me. Frustrated, I climbed out of bed and meandered through the stillness of the house with steps that followed the minutes on the clock. I searched aimlessly for sleep that refused to be found or, subconsciously, I was searching for Barry, as I had many times since his death.

Everything in the house appeared exactly the same. Except nothing was the same. Previously overlooked mementoes of his love for me were in every room, and memories taunted my pain. The kitchen counter held a unique canister set Barry had bought at the craft fair

Powers Crossroads because I'd admired it. The antique hall tree I'd loved stood at the back door as a coat check. And in the corner of the breakfast nook sat the handmade, flip down writing desk with drawers and divided slots he'd brought home years ago as a surprise for me. I detested clutter and loved organization, which had made his gift even more thoughtful. To the contrary, clutter belied my organizational proclivity as bills, stamps, paper clips, and receipts lolled in disarray on the desktop. I picked up a bill from the stack and saw that the water department had made an error. Rather than the usual monthly charge, there was a credit for almost three hundred dollars. I scribbled myself a note to call city hall and clear up the mistake.

My insomnia was relentless. I was wide awake and as agitated as the wind that howled and prowled its way through the tall pines. I sought refuge from the all too familiar pain of an oncoming grief attack. I didn't want to take Xanax to get through the long, lonely night, but I reasoned that the drug would not only put me to sleep but would also temporarily dull the pain of losing Barry. I reached in the back of the bathroom medicine cabinet, retrieved the bottle, and shook out one pill. I stared at the refilled prescription bottle, and the awareness that I could permanently end my pain was right in front of me, tempting me to succumb to the relief I desperately wanted. Death would have to be easier.

However, when I filled a Dixie cup with water and dumped all of the pills into the palm of my hand, I had an uncanny sensation that Barry was in the room with me. I turned and fully expected him to be standing right behind me, but I was met with only thin air and disappointment. Resigned to heartache I replaced all of the Xanax except one and added a reminder to the "call city hall" note: "Call Dr. James and schedule an appointment ASAP."

I'd never before gone to therapy and wasn't sure what to expect, but Patty, who preferred I used her first name, immediately put me at ease in the comfort of her smile. During the course of our session I mentioned the Xanax, and she insisted on no more pills. Patty was adamant that drugs were not the solution. She explained the only way out of the pain was through it and that grief was a healing process which would take time. Rather than mask the pain with drugs, I would have to allow the pain to ebb and flow or recovery would take years. Patty also helped me understand the survivor's guilt that plagued me was normal and would eventually pass, as would the anger—unreasonable anger at Barry for dying and more so at God for letting him die.

In that first of what became weekly sessions she asked me to consider my marriage. "Sheila, would you have exchanged the life you shared with Barry for another if it would have spared you the pain of losing him?"

I didn't respond immediately. Cancer had taken my husband but not our love or the memories that would keep me company in my old age. Until that question waited for an answer, I hadn't given much thought to the deeply meaningful lyrics of Garth Brooks' megahit "The Dance." As the song came to mind I answered honestly, "No, not even one day."

"Then rather than dwelling on his death, I want you to appreciate your life, an amazing life with a man who loved you." She chose her next words carefully but stressed, "Sheila, you have to let him go and, in time, get on with your life."

I wasn't sure Patty understood the futility of her advice and changed the subject. I discussed with her selling my house and running away. Away from echoes of the past, away from the dark cloud of grief, away from everything Barry and I had shared. Patty confirmed what I already knew. There was nowhere my grief wouldn't be with me. She pointed out that if I packed a bag and left town, with grief as my fellow traveler, I wouldn't have the love and supportive network of family and friends. Patty advised me not to make any life-changing decisions until the grief abated, and I would be able to see beyond the skewed picture of loss. She recommended at least a year and reminded me, "No more prescription crutches."

Without Xanax the raw pain of grief coursed through my veins and was insufferable. More than once I'd almost succumbed to temptation before I threw the pills away. I had to take Patty's advice to feel the pain. Inexplicably, the periods when my grief was at its worst were when I sensed that Barry was still with me.

At Christmas I'd put up only a small tree in the den with white doves as ornaments, saved from the funeral floral arrangements. On Christmas morning I sat in what had become my usual place, Barry's chair, and watched a Celine Dion Christmas special that included her poignant, "Because You Loved Me." Sobs choked me, and pain ripped through my heart.

Brad suggested we change the channel, but I declined. I needed to let pain flood my soul in order to heal. Relentless grief threatened to engulf me when a single dove glided from the tree to the floor. Although there was no movement or draft, nothing that would have propelled the Christian symbol of love and peace from its perch. Nonetheless, the dove fluttered in front of me.

When Cathy gave me her Christmas gift, there was an angel in the decorative bag. I rescued the angel ornament, and Cathy was surprised. She explained that the glittered angel was not part of my present and that it must've fallen from her tree into the bag. I offered her the angel to replace on the tree, but she refused. "No, absolutely not. There were dozens of bags under my tree, but the angel dropped into *your* gift bag. I believe Barry sent it to you."

Even with those nudges towards recovery, the grief attacks were like a tunnel of darkness that was grueling to get through. However, I took Patty's advice to allow the pain to wash over me, wave by crashing wave. As painful as they were, the frequency and severity of those assaults on my heart lessened with time. The turning point came on Valentine's Day when I left the preferred seclusion of my bedroom and took my grief for a walk in the afternoon sunshine. Tears streamed down my cheeks, and I prayed for strength and guidance. I was still angry and confused as to why God had ignored the many prayers and had taken Barry. But I had to know without a doubt that he was at peace and in God's arms, and I prayed for that blessed assurance.

I finished the mile long block and walked towards the driveway where one of neighbors Ricky and Jan's little girl was jumping up and down. She excitedly pointed to the upturned rainbow that lounged in a colorful smile above my house, though there had been no rain for days and there was no hint of moisture in the air. As I regarded the upside down rainbow, I felt…something. It wasn't exactly one of those "Aha moments" that Oprah Winfrey talked about on her t.v. show. Nor was the feeling nearly as dramatic as Ebenezer Scrooge's transformation after his trio of ghostly visitors. And my heart didn't grow "three sizes that day" as did Dr. Seuss' Grinch. What stirred inside me was more subtle, a whisper that all was well. Regardless of my anger and loss, God was still God. And I had to make my peace with Him.

Despite the inspiration the process of healing wasn't nearly complete, and my road towards healing had not been without setbacks. There were countless of sleepless nights when I retrieved dozens of albums and scrutinized hundreds of photos until my heart ached with longing for days that had slipped through my fingers. I concluded the adage "this too shall pass" was not limited to the bad things in our lives, but to the good as well. It was a painful lesson.

There was the day Pat came to see me and noted the lack of housekeeping on my part. She didn't know how not to be busy, and over my objection she sorted the laundry and began to clean everything that needed to be cleaned, even changed the sheets and threw the used ones in to wash. I didn't realize until the sheets were in the dryer that Barry's t-shirt, and the last of his fading scent, had been thrown into the washer along with the sheets. I cried inconsolably as Pat apologized and held me until there were no more tears. We both understood my tears had nothing to do with the laundered t-shirt.

Other painful episodes included the day I poured his cologne down the bathroom drain and the morning I cleaned out his closet. I found a small cedar box filled with love letters from our teenaged dating years. I had no idea Barry had saved those letters written by a young girl in love. I slid the yellowed sheets of paper from frayed envelopes and read immature scribbles. Surrounded by tattered remnants of the past, I huddled for hours on the closet floor before I was able to pull myself together and finish what I'd started.

As I completed the task, I almost heard Barry say, "Sheila, I'm not coming back." I packed up bags of clothes and delivered them to the local men's shelter for donation to those in need, which is what Barry would have wanted. I later received the sincerest card of gratitude from the center, from men who had very little and were grateful for the "nicest clothes" they'd ever owned. For whatever reason it'd been difficult to part with his clothes, but it was the right thing to do.

Each heartbreaking step was a reminder that he was gone, and I was grateful for a job that filled my week days and for compassionate coworkers. Cyndie always had a sympathetic shoulder for me to cry on—as did Carla and BJ. In addition to empathetic friends and family, the community as a whole was supportive as customers continued to patronize our business. When I'd contacted city hall regarding the credit on my water bill, I was told an anonymous source had paid three hundred dollars on my account. It was evident that running away to the unknown was no more a solution than was

Love, Life, & Broken Rainbows

the temptation to overdose on sedatives. I'd lost my husband, but I was fortunate to have family and friends in my life who loved me.

Although it took a few months for me to realize they had a rotation schedule of support that pulled me from grief's harsh grip and forced me to move forward. Several friends were only a phone call away, and each of them took time to drop in and check on me. Jerry and Jerline took me out to dinner a couple of times during the week; Cindy's turn was Friday nights, when a long weekend loomed before me. We would go out to dinner and a movie or shopping to fill my empty hours.

Kim appeared on a Saturday, marched into the bedroom, and punched the "off" button on the cassette player that halted Celine Dion's beautiful voice. She opened the blinds, and pulled the covers off the bed. "It's almost two o'clock, and you've grieved long enough for today. I made you an appointment with your hairdresser. You've had root rot for weeks, and you gotta choose a color, either blonde or dead rat brown—but not both. Now grab a quick shower, and I'll find something in your closet to fit your scrawny ass. Get up!" She was not there to coddle me.

I complied because she didn't leave me room to argue. Kim had also helped me shop for a replacement for Barry's recliner so that the first thing I saw when I entered our home was not his vacant chair, void of his happy smile. I was thankful I'd heeded Patty's advice not to do anything irreversible. Likewise, she'd been right about the importance of caring friends and family, and I was indebted to them. Despite my gratitude for their vigilance, there were times I wanted the merry-go-round to stop. I also became aware that over the past few months their lives had been unfairly disrupted by my loss.

Consequently, I opted to take myself to a restaurant for dinner on a Saturday night, alone. The Applebee's hostess was polite when I requested a table for one, as was the waitress who asked if anyone would be joining me and removed the extra place setting when I answered, "No." It was evident from their demeanor they were unaccustomed to a woman dining solo.

After I ordered I laid my book aside and took note of the other diners. It was the couple two booths over that first captured my attention. They ate in silence, no smiles or laughter, no hand touching or conversation took place during the ten minutes or so I observed them. It was the desolation on the woman's face, a mirror image of my own, that led me to the conclusion that she was as lonely as I—even though her husband sat less than two feet in front of her. The woman at the table, who ordered a second daiquiri, and I were strangers linked by our mutual melancholy.

My attention was then drawn to an elderly woman at the next table. She was dressed in a lavender polyester pants suit that matched her gray, tinted hair. I eavesdropped on the one-sided conversation as she was bending the ear of an uninterested waitress considering her escape. "I live by myself, you know, so it's nice to get out once and awhile and talk to others. My husband died more than three years ago, but I miss him every day. I have four children, but they're all grown and live out of state, scattered across the country. I realize they're busy with their own lives, but I do miss them and the grandchildren so very much. Would you like to see pictures of them?" She was talking to a vacant space because the impatient waitress had made her getaway.

As I continued to observe other diners, an old sixties tune about lonely people, The Beatles' "Eleanor Rigby," drifted through my sadness. I noticed that regardless of their exaggerated laughter, lonesomeness was painted on several faces at the horseshoe bar where they sought a sense of camaraderie, a human connection over a cold beer. The weary, middle-aged bartender wore a mask of interest with a pasted on smile as she mechanically wiped the bar, dumped the ashtrays, and gathered her tips. No doubt she grew tired of listening to the problems of others when her worry lines revealed she had problems of her own. I scanned the restaurant once more before my meal arrived. It was obvious that loneliness didn't always show up dressed in black.

I nibbled on a crispy chicken tender from the appetizer sampler, although I had no appetite, and thought about Patty's advice to focus on what I'd had instead of on what I'd lost. Perhaps her advice was not as senseless as I'd first thought. Patty recommended that I find new dreams, dreams that didn't include him. But how was that possible when our lives were as one? I was lost without Barry, but he'd told me on our last day in the ICU that I had to let him go. Somehow, I had to get past my misery and let go of "us." I recalled that Patty had explained the stages of grief, which often came in a different order, with one exception. The last stage was always acceptance. Would I ever reach that last stage?

With a heavy heart I paid the check and headed for home where solitude, my loyal companion, waited to greet me. During the drive I reflected on my unexpected and unwelcomed status. No longer defined by my role as a wife, I was an extra piece of society's puzzle trying to "fit." I didn't belong with young, single women. Nor was I in the classification of divorcée. I certainly didn't blend in with our town's numerous, blue-haired elderly widows. I was having an identity crisis, but the love Barry and I had shared and the agony of losing him were forever interwoven in my heart, polar opposite emotions that had become a part of who I was.

But who was I? I struggled daily to find myself without Barry. No one had explained that when we lose our spouse, so, too, do we lose our shared dreams for a future that could no longer be realized. Those dreams had unknowingly been as fragile as Waterford crystal—and just as easily shattered. Years of precious moments were as irretrievably lost as footprints in the sand. I had to accept the steps behind me couldn't be retraced, and the road to a future with Barry was forever closed. The new road before me was filled with mountains and valleys that blocked my view of whatever waited on the other side of limbo.

Those thoughts clamored for attention as I arrived home and let myself inside. I pushed my confusion aside and sorted through the mail. There was a letter from the State University of West Georgia, the Dean's office, and more out of curiosity than interest, I opened it. The notice was brief and to the point: if I didn't complete the coursework for my degree by the end of summer quarter, my diploma would fall under new catalogue guidelines for graduation, which would mean additional classes. The letter further stated that the only courses I was lacking were two quarters of Spanish, and I qualified for a program that would allow me to earn those two quarters in only four weeks.

I could elect to become a full-time student at a university approved school in Cuernavaca, Mexico, during the month of July. The contact information and deadline for registration were provided. I checked the calendar and confirmed that Brad's wedding was planned for the week before I would leave the country, and Chuck's wedding wouldn't take place until two weeks after I returned. I would be off from work for six weeks during summer break. The timing was perfect, maybe even a godsend.

I picked up the letter again and remembered my promise to Barry that I would finish college. I wouldn't be running away, not permanently. Although a month in Mexico, living with a host family and spending my days in Spanish classes, would serve a dual purpose. I would graduate, and my unfilled summer weeks would be busily occupied. The trip would be a respite from everything that reminded me of Barry and our lives together, a temporary distraction from grief. My husband would have been the first one to encourage me to get on with my life. He knew when I hadn't there would be new memories, new footprints in the sand. Those footprints awaited, but I had to take the first step. The easier choice was to wallow in self-pity, as if I were the only woman who'd ever lost her North Star.

But Mexico? Due to a significant loss of income, a casualty of his death, my purse strings were tight, and I wasn't eligible to collect Social Security widow's benefits. I was nowhere near the age requirement of sixty, and neither of my sons was enrolled as a full-time student. Nevertheless, I could afford the program because my scholarship would cover the costs of tuition and books, and the living expenses were manageable. I considered that a college degree could lead to a better paying job. Before doubt dissuaded me I reached for the phone, dialed the number for the coordinator's office, and left a message regarding the Mexican sabbatical. I had to climb out of the quicksand, and the educational excursion would be a crucial first step.

Life has taught me there are things that happen in our lives we don't want to happen, but we have to accept. And there are people we think we can't live without but whom we have to learn to live without. It has been said that which does not kill us will make us stronger. Whether I agreed or not, I'd heard repeatedly the proverb that time heals all wounds. Was it really darkest before dawn? Poet Robert Frost said he could sum up everything he had learned about life in three words: "It goes on."

But I very much needed to find out for myself if life goes on....

Made in the USA
Lexington, KY
31 January 2017